Working children in the informal sector in Managua

Aida Aragão-Lagergren

UPPSALA 1997

Doctoral dissertation for the degree of Doctor of Philosophy in Social and Economic Geography at Uppsala University, 1997

ABSTRACT

Aragão-Lagergren, A. 1997: Working children in the informal sector in Managua. *Geografiska Regionstudier* 31, 311 pp. Uppsala.
ISBN 91-506-1201-8.

This thesis deals with a group of working children in the informal sector in Managua, Nicaragua, engaged in those "visible" activities considered to be typical of child work in this sector of the economy: vending, warding and washing cars, shining shoes, working as "helpers", or loading and carrying goods.

Methodologically, an important decision has been to let interviews with the children at their places of work provide most of the information about themselves and about their household. All over Latin America, the informal sector has expanded at a rapid rate. In Managua, that expansion has led to stiffer competition, new barriers to entry into the sector, within-sector structural changes—and this has adversely affected the situation of the working children.

The study focuses upon two main issues: the economic and social aspects of the work of the children and their role in the informal sector, and, secondly, the living conditions of the children. With regard to the first issue, the conclusion is that children's work is a well-organized activity, that it is of considerable economic significance for their households and for themselves, and that the working children came from households with varying socio-economic characteristics.

Three distinct everyday life patterns were identified through an analysis of the spatial and temporal characteristics of and interdependencies between the children's activities. In particular, the spatial relationships between school, work and home had a major impact upon the children's daily and weekly activity patterns.

Key words: child work, informal sector, urban geography, interview method, Latin America, Nicaragua.

Aida Aragão-Lagergren: Department of Social and Economic Geography, Uppsala University, Norbyvägen 18 B, 752 36 Uppsala, Sweden

© Aida Aragão-Lagergren 1997

ISBN 91-506-1201-8

Printed in Sweden by Gotab, Stockholm 1997

Distributor: Uppsala University, Department of Social and Economic Geography, Norbyvägen 18 B, 752 36 Uppsala, Sweden

To the working children of Managua

Contents

Preface		7
Part One		11
1	Introduction	15
	Objectives of the study	19
2	Theoretical background	21
	Child work and the city	21
	Urbanization processes	23
	The global context and inequality in the city	25
	The formal and the informal sectors of the urban economy	28
	Policies toward the informal sector	36
	The informal sector and development theories	40
3	Child work	47
	Child work in the literature: some general characteristics	50
	The legislative approach	56
	From adult- towards child-oriented research?	59
	Literature on child work in Nicaragua	64
	Child work in the urban informal sector	65
	Child work activities in the urban informal sector in Central America	73
4	The case of Nicaragua	77
	The living conditions of the urban population	78
	Increasing poverty	78
	The urban informal sector	81
	Characteristics and changes	82
	Expansion at what price?	87
	Poverty and the urban informal sector	88
	Strategies of the households	89
	Child work—the last resort?	90
5	Methodology	93
	Rationale for the selection of a research methodology	93
	The Methodology of the Study	99
	Research strategy	101
	Other Sources	102

Part Two		103
6	The case study	107
	The field work	107
	The interviews with the children	108
7	The study area	113
	The selection of the working places	113
	The sample of parking areas	114
	The sample of markets	114
	Portrayals of the places of work: spatial activity patterns, organization of work and work milieu	116
	The Galeria Internacional parking lot	117
	San Judas market	120
	Israel Lewites market	122
	El Mayoreo market	124
	Roberto Huembes market: the parking lots and the market	126
	Concluding remarks: the struggle over urban economic space	131
8	Selection of the sample of working children	135
	Child work activities investigated in this study	135
	Patterns of gender differentiation	135
	The sample of working children	138
9	Living conditions of the children	141
	Housing	141
	Where do the working children live?	143
	Place of residence and housing situation	144
	The household and the family	147
	Structure and size of the households	150
	Family type	152
10	The economic role of the children	159
	The occupations	159
	Selling: a sign of poverty	160
	Occupational categories	166
	Occupational categories and activities	170
	Principal and secondary activities	171
	Occupational mobility	176
	The income	181
	Income determinants	185

	Places of work and activity types	185
	Occupational categories and modes of payment	188
	Income types	192
	The monetary income	197
	The size of children's daily income	197
	Income classification	201
	The destination and use of the monetary income of the children	201
11	The households of the children in an economic perspective	209
	The activities of household heads and their partners	209
	Income classification of heads of household and their partners	212
	Is there a typical "working child household" in Managua?	215
12	The working children's everyday life	223
	Classification of activities	224
	Place and time allocation of activities	231
	Playing and sports	232
	Mobility	234
	Activities at home	236
	Self-directed and household-directed work	236
	Schooling	238
	The educational situation of the interviewed children	242
	Work in the Labour Market	248
13	The spatial organization of the everyday life of the working children—a missing link?	253
	The everyday life patterns	255
	Combining school and work	260
	The role of the spatial patterns of activities in shaping everyday life patterns	264
14	Risks at work	269
15	What the children think about child work	277
	...and dreams of the future?	282
16	Summary and conclusions	287
	Child work: a new field for geography	299
Bibliography		301
Appendix		310

Figures

Fig. 1	Shoe-shiners at the Roberto Huembes market	12
Fig. 2	The boy who sold used newspapers, with a friend	104
Fig. 3	The location of the selected places of work in Managua	115
Fig. 4	The parking lot at Galeria Internacional	118
Fig. 5	The San Judas market	121
Fig. 6	Israel Lewites market	123
Fig. 7	El Mayoreo market	125
Fig. 8	The Roberto Huembes market: the smaller parking lot	127
Fig. 9	Another view of the Roberto Huembes market	130
Fig. 10	The sample of working children by age, sex, and place of work.	140
Fig. 11	The place of residence of the sample of children by district type and place of work	146
Fig. 12	The sample of children by family type	154
Fig. 13	Presence of parents in the households of the children	156
Fig. 14	Distribution of the sample of children by occupation, gender and place of work	161
Fig. 15	Lemon sellers at the San Judas market	163
Fig. 16	Sellers by occupational category and type of products	166
Fig. 17	Sellers in front of the bus station area at Israel Lewites market	168
Fig. 18	Occupational category of the children by sex	169
Fig. 19	Principal and secondary activities	173
Fig. 20	Location of principal and secondary activities	175
Fig. 21	Car wards at the Roberto Huembes market	178
Fig. 22	Occupational mobility	179
Fig. 23	Age and work career of children who had changed occupation	180
Fig. 24	A boy who sold vegetables at El Mayoreo market	187
Fig. 25	A boy who wards and washes cars at the Roberto Huembes market	190
Fig. 26	Type of income by occupational category	194
Fig. 27	Mixed income by activity type and occupational category	195
Fig. 28	Type of income by activity and occupational category in per cent	196
Fig. 29	Children's mean daily income in Cordobas by occupational category and activity type	199
Fig. 30	The income of the children	202
Fig. 31	Sellers at the Roberto Huembes market	203
Fig. 32	The destination of the children's monetary income	205
Fig. 33	Car wards at Galeria Internacional	206
Fig. 34	Occupation and place of work of female and male household members	212
Fig. 35	The income of female household members	214
Fig. 36	The income of male household members	215
Fig. 37	Socio-economic characteristics of the households	220
Fig. 38	Relationship between the drop-out rate, illiteracy and work in Central American countries (Nicaragua excluded)	241
Fig. 39	The weekly work schedule of the children	249
Fig. 40	Distribution of children's working hours/day by working days/week	250
Fig. 41	Time allocation in the everyday life of children in pattern A during school days and work days	256
Fig. 42	Time allocation in the everyday life of children in pattern B	258
Fig. 43	Time allocation in the everyday life of children in pattern C	259
Fig. 44	The three patterns of weekly time allocation	261
Fig. 45	Time allocation of each child in the everyday life pattern B	262
Fig. 46	Time allocation of each child in the everyday life pattern C and A	263
Fig. 47	The children really enjoyed to use the tape recorder!	275

Preface

My interest in child work originated during my four year stay (1987–1990) in Managua, Nicaragua, where I worked as a United Nations associate expert in a household survey programme at the Nicaraguan Statistical Institute (INEC). The methodological difficulties encountered in trying to obtain information about the working children in the city led to my decision to undertake a study by myself.

When the study now has been completed, I want to thank some of the people and institutions that have provided the help and support without which this work would have been impossible to carry out.

First of all, I want to thank all the children which I interviewed in Managua - they made this work possible. Their belief in the significance of their work for themselves and their families, their pride in this work, and the genuine enthusiasm with which they participated in the study make it very important for me to try to pass on others this account of who they are and what their lives are like.

I want to thank Maria Rosa Renzi at the FIDEG institute in Managua for her valuable collaboration and generosity. She was both my "steady point" in Nicaragua and a great source of knowledge that she kindly shared with me. I also want to thank my Nicaraguan colleague Aida Guillén who assisted me during the field work interview periods.

The Institute of Latin American Studies in Stockholm was my most important link to Latin America in Sweden. I am greatly indebted to Weine Karlsson for his collaboration and for making me always feel welcome. Thanks also to other colleagues at the institute with whom I have had the opportunity to discuss and share experiences in the continent of our common interest.

Birgitta Ling at Rädda Barnen, Stockholm, was my first contact with the issue of child work. She has always shown her interest when I needed to talk to someone with a profound and professional knowledge of child work coupled with a realistic and humanitarian understanding of the life situation of working children. I thank her for valuable comments on some chapters of this book.

William Meyers, who has dedicated a great part of his professional life to child work issues, first at the United Nations Children's Fund (UNICEF) and later at the International Labour Office (ILO), is a respected authority in this field; he has been a source of inspiration and has given me good advice. I want to thank him for giving me some of his time and also for valuable comments on some chapters.

The presence and fellowship of my friends and colleagues at the Department of Social and Economic Geography in Uppsala have been very important to me during this period of my life. I want to thank them all for constructive discussions and good times together.

Some of my colleagues have been especially important in the course of my research. Sune Berger has been my supervisor from the very first beginning of this project. He helped me to begin, he has encouraged me to go on, and he has always been there when needed. Hans Aldskogius has tried his best to improve the language in the book, and has made many suggestions on substantive matters. Roger Andersson has read my manuscript with great care; I appreciate the interest he has shown, and I am very grateful for his many valuable comments. Jan Öhman has read and commented upon some parts of the manuscript.

I am also very grateful to professor Göran Hoppe for his careful reading of and many useful comments on the final manuscript.

Thanks also to Jon Hogdal who drew the map of Managua and the sketch maps of the places where the children worked, to Mats Lundmark who has helped me with the graphs, and to Gerolf Nauwerck who did the layout work. I have had the good fortune to get much help from Åsa Larsson and Lise-Lotte Isaksson in the "Geo Library", and from Ewa Hodell in the departmental office. I am indebted to them for their support in many practical matters.

Most of all I must thank my family. My husband Lars and my wonderful children Maya and Micael have been most understanding and willing to accept the sometimes peculiar behaviour of a thesis author, and they have always given me the necessary support and encouragement when I best needed it. Finally, I want to thank my mother in Portugal who always, despite our spatial separation, has been within reach and willing to help me solve many practical problems. With this book I also want to honour the memory of my grandmother and of my father.

I received financial support for the first field work period in Managua from the Department for Research Cooperation of the Swedish International Development Cooperation Agency, and from the Swedish Society for Anthropology and Geography. The second field work period was in part supported by the Institute of Latin American Studies in Stockholm.

Uppsala in February 1997

Aida Aragão-Lagergren

Part One

Figure 1   Shoe-shiners at the Roberto Huembes market

A Shoe-shiner in Managua

He is ten years old and born in Managua. He lives with his mother and three brothers. Every morning he gets up at six, and after the morning meal he walks to the school that is situated very close to his home. At twelve, when school has finished, he returns home, has something to eat, changes his clothes and picks up his box with shoe-shining tools. He lives quite far away from the Roberto Huembes market where he works and has to travel fifteen minutes by bus to get there. Usually he begins work at one o'clock.

He has been a shoe-shiner for about one year. Earlier, he worked as a seller. He sold handkerchieves and razor blades, but that job did not give much profit so his mother decided that it would be better for him to find another job. He began to save his earnings together with one of his brothers, and eventually they were able to buy a tool-box for shoe-shining. He works in the afternoon after school, and his brother in the morning before school. He enjoys his job, because he likes to earn his own money, he says. But he gives everything he earns to his mother, who is an ambulatory seller of razor blades. He usually works until six o'clock in the afternoon and then takes the bus back home.

Once at home he helps to sweep the floor and usually he has some time for play before he goes to bed. He works every day according to this schedule except on the weekends when he usually works for longer hours, because these are "good business days". He confesses that he is quite afraid of being out in the city, working, because "in the street anything can happen". If he did not have to work at the market, he says, he would like to stay at home and work there. In his opinion, however, it is good that children work so that they can get enough to eat. He does not want to have the same job when he has grown up. He wants to be a car mechanic.

Chapter 1

Introduction

Every day, every month, every year, they are there in the streets of Managua - working children. They are a permanent feature of the city, an abiding and constantly renewed group. What would the city look like without the presence of these children? Would anyone even notice their absence in the event that they would suddenly vanish from the streets, and wonder why no child has to work, for whatever reason? I can hardly believe that, because even when they are there for all to see, they seem to be invisible to people in general and to public authorities, which fail even to recognize them for what they are - members of the largest group of workers in the city - the workers in the informal sector.

They wake up with the city and go to work, like so many other workers do. Their places of work are wherever they can find an accessible spot where they can offer their services, struggling everyday against a multitude of other informal workers in the city for the right to work: in the middle of the traffic in the streets, in parking lots, in the markets and outside the malls and supermarkets. No one knows how many they are or where they come from, if they have a home to return to after the working day is over, or if they live in the streets. No one knows whether they face danger in their work, if they are exploited by others, if they attend school, and what their everyday life is like. No one knows what they think about their present life and what they wish that their lives as adults will be like.

To understand the situation of the urban working children it is necessary to consider a complex set of social, economic and political aspects at the local as well as at the global level. It is also indispensable to keep in mind that first of all they are children, but that they work. And finally, that the dominant arena of child work in the informal sector is the city.

The urbanization processes in the cities of Latin America are reflections of changes over time in global, national and regional economic policies. Relationships between the three levels have been interpreted by social and economic scientists in different ways, and different formulas have been thought out as solutions to the problem of poverty in most of the countries in the region. However, the poverty problem has not been solved and during the present decade the gap between rich and poor has become more accentuated within the countries of Latin America. Although there has been some progress in the establishment and development of new democracies in many countries during the last few years, internal conflicts have not been resolved, and violence is a daily worry for people in the urban as well as in the rural areas. Social and political instability basically have their roots in the uneven access to basic resources. In the city, the lack of stable income is a major factor behind social instability.

The debt burden from the economic recession in the 1980's in most countries in Latin America has led to the introduction of severe Structural Adjustment Programmes in the 1990's, imposed by the World Bank, which imply drastic changes in national economic and social policies. In the case of Nicaragua, these policies have indeed made it possible to halt the hyper-inflation of the 1980's, but have not succeeded in increasing production or in creating employment. Instead, and mainly in the cities, the recession of the formal economic sector – in terms of privatization of state enterprises and cuts in health and education programmes – has resulted in fewer jobs and the dismissal of many workers. Those who have been laid off, as well as new labour in the city, have no other alternative but to find or create a job by themselves in the informal sector of the economy.

In Managua, more than half of those who have a job work in the informal sector.[1] They work in the markets and in the street, but it is at home that most of the work in fact takes place. They are not only street sellers or shoe-shiners, they are also domestic servants, owners of workshops, small manufacturers, hairdressers, car mechanics, in fact they are involved in the production of all kinds of goods and services, not only for the low income households in the city, but for the urban population in general.

They work long hours each day and often all days of the week, but their jobs are poorly paid and their incomes are highly unstable. It is precisely these two factors - lack of regular and sufficient income - that explain why the majority of the households of these workers live in poverty and why their children are forced to work. It is true that not only poor children work, but only poor children *have to* work. Their work may not be so important in real capital terms but it certainly helps to raise desperately low household incomes and to improve the living conditions of the children themselves.

Child work is a complex issue because it involves a great number of moral, human rights, legal and economic aspects. Although the importance of the work of children is widely recognized, child work is usually not studied in economic terms and the role of children as income suppliers tends to be neglected. Instead, child work is often categorically condemned as morally unacceptable, without any real attempts to take into consideration the living conditions of the children who work. If the work of the children was taken seriously, it would become part of economic plans and programmes. There is a paradox here: the work of the children has seldom been included in economic plans or programmes by international and national labour organizations, or by financial institutions and foundations. On the other hand, economic plans and programmes at all levels have a significant impact on the situation of the children.

Exactly what role the work of children plays in the evolution of the informal sector is not known. Until recently, the informal sector has

---

[1]. In 1995 in Managua, 59 per cent were employed in the informal sector. Source: Fundación Internacional para el Desafio Económico Global (FIDEG). El Observador Económico. No. 48. p. 34.

been absorbing that part of the labour force for which there are no jobs in the formal sector. However, it is an open question for how long the informal sector will be able to solve, in a sense, the problem of employment in the city. There are signs that the sector is becoming saturated, and one may well ask in what way this process will affect the living conditions of working children.

This study will deal with a group of working children in the urban informal sector of Managua. They work in different places in the city and are engaged in activities which are considered representative or typical of child work in the informal sector: vending, warding and washing cars, shining shoes, and working as "helpers", or loading and carrying goods.

There were three main reasons for the selection of this group for the present study. Firstly, the children who work in the urban informal sector comprise one of the largest groups of working children in Latin America. In Managua, they represent the great majority of the working children. However, and despite that magnitude, relatively little is known about this group. Hence, detailed knowledge about their working and living conditions is urgently needed in order to make possible the design of child-oriented policies and programmes.

Secondly, because the streets or other open places adjacent to the streets usually constitute the visible work places for children and because of the nature of the activities they perform, their work has largely gone unnoticed both by the public (consumers) in general and by the authorities. Consequently, their status as workers is poorly defined and their contributions to the economy little known. To study their working conditions would therefore shed some light on the economic significance of children's work, through which they not only earn their own bread but which often contributes more than so to family or household income.

Thirdly, it is of vital importance to increase awareness, on the part of the general public and of institutions, of the living and working conditions of children in order to secure their right to protection from dangers related to work, as well as to put the issue of the human rights of working children at the forefront. Child workers in the urban informal sector are such a familiar sight in the city of Managua that they have become invisible in their role as workers. This paradox has serious consequences for the children in several ways. It means, for instance, that they are often regarded as vagabonds and thieves, threatened and maltreated, and that the risks they face tend to be ignored.

Objectives of the study

The overriding purpose of this study is to contribute to a deeper understanding of the conditions of life for working children in Managua, Nicaragua. It is hoped, also, that this case study will make a contribution to general knowledge about the situation of children in similar circumstances, in their two roles as workers in the informal economic sector and as children.

Although the theoretical framework of the study includes elements from social science in a broad sense, the perspectives of social and economic geography have been particularly important in two respects.

Firstly, this work can be positioned in the tradition of "place" studies, which focus upon the interrelationships between different subsystems - physical, social and economic - within a region or a "place". At one level, the study is concerned with relationships between the built-up urban environment in Managua and patterns of social differentiation and economic activities. At another level, perhaps best described as "micro-geographic", the analysis focuses upon the relationships between the physical characteristics of different places of work and the type and organization of child work in those places.

Secondly, the tradition of spatial analysis, with its emphasis upon how spatial relations across space impact upon social and economic organization, has been important. In particular, this perspective has guided the investigation of how the everyday life of working children is shaped by the spatial relationships between home, school and place of work.

The organization of the study reflects the attempt to investigate two central and interrelated issues with regard to child work in the urban informal sector in Managua. The first issue relates to the economic and social aspects of the work of the children, and should be seen in the context of widespread poverty and increasing economic inequalities in the country. This analysis will focus upon the role of the children's work in the informal sector and the significance of their work for the economy of their household and consequently for themselves. The assumption is that, contrary to what is sometimes believed, the work of the children is a significant component of strategies used by households in order to cope with a lack of resources and to increase their income. Also, it is assumed that child work in the informal sector should be viewed as a well organized activity rather than sporadic undertakings aimed to provide capital for non-essential consumption.

The second issue is connected to the living conditions of the children, and should be seen in the context of children's right to be assured of certain basic rights and privileges, just as any other human being. In the case of working children, two particularly important aspects are the right to receive a free and appropriate education and the right to be protected from hazards at work. This issue will be dealt with through an analysis of how the everyday life of the children is organized in time and space.

More precisely, the following objectives for the study have been defined.

– To describe and analyse the spatial patterns of the activities of working children in order to identify some of the conditions that facilitate or restrict entrance into the urban informal sector and which have an impact on the position in which child workers find themselves in their struggle for access to and use of urban economic space.

– To analyse the economic role of the children by examining the characteristics of their work and their role as contributors to the economy of their households.

– To analyse the living conditions of the children with respect to housing, household situation and family bonds.

– To describe and analyse the everyday life of the children in a temporal and spatial context, focusing in particular upon the relationship between school attendance and work.

Chapter 2

Theoretical background

Child work and the city

No one can deny that child work exists in the world today. And no doubt children have worked, in one sense or another, since the dawn of mankind. But child work has taken very different forms through the centuries and the work of children has served different purposes and has thus changed in its characteristics. In the West it is common to distinguish between forms of child work before and after industrialization. This puts the emphasis upon the different character of child work in rural and urban areas. Before industrialization, children worked within the family sphere, and the tasks that children were engaged in were age and sex related. Children's work was almost as essential for the economy of the household as that of adults, and was an integral part of the socialization processes which prepared the children for an adult life.

In the period of proto-industrialization, small pre-industrial units of production came to dominate the economy of an increasing number of villages in many countries, and children's work became an important factor in this production. Some authors argue that it was in this period that children became more severely exploited as workers.[1] With industrialization and the accelerated growth of cities, the work of children gravitated towards urban areas. Together with women, children became a key element in labour-intensive, low-cost production in eighteenth century manufacturing. Industrialization led to mass

---

[1.] Levine, D. (1987): *Reproducing Families*. Cambridge University Press. Cambridge.

exploitation of child labour on a scale never experienced before; no consideration was paid to the age of the children, children were taken away from their families and placed in factories where they worked long hours and lived in conditions not imaginable in previous centuries. The works of Charles Dickens stand out as some of the most graphic descriptions of the appalling living conditions of the child workers of that time.[1] Among other more recent accounts on children in the city, Jo Boyden's "Children of the Cities", while not specifically focusing on working children, reviews different aspects related to the conditions of the life of the children in the South, including child work.[2]

Child work in Latin America has a different historical background, but resembles that of the West with respect to the recent relocation of child work from the rural areas to the cities. Although there are striking differences between countries, it has been argued that, generally speaking, the more exploitative forms of child labour are closely linked to colonial and pre-capitalist conditions in each country.[3] Salazar refers to historical research of several authors.[4] Child work during the early colonial era has been described as severe exploitation under conditions akin to feudal servitude and slavery.[5] Young slaves were used in domestic work, in mines, sugar mills, and on *haciendas*. In the late 19th century, with incipient industrialization and urban growth, children's work became a component also in the city's scenario.

There are some passages in novels and biographies which describe child work in textile factories, but in the cities in Brazil, Peru and Colombia, children were mostly found working as newsboys, shoe-

---

[1] Dickens, C. (1965): *Great expectations*. Calder, A. (ed.). Harmondsworth Penguin. (First edition 1860-61). London; Berg, M., Hudson, P. and Sonescher, M. (1983): *Manufacturing in town and country before the factory*. Cambridge University Press. Cambridge; Hudson, P. (ed.) (1989): *Regions and Industries*. Cambridge University Press. Cambridge; Garcia, R. (1989): *Incipient Industrialization in an "Underdeveloped" Country. The case of Chile, 1845-1879*. Institute of Latin American Studies. Monograph No. 17. Stockholm.

[2] Boyden, J. with Holden, P. (1991): *Children of the cities*. Zed Books. New Jersey.

[3] Salazar, M.C. (1994): *The social significance of child labor in Latin America and the Caribbean*. Paper prepared for the 48th International Congress of Americanists. Stockholm.

[4] Schibotto, G. (1990): *Niños trabajadores. Construyendo una identidad*. IPEC. Lima.

[5] Ortiz, F. (1987): *Los negros esclavos*. Editorial de Ciencias Sociales. La Habana. Cuba.

shiners, water sellers, waste carriers, beggars, coffee vendors, bricklayer's assistants and so forth. Referring to the work of Esmeralda Balsonaro[1] on child work in São Paulo, Brazil, and the attitude towards the work of the children in the city in the late 19th century, Salazar says:

> Then and now, in Brazil and elsewhere, many people justified the use of child labour in the manufacturing industry as a way to 'reduce the number of young vagrants on city streets', ...many employers in the region felt that the system was actually of benefit to working children.[2]

She also mentions that:

> An official report of 1893 speaks of their homes as squalid 'holes'. It also refers to 'absolute poverty' (currently a much used term) and to the need to supplement family income through the work of women, adolescents and children.[3]

Urbanization processes

The process through which child work has been relocated from rural areas to the city is not an isolated phenomenon. It must be understood within the context of more general urbanization processes. In Latin America, "the urban explosion"—as it is often referred to—has led to profound social transformations. Until the 1950's the majority of the population lived in rural areas, but during the 1960's and 1970's the urban population in cities of Latin America grew at a much more rapid rate than the total population.[4] From 1950 to 1980, 27 millions of people migrated from rural to urban areas in Latin America, and the

---

[1] Balsonaro de Moura, E. (1982): *Mulheres e menores no trabalho industrial: os factores sexo e idade na dinamica do capital.*Vozes. Petrópolis.
[2] Salazar, M.C. (1994). p. 6.
[3] Ibid. p. 5.
[4] Roberts, B. (1978): *Cities of Peasants: the political economy of urbanization in the Third World.* Edward Arnold. London.

continent is one of the most urbanized parts of the South.[1] The urbanization process in Latin America has been studied quite intensively by geographers as well as by other social scientists.[2] In particular, the economic and social problems resulting from the concentration of people to the cities has drawn the attention of scholars. Urban changes in Latin America have been expressed mainly in the growth of slum and squatter settlements, where social and economic problems are most severe, and in the emergence of a small, economically privileged, elite. These features of urbanization are typical of the whole region, but at the same time they vary a good deal from country to country. In fact, not all of the continent has experienced the same rhythm of urbanization, and in the case of the Central American countries, urban growth on a large scale has come rather late as the pace of industrialization has been relatively slow. In some countries other factors than economic ones have been particularly important for urban growth. In the case of Nicaragua, industrialization has not been as significant a factor behind migration from rural to urban areas as the civil war has been. However, the negative effects of urban growth in Nicaragua—lack of adequate housing, employment, and infrastructure—are similar to those found across Central and South America, although on a smaller scale.

---

[1] Hurtado, M. (1986): *Teeming cities: the challenge of the urban poor.* Latin America and Caribbean Review. World of Information. Quoted in Cubbit, T. (1995): *Latin American Society.* Longman. England. p. 150.

[2] See e.g. Gilbert, A. (1994): *The Latin American city.* London; Gilbert, A. and Ward, P. (1985): *Housing, the state and the poor.* Cambridge University Press. Cambridge; Preston, D. (1987): *Latin American Development. Geographical Perspectives.* Longman. Harlow; Santos, M. (1978): *O espaço dividido: Os dois circuitos da economia urbana dos paises subdesenvolvidos.* (original title: L'espace partagé . Les deux circuits de l'économie urbaine des pays sous-développés). Alves Editora. Brazil; Castells, M. (1983): *The City and the Grassroots.* Edward Arnold. London; Roberts, B. (1995): *The making of Citizens: Cities of Peasants.* Revised. Edward Arnold. London; Chatterjee, L. (1989): *Third World Cities. New Models in Geography.* Peet, R. and Thrift, N. (eds.): Vol. two. London; Datta, S. (1990): *Class Dynamics, Subaltern Consciousness and the Household Perspective. Third World Urbanization: Reappraisals and New Perspectives.* Urban Studies. Swedish Council for Research in the Humanities and Social Sciences. Stockholm.

The global context and inequality in the city

Although urbanization processes principally have a national dimension and vary from city to city, they have never been contained solely by national or regional borders. During the last few decades it has become increasingly obvious that these processes must be understood in the context of broad international trends. The UN report on Social Development identifies six trends which together go a long way to explain changes in most societies during the last few years of the "global era".[1] They are: the spread of liberal democracy, the speed of technological change, the media revolution and consumerism, the dominance of market forces, the integration of the global economy, and the transformation of production systems and labour markets. Three of them, in particular, have had an impact upon urbanization processes in developing countries and partly explain the growth of the urban informal sector: the dominance of market forces, the integration of the global economy, and the transformation of production systems and labour markets.

The first trend, the resurgence of economic liberalism, had its origins in the industrialized countries in the second half of the 1970's, and came as a response to the recession after the first oil crisis in 1978. The liberalism drift took shape in various radical reforms, such a reducing state intervention in the economy, privatizating public enterprises, liberalizing prices, deregulating services, and controlling inflation. Such structural adjustments in fact started in the North, in the United Kingdom and USA. However, liberal policies—the main feature of which is a shift in favour of market forces and private enterprise—have been transmitted by the wealthy countries to the poor through their dominance of international finance and trade. Today, the impact of these policies it felt in a large number of developing countries, many of them in Latin America. Liberalism has resulted not only in shifts in the power structure at the international level—with investor and creditor countries, as well as the two major multilateral finance institutions, the International Monetary Fund (IMF) and the World Bank, in leading positions in the global economy—but also in a strong competition

---

[1]. UNRISD (1995): *States of Disarray. The social effects of globalization.* Report for the World Summit for Social Development. UNRISD. London. p. 9.

between and within countries. Not only, but mainly within developing countries, this competition has made capital owners richer, while the poor have become poorer due to declining wages and lack of employment.[1] In the cities, where most of the state institutions and public enterprises are located, the dismissal of workers from the formal sector and an expansion of employment in the informal sector is a very visible result of liberal policies.

Lack of employment is also the result of another expression of the globalization of the world economy: the changing methods of production which have reinforced the trend from large to small units of production, from full-time to part-time employment, and in general towards less employment. In other words, the present trend is towards more informal and less secure forms of employment. The UN report stresses that the new methods of work weaken the positive relationship between expansion of output and growth in employment, leading to "jobless growth"; even if cycles of new growth in production will emerge, there will be no growth in terms of employment. With respect to developing countries the report states that:

> In developing countries, this change in production methods is reflected in an ever expanding informal sector whose greater flexibility and cost effectiveness seem to catch the mood of the times. ...But while informal enterprises may seem dynamic, in fact they often serve merely as the employer of last resort, a holding ground for the reserve army of the unemployed.[2]

Especially in the city, a lack of employment and growing underemployment have changed the urban patterns of life and have accentuated the dualistic structure of the urban economy—characterized by a declining formal sector and a growing informal sector.

Although it is becoming increasingly difficult to generalize about Latin America because of the growing differentiation between countries, and within countries, it is possible to argue that the three trends discussed above have affected a majority of countries in Latin America. The main consequence of the globalization process is a much

---

[1.] Ibid.
[2.] Ibid. p. 28.

more polarized society, with a small upper class that has been able to take advantage of the new liberal policies, and has been doing very well, and the large majority of the population which, by contrast, has not been experiencing any progress—in fact it is reduced to try to just survive each day. This polarization can be seen in terms of urban vis-à-vis rural areas, but within the cities it is more visible, because there the income distribution is so extremely polarized. The gap between the highest and the lowest income in urban societies is wider than ever. Inequality and social injustice for long have been facts of life, and in many cases the situation in these respects seems to have become progressively worse not only in periods of economic recession but at times of economic boom as well.[1]

Thus, although poverty is more acute in rural than in urban areas, two thirds of the population in Latin America live in the cities and here the contrast between rich and poor is most evident. The rapid rate of natural population growth since the 1960's, and a strong rural-urban migration during the last few decades have led to a veritable urban explosion and grave housing and environmental problems. Social deprivation in the city is of course related to lack of employment and low incomes. Lack of employment is the central cause of poverty in the city. Those who can not find a job have simply been obliged to invent their own jobs in order to survive. These people, their activities and their way of life constitute the informal sector of the urban economy. The informal sector, in fact, must be regarded as the foundation of a widespread mode of life for a large part of the majority of the urban population. The poor seek to cope with economic crisis at the household level by the use of so-called coping strategies, e.g. to adopt multiple survival strategies which involve the integration of children as workers in the informal sector. In Latin America, where most countries have been facing difficult economic problems in the wake of the so-called debt crisis, and more recently the adjustment crisis, the informal sector has grown at an annual rate of 6.8 per cent during the 1980´s and there is no evidence that the informal sector should be regarded as a transient phenomenon.[2]

[1.] Preston, D. (1987): *Latin American Development. Geographical Perspectives.* Longman. Harlow.
[2.] PREALC (1987).

The formal and the informal sectors of the urban economy

The complex life patterns of the poor, and in particular the role of the informal sector, have been the subject of much research since the 1970's. Today, it is a well established fact that informal economic activities provide the main source of income for a majority of the poor households in cities in developing countries and that this sector does not show any sign of disappearing in the near future. These types of activities have been interpreted in different ways and have been called by different names. It was not until the early 1970´ s, however, that they began to be understood and analysed in a more serious way as an integral part of the economy, with their own characteristics and structure.

The dualistic nature of the urban economy in developing countries has been the common point of departure in the search for basic concepts. Milton Santos used the terms *upper* and *lower* circuits of the economy.[1] Geertz wrote about the *firm* and *bazaar* economy.[2] Already in the 1960's, *traditional* and *modern* economy and later *informal* and *formal* sectors of the economy became common concepts. During the 1960's, theories of development came to rely upon a model based upon Lewis' work. In this, economic activities were divided into two sectors: the modern (for industry) and the traditional, which was characterized in terms of artisanship and was linked to rural poverty.[3] According to this model, the surplus of labour in the traditional sector would be gradually absorbed by the modern sector, a process which was seen as synonymous with development. Unemployment, under-employment and poverty were viewed as temporary phenomena which eventually would disappear. Rural migration into the city was regarded as the root of social and economic problems. The dualistic interpretation of the complicated urban social and economic structure

---

[1] Santos, M. (1978): *O espaço dividido: Os dois circuitos da economia urbana dos paises sub-desenvolvidos.* (original title: *L'espace partagé . Les deux circuits de l'économie urbaine des pays sous-développés).* Alves Editora. Brazil.

[2] Geertz, C. (1963): *Peddlers and Princes: Social change and economic modernization in two Indonesian towns.* Chicago.

[3] Lewis, W.A. (1954): *Economic Development with Unlimited Supplies of Labour.* Agarwala, A.N. (ed.): *The Economics of Underdevelopment.* Oxford University Press. New York.

was soon called into question, when it was demonstrated that it was not a sufficiently comprehensive framework for an analysis of all the different types of economic activities and forms of employment that exist in cities. At the same time, the optimistic view that development in the developing countries would follow the course of western industrialization faded, because, in spite of a real growth in industrial production in some countries, poverty, unemployment and other social problems did not disappear, but were intensified.

The shortcomings of this dualistic explanation have been pointed out by many authors, e.g. Joseph Gugler who wrote:

> In the 1960's renewed attention was drawn to the "murky' sector because in country after country substantial additions to the urban labour force failed to show up in employment statistics. While there was concern about unemployment, there was also an increasing recognition that a large and growing number of people were engaged in non-enumerated activities. They were thought to be working in the service sector. However, statistical enumeration is primarily a function of the size of a firm's work force, and small enterprises in the primary sector, e.g. peri-urban gardening, and in the secondary sector, shoe-making for example, are just as likely to go non-enumerated as are street vendors.[1]

Because of such criticism the need for a new concept became obvious. In the beginning of the 1970's such a new concept emerged. In a study of a low income neighbourhood in Ghana, Hart introduced a new terminology.[2] In his paper, presented in 1971, Hart emphasized the great variety of both legitimate and illegitimate income opportunities available to the urban poor, and distinguished between the formal sector and the informal sector of the economy. This terminology was later used by the International Labour Office (ILO), and in a report about Kenya by the United Nations Development Programme (UNDP) the two sectors were characterised as follows:

---

[1］ Gilbert, A. and Gugler, J. (1982): *Cities, Poverty and Development. Urbanization in the Third World*. Oxford University Press. New York. p.72.
[2］ Hart, K (1973): *Informal income opportunities and urban employment in Ghana*. Journal of Modern African Studies. No.11.

Informal activities are not confined to employment on the periphery of the main towns, to particular occupations or even to economic activities. Rather, informal activities are the way of doing things, characterised by :
–ease of entry
–reliance on indigenous resources
–small scale of operation
–labour-intensive and labour-adapted technology
–skills acquired outside the formal school system
–unregulated and competitive markets
Informal activities are largely ignored, rarely supported, often regulated and sometimes actively discouraged by the Government.

The characteristics of formal-sector activities are the obverse of these, namely,

–difficult entry
–frequent reliance on overseas resources
–corporate ownership
–large scale of operation
–capital-intensive and often imported technology
–formally acquired skills, often expatriated, and
–protected markets (through tariffs, quotas and trade licenses).[1]

This classification was widely accepted and it is still adopted by many institutions and organisations, as well as by the majority of scholars involved in studies of the informal sector; however, it has been constantly subjected to a great deal of criticism. Alejandro Portes has made important contributions to the theoretical discussion of the informal sector in general and specifically to the debate about this sector in Latin America. He emphasizes the dynamics of this sector and explains this feature in the following way:

> The informal sector is dynamic because there are few overhead costs, such as social security or the observance of health, safety or zoning ordinances. It is attractive both to those who seek to set up

---

[1] ILO (1972): *Employment, incomes and equality: a strategy for increasing productive employment in Kenya.* Geneva. p. 6.

an enterprise but are without capital reserves, as well as to those formal sector firms that wish to cut cost and gain flexibility by pulling-out work.[1]

This last aspect, "attractive to formal firms", raises questions about the relations between the two sectors. Portes sees this relation as a crucial factor that helps to maintain the low wages in the urban economy. There has, in fact, been a lively debate about the degree and nature of this interrelationship between the two sectors. There is plenty of evidence to support the conclusion that people tend to move between the two sectors, as they adapt to new life situations, from the formal to the informal and back again to the formal, and that many work in both sectors at the same time.

> Workers move easily from one sector to another or simultaneously work in both, while urban poor households generally include workers in both sectors. It is now generally recognized that the informal economy does not develop simply in the interstices of the economy in traditional activities regarded as unprofitable by the formal modern sector. On the contrary, far from being a residual sector, it is a dynamic sector, constantly being recreated and reorganized in response to changing conditions in the formal sector.[2]

Roberts maintained that economic dualism is only a tendency. He stressed the fact that most firms, large and small, operate both formally and informally depending on their product or service, the economic climate and market demand, and that informal employment is found throughout the economy.[3]

This phenomenon is now being understood as a structural and successively more permanent characteristic of current patterns of economic development in Latin America as well as in other parts of the

---

[1]. Portes, A. and Walton, J. (1981): *Labour, Class, and the International System.* Academic Press. New York.

[2]. Safa, H. (1987): *Urbanization, the Informal Economy and State Policy in Latin America.* Smith, M.P. and Feagin, J. R. (eds.): *The Capitalist City. Global Restructuring and Community Politics.* Basil Blackwell. New York. p. 257.

[3]. Roberts, B. (1989): *Employment Structure, Life Cycle, and Life Changes: Formal and Informal Sectors in Guadalajara.* Portes, A., Castells, M., and Benton, L. (eds.): *The Informal Economy. Studies in Advanced and Less Developed Countries.* Johns Hopkins University Press. London.

Third World. The ILO report from 1972 pointed out the existence of these relations and recommended strengthening the linkages between the two sectors as a strategy for promoting the informal sector.[1] Research done in the last few years shows, however, that these linkages do not promote development of the informal sector. If we return to Portes' definition of the informal sector, he distinguishes three modes of production within it: direct subsistence, petty commodity production and exchange (based on the labour of those self-employed who produce goods and services for the market), and backward capitalistic production which includes small enterprises employing unprotected wage workers (i.e. hired by larger firms on a casual or subcontracting basis).[2] He points out that originally those three forms of production in the informal sector served to satisfy the needs of the poor, providing them with goods and services at lower prices than in the formal sector, and that petty commodity production and direct subsistence production were the most important forms.

Over the last few years, the relationship between these modes of production have changed. As relations to the formal sector have increased in importance, an expansion in the more backward forms of capitalistic production in the informal sector has taken place. This has not improved the situation of the poor, but rather come about in order to fulfil the needs of the formal sector. These interrelations have been studied by several authors, for instance by Roldán in her study of industrial homework in Mexico. She described this as linked to the formal sector, through several stages of subcontracting from small, through larger, and finally to multinational enterprises. Seventy per cent of the studied enterprises had linkages with multinational firms. Portes sees these relations primarily as an expansion of the informal sector, which he does not regard as totally dependent on the formal sector. Roldán, however, goes further and points out that:

> The formal/informal dichotomy assumes that the two sectors are autonomous, when in fact the nature of their relationship is one of

---

[1]. ILO (1972): *Employment, incomes and equity—a strategy for increasing productive employment in Kenya*. Geneva.

[2]. Portes, A. and Walton, J. (1981): *Labour, Class, and the International System*. Academic Press. New York.

domination/subordination. This is shown by empirical studies that revealed the comprehensive networks of economic relations which bind the ostensibly independent informal sector to the industrial, modern economy, and its contribution to the daily and generational reproduction of its work force.[1]

Portes primarily sees the relationship between the two sectors as a result of the institutional boundaries of the economy:

> The informal economy is thus not an individual condition but a process of income-generation characterized by one central feature: it is unregulated by the institutions of society, in a legal and social environment in which similar activities are regulated. Any change in the institutional boundaries of regulation of economic activities produces a parallel realignment of the formal-informal relationship. In fact, it is because there is a formal economy that we can talk of an "informal" one. In an ideal market economy, with no regulation of any kind, the distinction between formal and informal would lose meaning since all the activities would be performed in the manner we now call informal.[2]

Not just the concept of, but also the very term informal sector has generated, and is still generating considerable debate, although it has been widely accepted and used for more than two decades. The principal critique is that it is impossible to incorporate within one single sector so many different types of production. This heterogeneousness is the major impediment to efforts to develop a conclusive definition.

> It has to be realised that there is no one single definition of the "informal sector", because it constitutes a complex of productive

---

[1]. Roldán, M. (1987): *Yet Another Meeting on the Informal Sector? Or the Politics of Designation and Economic Restructuring in a Gendered World*. Proceedings from a conference in Denmark. *The Informal Sector as an Integral Part of the National Economy. Research Needs and Aid Requirements*. Roskilde. p. 29.

[2]. Portes, A. and Castells, M. (1989): *World Underneath: The Origins, Dynamics, and Effects of the Informal Economy*. Portes, A., Castells, M., and Benton, L. (eds.): *The Informal Economy. Studies in Advance and Less Developed Countries*. John Hopkins University Press. London. pp 12-13.

and reproductive processes which cannot be contained in one single definition.[1]

Norlund partly criticizes Portes' definition because he does not take reproductive activities into account, and consequently not gender relations. Norlund chose to use the term "informal work" instead of informal sector, and argues:

> When I refer to informal work and not the informal sector it is in an attempt to indicate that informal work can comprise many different kinds of work: productive or reproductive, paid or unpaid, work which is related to the capitalist sector/state sector or independent work (petty commodity production). If non-income generating or reproductive activities are to be included, it is necessary to move closer to the base of society, to the household level.[2]

The case for rejecting the informal sector as an analytical category has been summarized by Martha Roldán.

> The concept of informal sector, rather than providing an explanation, offers a merely descriptive insight into certain occupational categories. The concept offers no specific criteria which allow the identification of a particular activity with one, rather than the other sector (i.e. without defining activities in one sector except by reference to their lack of characteristics exemplifying activities in the other sector). The conceptualization therefore does not offer any internal theoretical coherence, but it comprises an agglomeration of arbitrarily chosen social phenomena whose selection and promotion may vary according to specific institutional priorities.[3]

Also, Sethuraman comments that:

> Though it has gained wide currency the concept has remained elusive and controversial and sometimes acted as a deterrent for initi-

---

[1]. Norlund, I. (1990): *Informal Work: Textile Women in Vietnam and the Philippines*. Datta, S. (ed.): *Third World Urbanization: Reappraisals and New Perspectives*. Swedish Council for Research in the Humanities and Social Sciences. Urban Studies. Stockholm. p. 118.

[2]. Norlund, I. (1990). p. 124.

[3]. Roldán, M. (1987). p. 29.

ating further action. It should be stated at the outset that the terminology 'informal sector' is but a shorthand connotation to describe a variety of heterogeneous activities.[1]

Another strong flow of criticism has come from scholars with a gender perspective. They criticize the concept for not taking into account the gendered forms of production and reproduction in the sector and the subordination of women in these processes.

In spite of such criticisms, the majority of those who have discussed this matter agree that, in the absence of a better term, we should continue to use the term informal sector. Sethuraman, despite his criticism, comes to the conclusion that, though the informal-formal terminology was not satisfactory from all points of view, it had gained wide currency both in the literature and development programmes and that he thought that it had come to stay.[2]

Since that was written in the early 1980's, the debate has continued, and some scholars have preferred to use the term *informal activities* within the context of *informalization processes*.

A large number of studies have focused upon the central role of the informal sector as a part of the survival strategies of the poor in the cities of developing countries, and the movements of workers between the two sectors have been seen as important components of these survival strategies.[3] As part of these survival strategies, the informal sector has been viewed not only as a set of purely economic activities, but as an entire way of life or an informalization culture, as Brian Roberts[4]

---

[1]. Sethuraman, S.V. (1987): *The Informal Sector and the Poor in the Third World*. Proceedings from a conference in Denmark. *The Informal Sector as an Integral Part of the National Economy. Research Needs and Aid Requirements*. Roskilde. p. 136.

[2]. Sethuraman, S.V. (ed.) (1981): *The Urban Informal sector in Developing Countries. Employment, Poverty and Environment*. ILO. Geneva.

[3]. Gonzalez, A. (1990): *Informal Sector and Survival Strategies: An Historical Approach. Third World Urbanization: Reappraisals and New Perspectives*. Urban Studies. Swedish Council for Research in the Humanities and Social Sciences. Stockholm; Peattie, L. R. (1975): *Tertiarization, Marginality and Urban Poverty in Latin America*. Latin American Urban Research. Vol. 5. Sage Publications. London; Pahl, R. (1980): *Employment, work and the domestic division of labour*. International Journal of Urban and Regional Research. Vol. 1. London; Pahl, R. and Wallace, C. (1985): *Household work strategies in economic recession*. Redclift, N. and Mingione, E. (eds.): *Beyond Employment: Household, Gender and Subsistence*. Basil Blackwell. Oxford.

[4]. Roberts, B. (1978): *Cities of Peasants: the political economy of urbanization* in the Third World. Edward Arnold. London.

has called it. Within this context, the informal sector also includes the local relationships and social networks expressed in kinship and community relations, which together form a kind of protective net for the workers in the informal sector. This defence mechanism protects the poor in the city who do not have the individual skills and qualifications, such as formal education, needed for entering the competitive formal sector. Jobs in the informal sector are often filled through kinship and community connections and it is often very difficult for outsiders to become part of these networks. [1]

Policies toward the informal sector

Originally the term informal sector was introduced in order to emphasize the significance of self-employment and small-scale enterprises in providing work in developing countries. A main problem, however, has been to distinguish between the formal and informal sector, and a clear distinction with regard to the type of activities has not always been easy to maintain. Many activities are related in various ways to the formal sector, for instance. This difficulty has always impeded adequate policy formulations towards the informal sector. However, because of the magnitude of the informal sector in the cities of developing countries and its significance in a short time perspective as the major source of income for most of the poor, a different attitude on the part of governments has slowly been emerging. The ILO report from Kenya played an important role in this process, because it recommended the Kenyan government to promote the informal sector by increasing the demand for products and services from this sector.[2] According to ILO, informal sector activities make a valuable contribution to the overall urban economy and, because of the modest capital requirements, should be seen as a significant and cost-effec-

---

[1]. Mingione, E. (1987): *Urban Survival Strategies, Family Structure and Informal Practices. The Capitalist City. Global Restructuring and Community Polities*. Basil Blackwell. New York.

[2]. ILO (1972): *Employment, incomes and equity—a strategy for increasing productive employment in Kenya*. Geneva.

tive way in which the rapidly growing urban labour force could be absorbed.

The World Commission for the Environment and Development, appointed by the United Nations in 1987, also put special emphasis on the informal sector, linking it to urban development.

> In most of the developing countries, between 25 and 50 per cent of the economically active population in the cities can not find a satisfactory and stable income. When only a few job opportunities exist in the formal sector, these people are obliged to create their own jobs. This led to a rapid growth in the so-called 'informal sector' which accounts for a large part of the low-priced goods and services that are needed for the city's economy and consumers." And, "Governments should give greater support to the informal sector and recognize its vital role for urban development.[1]

Several examples of concrete measures intended to provide such support can be found, but so far they can not be said to have contributed substantially either to the improvement of the informal sector or the conditions of the people involved in its activities. Governments have chosen to reinforce and support primarily those activities in the informal sector which are characterized by small-scale production and which are connected to the formal sector.

Helen Safa has suggested that this change in governments' attitude towards some informal activities in part can be explained by the characteristics of the sector itself.

> Because of its capacity for labour absorption and cost advantages in a highly competitive international market, the informal economy is receiving increased support from both the private and public sector in terms of credit, access to raw materials and foreign exchange, and other privileges formerly reserved exclusively for the formal sector. This represents a clear change in attitude on the part of government agencies, who formerly tended to regard the informal sector as an

---

[1.] Hägerhäll, B. (ed.) (1988): *Vår gemensamma framtid*. Rapport från världskommissionen för miljö och utveckling. Prisma/Tiden. Stockholm. p. 272. (Free translation from the Swedish version of the report).

obstacle to development and treated it with benign neglect or outright repression.[1]

Safa presents several examples of such support from Colombia and the Dominican Republic, where governments directly supported industrial homework as a form of subcontracting to firms in the formal economy which were further linked to the international economy. As Roldán did in the case of Mexico, Safa concluded that this form of support in fact is a form of exploitation, because wages are kept below the minimum rates, and the fringe benefits and the general working conditions are poor. Portes has pointed out that this kind of support tends to encourage expansion of the informal sector.

> In general, informal activities appear to expand most rapidly in those countries where state regulation of the economy is extensive and cost differentials between the two sectors are significant. On the other hand, in countries where the state has consistently adopted anti-labour and deregulatory policies, the distinction between formal and informal sector becomes blurred.[2]

Another consequence of this type of economic support, which furthers the interests of firms in the formal sector by reducing their production costs, is that it leads to a weakening of the collective bargaining power of labour. Thus it is an open question whether this change in the attitude of some governments towards activities in the informal sector has predominantly negative or positive effects for those who work in this sector or for urban development in general.

The uncertainty as to which occupational categories and types of activities should be included in the informal sector, and the disagreement among scholars about the very validity of the concept, have also meant that governments and aid agencies have become hesitant as to which actions to take in order to support this sector. Doubts about whether economic support should be channelled to enterprises, households, or individuals have led to a lack of well-defined aid pro-

---

[1]. Safa, H. (1987): *Urbanization, the Informal Economy and State Policy in Latin America.* Smith, M.P. and Feagin, J. R. (eds.): *The Capitalist City. Global Restructuring and Community Polities.* Basil Blackwell. New York. p. 261.

[2]. Portes, A. and Benton, L. (1984): *Industrial development and labor absorption: a reinterpretation.* Population and Development Review No. 10: 4. p. 615.

grammes. Roldán includes this aspect in her critique of the informal sector concept :

> ...finally the theoretical stance implicit in the informal sector perspective encourages the formulation of generalized and undifferentiated policies whose impact is either neutral or prejudicial for the majority of individuals and enterprises found in the local informal sector. In fact, membership of this sector extends to several classes and class fractions whose interests are neither identical nor necessarily complementary.[1]

In a conference in Denmark in 1987,"The informal sector as an integral part of the national economy. Research needs and aid requirements", the participants came to the conclusion that no effective forms of support to the informal sector exist. There was general agreement that a primary goal should be to improve education, not only in terms of technical skills but also with respect to basic social and political organisation. It was also generally agreed that it is very difficult to give direct support at the household level because of the diversity of activities and work relations of households. Furthermore, the fact that aid is usually given through state agencies, and generally is given directly to production units, was pointed out as an impediment to the introduction of new forms of support. It seemed to be a common and accepted idea that aid policies must be part of a global economic plan in order to be integrated in the country/city development process.

It is in fact possible to find many examples of support to informal activities both through credit and through direct financial assistance, especially to small-scale production units. However, new difficulties have arisen when it comes to identify target groups for support projects. New forms of employment strategies by the low income households in the city, which sometimes transcend the traditional definition of the sector, in particular regarding its separation from the formal sector, have made the definition if not meaningless, at least

---

[1]. Roldán, M. (1987). pp. 29-30.

somewhat obsolete. With respect to this new situation the UNRISD 1995 report states:

> Intra-group divisions have also become sharper and deeper in the informal sector. A relatively small group of informal entrepreneurs with skills, capital assets and, in some cases, political connections has been able to exploit new market opportunities. Thus, when governments have tried to support the informal sector by creating targeted credit schemes, the benefits have frequently been captured by middle-class individuals who are more adept at dealing with officials. Meanwhile, most informal workers face increasing competition and are struggling to survive.[1]

The informal sector and development theories

The informal sector has been described as illegal, parasitic, speculative and anti-revolutionary, it has been accused of provoking hyper-inflation and social inequality in the city, and it has been regarded either as a menace to or as essential for the formal sector. These dissimilar and even antagonistic perspectives have to be understood against the background of prevailing theories of development. The question is if the informal sector contributes to growth or if it is an impediment to development.

In the 1950's and 1960's the liberal theories of growth and modernization conceived of development as a unilinear process of change from a traditional state to a modern state based on industrial models of development. A major aspect of that development process was the diffusion of social, political, and cultural forms associated with modern industrial societies. That diffusion would take place through a "trickle-down" effect, and social conflicts associated with rapid urbanization were expected to be transient. Unemployment, underemployment, squatter settlements and poverty in general should disappear when migrants become part of the modern economy. These theories recog-

---

[1] UNRISD (1995): *States of Disarray. The social effects of globalization*. Report for the World Summit for Social Development. UNRISD. London. p. 48.

nized the dualism of the economy but regarded this as a transitory phenomenon. The informal sector was seen as a practice of migrants and backward rural people, and therefore as a parasitic sector which should be absorbed by the modern one.

This view of development was mainly based on dualistic theories, and influenced by the work of Oscar Lewis[1] and also by that of Rogers[2] who regarded the poor as a sub-culture; in the case of the former –the culture of poverty, and in the case of the latter –a peasant sub-culture. Both considered the poor to be impassive actors, lacking the initiative necessary to improve their situation, in fact responsible for being in a state of poverty. These approaches have been broadly criticized because they have spread through the world an image of the poor as apathetic masses without ambitions and therefore unable to participate in development processes.

It is important to keep in mind that the emergence and prestige of the dualistic theories coincided with a period when Latin America experienced fast rates of industrial growth, with the support of foreign capital. That partly explains why other forms of production but the "modern" were seen as parasitic and not contributing to development. For W.A. Lewis, development was related to industrial development. The modern industrializing sector should absorb labour surplus in the traditional sector, and it that way the problem of poverty should be solved.[3] The work by Geertz and Santos within the framework of dualistic theories had another and very different view of the role of what they termed the bazaar or lower circuit sector of the economy, respectively. They stressed the importance of the interplay between these sectors and the modern or upper circuit and the positive role that these sectors could play in the creation of jobs.

Dependency theories and Marxist theories in part were a reaction to the failure of modernization theories. In the 1970's the expectations that these theories had raised, had not, despite industrial growth, been realized. The diffusion of wealth by trickle-down processes had not

---

[1]. Lewis, O. (1970): *The Culture of Poverty*. Anthropological Essays. Random House.
[2]. Rogers, E.M. (1969): *Modernization among Peasants*. Michican State University.
[3]. Lewis, W.A. (1954): *Economic Development with Unlimited Supplies of Labour*. Agarwala, A.N. (ed.): *The Economics of Underdevelopment*. Oxford University Press. New York; Lewis, W.A. (1955): *The Theory of Economic Growth*. Allen and Unwin. London.

come about and the gap between rich and poor had widened. The failure of modernization models of development was interpreted in terms of the relationship between underdeveloped countries – the periphery, and developed countries – the centre, in which the dependent position of the periphery meant that it basically just contributed to the wealth of the centre. These theories rejected the dualistic view of the economy in developing countries. The urban economy was seen as a whole with a dominant capital intensive production sector. Activities and labour which could not find a place in that sector were regarded as marginal and as an impediment to development.

Quijano, emphasizing the importance of different modes of production, argued that petty commodity production was independent of capitalist production, and that the relationship between capitalist and non-capitalist production resulted in the latter being exploited by the former. In this process, the poor engaged in non-capitalist modes of production remain poor because they provide the capitalist production sector with cheap labour.[1] Tokman approached the question of dependency in another way, and regarded the informal sector as an integral part of the urban economy but at the same time an exploited one.[2] Within this context, special emphasis has been put on the relations between the formal and informal sectors, and also on the impact of the new international division of labour.[3]

Neo-modernization theory in the 1980's saw the role of the informal sector in development as a positive element, and viewed the sector as a dynamic factor in development processes. ILO's call to all countries for support of the informal sector was an important step

---

[1.] Quijano, A. (1974): *The marginal pole of the economy and the marginalised labour force.* Economy and Society. No. 3; Quijano, A. (1975): *The Urbanization of Latin American Society.* Hardoy, J. (ed.): *Urbanization in Latin America.* Anchor Books. New York.

[2.] Tokman, V.E. (1978): *An exploration into the nature of informal-formal sector relationships.* World Development. No. 6.

[3.] Schteingart, M. (1990): *Production and Reproduction Practices in the Informal Sector: The Case of Mexico. Third World Urbanization: Reappraisals and New Perspectives.* Swedish Council for Research in the Humanities and Social Sciences. Stockholm. Walton, J. (ed.) (1985): *Capital and Labour in the Urbanized World.* California.

towards the recognition of the significance of this sector for development. The neo-liberal De Soto[1] regarded underdevelopment as a direct result of state control which tended to impede development through free enterprise. He saw the informal sector as the main generator of development because it is independent of all formal bureaucratic systems.

During the first half of the 1990's, neo-liberalism seems to have dominated the discussion on development in Latin America. Market capitalism seems to be accepted as the only path towards development, and individual rather than collective achievement is encouraged. In practice, "Structural Adjustment Policies" developed by the International Monetary Fund and the World Bank are the dominant expressions of neo-liberalism.

Presently no consensus exists with regard to the role of the informal sector or the policies that might be implemented in order to improve the way in which it functions. On one hand, the optimistic view of the informal sector as dynamic, whether dependent or independent of the formal sector, is disappearing. The size of the sector is regarded as alarming, and there are signs that unemployment is spreading in the sector. Underemployment is certainly rising and the generally very low income of the workers in the sector is a matter of great concern. In the past, it used to be easy to get into the informal sector, but because of higher competition within the sector there are now many and new barriers that restrict entry, and the often unsuccessful struggle to create a job is resulting in increasing criminal activities in the city. On the other hand, the urban informal sector is estimated to make an important contribution to the regional and national domestic product. Two thirds of the urban population in Latin America are employed in the informal sector but the majority of them are desperately poor. Sethuraman talks about the marginalisation of the sector, referring to the increase in service and other activities that do not require capital inputs, and to generally falling incomes. He regards the magnitude of the sector as a matter of major concern, because as the sector is growing, the possibilities of lifting the workers above the poverty line are

---

[1]. De Soto, H. (1991): *El otro sendero*. Mexico. Primera edición peruana 1986. Instituto Libertad y Democracia.

diminishing. Furthermore, if output and employment in the public and in the modern private sector fail to show rapid growth, the pressure on the informal sector to create more jobs, especially for the poor, is likely to increase, and this will be accompanied by falling incomes and further deterioration of the living situation of the poor. In order to avoid involuntary expansion of the informal sector, which implies higher unemployment and falling incomes for the workers, it is imperative, according to Sethuraman, that a strategy to develop the urban informal sector be accompanied by growth-oriented strategies. The movement out of formal employment to informal employment puts even greater pressure on those who are already struggling to make a living in the overcrowded informal sector.[1]

Martha Roldán summarizes how the informal sector has been viewed during the last few decades:

> In sum, there is – in a period of 30 years, and with regard to discovered economic practices – a movement from derision/indifference (in the 1950's and 60's), to promotion with optimism, as a source of growth (in the 1970's), to promotion or acknowledgment with resignation, as survival strategies, (in the 1980's). There appears, therefore, an involution of thought. The old working poor of the 50's and 60's, transformed into capitalist entrepreneurs during the 70's are now returning to the poor. They are once again struggling for survival, rather than contributing to growth.[2]

Notwithstanding that there are different opinions as whether the dualistic view of the urban economy is or is not an appropriate way of studying and understanding the complexity of urbanization processes, this approach has not really been replaced by any other. The basic concept, and the terminology associated with it, has been the focus of discussion from the time when it was introduced until now – thirty years later – and still there is no equally well established alternative. Without doubt, the terms informal and formal sector have become very common and are broadly used by governments, policy makers, aid agen-

---

[1]. Sethuraman, S.V. (1994): *The Challenge of Urban Poverty in Developing Countries: Coping with the Informal Sector.* ILO. Geneva. (Working paper. Not published at the time of a personal interview with the author in April 1994).

[2]. Roldán, M. (1987). p. 41.

cies and scholars at both national and international levels. In the context of this study, which deals with child work in the urban environment, there is no doubt that a realistic conception of the character of the informal sector is fundamental.

However, child work in the informal sector has not been studied as much as the work of adults in the sector, although it is an integral part of that sector of the economy and therefore affects its evolution.. One might well argue that an increasing participation of children is bound to influence the process of marginalization and pauperization of the sector. Also, it seems likely that children will be the first victims of increasing competition and unemployment in this sector.

Chapter 3

Child work

The concentration of working children to developing countries reflects, in the first place, the poverty of themselves and their families, and must, in a broader context be seen as one result of economic processes and policies which have successively produced greater inequalities between North and South and increasing inequalities within countries.

It was not until 1979, which was proclaimed as The International Year of the Child, that the issue of child work really was brought to light, with the focus on the working children's living conditions in both rural and urban areas. No one knows how many children work. However, recent estimations by the International Labour Office (ILO) in 1996, suggest that in the developing countries alone, about 120 million children in the 5-14 age group are fully at work and around 250 million have work as a secondary activity.[1] About seven percent live in Latin America. The difficulty of estimating the number of children at work is often stressed both by ILO and other UN agencies as well as by individual researchers. They all agree that the estimations of child work are much too low, mainly because of the lack of reliable statistical data in most developing countries and because of various methodological problems in estimating the number of the working children. However, in my opinion a major hindrance for the production of reliable data is the lack of internationally accepted definitions of child work.

[1.] ILO (1996): *Child labour targeting the intolerable.* Geneva. p. 7.

Since the early 1980's, much has been written about child work. However, very little is still done, through global or national policies, in order to improve the generally poor conditions of life of the low income households and consequently of the children belonging to those households. Child centred policies have been required and recommended by organizations and agencies concerned with children's conditions of life, but only a start has been made. Structural Adjustment Programmes, external debts, market liberalisation and so forth have actually led to a more severe lack of employment, both in cities and in rural areas, and consequently to the impoverishment of new groups of the population, increasing the differences between rich and poor.

Child work might not always be an extreme alternative for poor households. In fact there are many exceptions to that situation. There are some data on non-poor children who want to work in order to become economically independent, and on others who prefer to work rather than to study. Many children work, not by necessity, together with their parents in family enterprises or workshops, and there is evidence that in one and the same country poor children do not work (mainly due to the lack of employment in their region) and that non-poor children work, e.g. in seasonal work. However, poverty and child work generally go together. Also, ILO's report showed that 95 percent of child work is found in developing countries.[1]

When children work because of their families poverty, child work has to be considered as one extreme alternative that low income households choose in order to cope with a critical lack of resources; children are often sent to work when all other possibilities have been exhausted. Child work is an expression of the second lowest level of poverty, when both the child and the household together, as a unit, search for ways to satisfy their daily needs; at that stage the child's contribution is indispensable to the household economy. The bottom level is the state of indigence, when the family structure disintegrates, and the child no longer has the support of a household but is left on

---

[1] ILO (1986): *Child Labour: A briefing manual.* Geneva. ILO (1983): *Report of the Director-General. Part I: Child Labour.* International Labour Conference. 67th Session. Geneva.

its own to fight for survival. Without the economic contribution of working children, the households would be poorer and the children would be even more seriously affected by poverty.

Child work is a complex issue to study. It involves moral, cultural, social, economic, civic, human rights, legal and political aspects. These aspects are often interpreted and acted upon in different ways by different actors – organizations, institutions and governments. Some authors draw parallels between child work and the work of women in terms of the availability of cheap labour as a pre-requisite for the survival of small-scale economic activities, both in goods and service production; both women and children are often self-employed or poorly paid and unpaid family workers. This type of work often lacks social recognition, is usually associated with very low payment, sometimes in kind, and long working days. However, children are even more exposed as workers than women, simply because of their status as minors and also because of the special characteristics of their work.

Today, child work is in fact illegal in the sense that it is not permitted by existing national labour legislation. However, only some countries have adopted the "Minimum Age Convention" of the ILO, that deals with admission to employment, and have included it in their national labour legislation.[1] The United Nations Convention on the Rights of the Child, 1989, Article 32, provides for a range of measures to be taken with regard to child work, including legislative measures.[2] The fact is, however, that there is an illegal labour force of more than two hundred million people in the world – the children – who in reality are

---

[1] The Convention No. 138, "Minimum Age for Admission to Employment", in article 2 establishes at least two minimum ages for admission to employment below which "*no-one under that age shall be admitted to employment or work in any occupation*". The general minimum age shall not *be less than the age of completion of compulsory schooling and, in any case, shall not be less than 15 years, 14 years for countries whose economy and educational programmes are not sufficiently developed.* 49 countries had adopted the Convention No. 138, until June 1996. A new ILO Convention on the most intorelable forms of child labour is under preparation to be adopted in 1999.

[2] Article 32 of *The Convention on the Rights of the Child* requires that states recognize the "right of the child to be protected from economic exploitation and from performing any work that is likely to be hazardous or to interfere with the child's education, or to be harmful to the child's health or physical, mental, spiritual, moral or social development", and the adoption of legislative, administrative, social and educational measures "to ensure the implementation of the present article".

not protected by the regulations on working conditions dictated by international and national labour laws, and who therefore are highly vulnerable to exploitation in the labour market.

Because of their status as minors, children are unable to effectively resist exploitation and to apply for justice. Children are not able to organize themselves in unions in order to defend their own interests as workers - in fact they are not supposed to work - and no labour union might represent them because they are minors. They are regarded as being under the guardianship of adults and not as responsible individuals who often play a vital role for their own economy and for that of their families. Finally, because of their age, children cannot effectively organize themselves as a political pressure group.

Child work is not only found in developing countries. Reports from the Anti-Slavery International have repeatedly denounced the miserable working conditions and the exploitation of working children also in so-called developed countries in Europe and in the USA, generally resulting from the increasingly uneven access to resources within these societies. However, in this section, the focus will be on child work in developing countries.

Child work in the literature: some general characteristics

Child work is a large subject and has been approached in many different ways. In this section, therefore, a broad picture of research on child work will be presented on the basis of a review of the literature. However, the literature is voluminous and it is beyond the scope of this study to do justice to all the aspects related to child work that it deals with. Rather, the intention is to try to give the reader a general idea about the focus and trends of studies on child work.[1]

The years around 1980 mark the beginning of a period in which interest in research on children has constantly increased in scope and

---

[1]. Relevant literature for the study area of the present work will be specifically referred to in Part Two.

intensity. In particular, a growing interest in studying children as social actors led to changes in the focus of research. Whereas children had previously been the subject of research particularly in medicine, pedagogy, demography and psychology, the attention of researchers in the social sciences was now beginning to be drawn to the category of children at work. From that time, much has been written about working children, although by no means all of the literature is actually based on research. In fact only a modest amount of child work studies have been done by social scientists. In the last few years an increasing number of sociologists, anthropologists and demographers have entered this field.

The review of the literature showed that it is quite difficult to talk about research on child work without mentioning some Inter-Governmental Organizations (IGO), with the ILO as the leading one. In fact, most of the research that is of particular relevance for the present study has been done under the auspices of ILO or has at least been published by this organization. Thus a distinction will be made in the following between work that has been done by IGOs, individual scientists, and Non-Governmental Organizations (NGO), for example Save the Children, Anti-Slavery International and other.

To begin with the last category, the NGOs, it is clear that their principal objective is not to undertake research on children at work. For these organizations, which typically work directly with children in various circumstances, children at work is only one category of concern and clearly not the one that has drawn most of their attention. Instead, their principal focus has been on homeless children and children in prostitution.

However, the NGOs have also produced a number of reports on child work, which can be broadly classified as attempts either to campaign for the civil and political rights of the children, or to bring to light in a more general way the unfulfilled needs of the children. Most of these reports have been produced by activists within these organizations without specific research skills or experience. With a few exceptions, they are descriptions of situations at the national or local level, often reflecting the author's personal experiences of working directly with children and a genuine interest in improving the conditions of life of children.

A major criticism that can be levelled at these studies is that they often uncritically use secondary sources, mostly from the media world, and seldom base the results upon own investigations. This has made them less useful in the attempts to develop meaningful indicators of the situation of children and as a result the reports are almost impossible to use for comparative purposes. However, despite their methodological shortcomings, such reports from NGOs have been of immense importance in bringing the life situation of children at work to the attention of the public in general, of aid agencies and governments. Some of them have been path-breaking by revealing the most severe situations of children at work such as in carpet-making, mining, in textile industries, in the streets in urban areas, in bondage and in prostitution.[1]

An example is the series of eight reports by The Anti-Slavery International for the United Nations Standing Committee on Modern Forms of Slavery, which deal with child labour in various industries and activities.[2] These reports were of a descriptive character and were mostly based upon secondary sources; no common aims or methods were established in advance and this render it almost impossible to compare results. However, the report on Jamaica[3] is an exception as it used a structured methodology which assured consistency in the data collection. It is quite possible that much more has been done in research by NGOs, but as the results have not been published or spread outside their respective countries, it is not available.

Research on child work undertaken by independent scientists is not as abundant as might be expected, and is sometimes presented as a part of an educational career and therefore difficult to obtain. The high costs of intensive field work and a lack of economic support for this kind of research – child work does not seem to be an attractive subject for research sponsors – and perhaps the lack of prestige in the subject area (because it is not a traditional research area), rather than a lack of interest, can explain the scarcity of original research. Individual

---

[1]. See reports of e.g. Anti-Slavery International, Save the children, Rädda Barnen.

[2]. Anti-Slavery International (1979-1987): reports on child labour in Morocco, India, Thailand, South Africa, Spain, Italy, Jamaica and the United Kingdom. London.

[3]. Ennew, J. and Young, P. (1982): *Child Labour in Jamaica*. Anti-Slavery International. London.

research on child work was first performed by anthropologists and focused on its role in the socialization processes which prepare the child for a useful and rewarding adult life. In a societal perspective, work has been seen to have implications for the transmission of skills, the evolution of attitudes to work, class consciousness, and the social division of labour. Socialization processes, rather than the economic significance of the work of children, were thus the focus of research.

With few exceptions, these studies concentrated on rural societies. Child work was studied from a demographic perspective, especially in the context of fertility, and not explicitly as a component of the rural economy. Two scholars are usually mentioned as pioneers in this kind of studies. Cain wrote in 1978 about child work in a village in Bangladesh and used a time budget approach in his analysis of the participation of children in work.[1] Schildkrout looked at the relationship between children's work and women's work in Kano, India.[2] Anthropologists occupy an important place in research on children but, here as well, street children have been the focus of attention, and cultural rather than economic aspects dominate the research. Still, anthropologists have often been pioneers in trying new and more sophisticated methods and are also often careful in describing their methodologies. In the economic sciences, research on child work has not been a high-prestige field, and in fact purely economic research is not abundant in the literature. Alia Ahmad's work on child labour in Bangladesh is an example of a purely economic study on child work. Tienda's study on the economic activities of children in Peru is a valuable contribution to the literature.[3]

The role of the IGOs in research on child work is of unquestionable importance. They are the largest producers and sponsors of studies. These organizations not only publish results of research undertaken by qualified experts on their own staff, but has also financed a great deal

---

[1.] Cain, M. (1978): *The Economic Activities of Children in a Village in Bangladesh.* Population and development studies.

[2.] Schildkrout, E. (1981): *The employment of children in Kano.* Rogers, G. and Standing, G. (eds.): *Child Labour, Poverty and Underdevelopment.* International Labour Office. Geneva.

[3.] Tienda, M. (1979): *The Economic Activity of Children in Peru: Labor Force Behaviour in Rural and Urban Contexts.* Rural Sociology.

of other research. They have also played an important role by directly or indirectly introducing new concepts and definitions which have come to be used both by independent researchers and by NGOs in their programmes and documentation, and thus have also directly or indirectly influenced the "trends" which dominate research. The United Nations (UN) agencies World Health Organization (WHO), United Nations Children's Fund (UNICEF), and ILO are the leading in child work issues, but the United Nations Development Programme (UNDP) has also played a significant role by supporting statistical surveys that have partly been aimed at producing information about the conditions of life of the low income households and consequently of the children of those households. WHO's contributions have naturally focused on health aspects of child labour, as in the 1987 report "Children at Work: Special Health Risks".[1]

UNICEF has had a much broader role than WHO in research on child work. However, child work has not had as predominant a place in these studies as the category of street children.[2] An important research contribution was the establishment of "Situational Analyses", to be performed in all countries where UNICEF is represented. These have already been carried out in many countries. However, the validity of some of the categories included can be discussed. These analyses are intended to produce comparable and cumulative information about the conditions of life of "Minors in Specially Difficult Circumstances" (UNICEF definition), with children at work included in various sub-categories of that group. They are based upon guidelines established or proposed in the agency's "Methodological Guide". This guide is a valuable contribution to the development of standardized basic indicators which can be used in research on child work. The idea behind these guidelines is that both NGO's and researchers sponsored

---

[1] WHO (1987): *Children at Work: Special Health Risks*. Technical report series. No. 756. Geneva.

[2] "Street children" is a definition of UNICEF that has drawn much attention and also criticism. It has led to the emergence of two other concepts, "children in the street" and "children of the street", distinguishing between the children who live in the street and those who work in the street but belong to a household. This distinction has in its turn also met some criticism.

by the agency should use them in research on variously defined groups of children.

These situational analyses have produced much useful data about working children in Latin America. "En la calle. Menores trabajadores de la calle en Asunción", about the situation of the children working in the streets of Asunción, Paraguay, is a good example of these publications.[1] Apart from these, there exist other publications which are the result of research sponsored by UNICEF and its International Child Development Centre in Florence. In general, however, studies about child work are less well represented than studies of other aspects of children's life.

Since 1979 ILO has run a research programme which has produced reports on child work. The first of these reports presented broad panorama sketches of the problem at the regional or country level, but based only upon secondary sources of an official character.[2] The work by Elias Mendelievich, "Children at work", is a good example.[3] The aim was to provide broad information on the problem of child labour in various parts of the world, both in developed and developing countries, embracing most of the issues related to child work, legislative framework, types of employment, sectors of employment and working conditions, without going very deeply into any of these aspects, and mainly concentrating on the formal sector of the economy. In 1982, a book edited by Rodgers and Standing, "Child work, Poverty and Underdevelopment", marked a turning-point in research on child work, and in my opinion it has still not been surpassed in terms of breadth and depth of its conceptual and methodological contributions.[4] The editors' article "The economic roles of children: Issues for

---

[1]. Espínola, B., Glauser, B., Ortiz, R.M. and Carrizosa, S.O.(1989): *En La Calle. Menores trabajadores de la calle de Asunción*. UNICEF. Serie Metodológica. Programa Regional. No. 4. Bogotá.

[2]. The list of this type of studies/reports is enormous. See e.g. Bossio, J.C. (1991): *Algunos planteamientos acerca del trabajo infantil en América Latina*. Seminario Regional Latinoamericano. OIT. Quito; OIT (1994): *El trabajo infantil en Argentina. Propuesta para un Programa Nacional de Acción*. Geneva; Bossio, J.C. (ed.) (1993): *El trabajo infantil en el Perú* . OIT. Geneva; OIT (1993): *El trabajo infantil en Venezuela. Bases para la adopción de un Programa de Acción*. OIT. Geneva.

[3]. Mendelievich, E. (1979): *Children at work*. International Labour Office. Geneva.

[4]. Rodgers, G. and Standing, G. (eds.) (1982): *Child work, Poverty and Underdevelopment*. International Labour Office. Geneva.

analysis" is the first ever attempt to classify the economic activities of children in an economic perspective and also highlights the difficulties of this task. The quality of the contributions to this book makes it a unique achievement even today, fifteen years after its publication.

Other types of reports have also been published, some at the regional level and others at the national level, in an attempt to obtain statistical data on child work, that would permit the establishment of National Programmes of Action in order to combat child labour. These reports and studies have often been made in collaboration with UNICEF and regional ILOs. A further contribution has been the elaboration of a guide for project design by Alec Fyfe (1993).[1] Because of these and other efforts it is within ILO's publications that so far the most complete and valuable research can be found.

3.2 The legislative approach

Child work has been an issue of major concern for the ILO. The principal goal of the organization has been the total abolition of child labour in the world, in accordance with ILO's Minimum Age Convention No. 138 from 1973.[2] The establishment in 1992 of the International Programme on the Elimination of Child Labour (IPEC) within ILO has further contributed to the promotion of research in a great number of countries. The point of departure was that all work is bad for children and that research efforts in the first place should explore the negative effects of work on child development. In the preamble to the programme, it is stated that " the time has come to establish a general instrument on the subject, which would gradually replace the existing ones applicable to economic sectors, with a view to achieving the total abolition of child labour".[3] ILO's "doctrine" to a certain extent reoriented the focus of research on child work.

[1.] Fyfe, A. (1993): *Child Labour: A guide to project design*. International Labour Office. Geneva.

[2.] ILO (1973): *Minimum Age Convention No. 138*. ILO (1986): *Child Labour: A briefing manual*. Geneva. p. 47–54.

[3.] Ibid. p. 47.

Emphasis was put especially on demonstrating the negative effects of work on children and with a focus on the most extreme forms of work. Possible positive effects of work on children were not mentioned. As a result, there has been a proliferation of studies and reports on some of the most degrading work situations that children can be exposed to, among which bonded work is one of the most appalling forms.

To have the legislative instruments needed to prohibit child work and to implement these instruments at the local level are two very different things. Time has shown that it is very difficult, if not impossible, to prohibit child work by laws and conventions, particularly if no economic alternative is provided for the child or the child's family. In fact, with a few exceptions, the Minimum Age Convention, although it has existed for a long time and is generally well-known, has not been implemented by authorities in the countries which have ratified the Convention and where abuse and exploitation of children through work indeed is a reality. Furthermore, traditional inspection systems have been shown to be ineffective since they only reach those children which work in the formal sector of the economy. Children who work in agriculture or in the urban informal sector are much more difficult to reach, because they are often not confined to specific places of work.

It appears to have been very difficult to abolish child work through laws or regulations, in spite of their long existence and the commitment of governments to implement them. It now seems to be finally understood that if no alternative is offered to the children and their families in order to alleviate the state of poverty in which they live, even the worst forms of work will continue to exist. A new, more "moderate" attitude towards child work seems to be emerging.

This new attitude is reflected in ILO's "Strategies, priorities and lessons for the future: A summary", in 1995.

> The starting-point for implementing ILO-IPEC's strategy in participating countries is the will and commitment of individual governments to address child labour in cooperation and consultation with employers' organizations, workers' organizations, other NGOs and relevant parties in society such as universities and the media. They

are supported to adopt measures which aim at *preventing* child labour, *withdrawing* children from hazardous work and providing *alternatives*, and *improving the working conditions* as a transitional measure towards the elimination of child labour.[1]

This strategy is an important step towards more realistic research on child work because it is no longer dominated by unqualified faith in the abolition of child work. In practice, there is already evidence that also severe forms of exploitation of working children can be resolved by the implementation of other measures, such as adapted school systems and regulated working time, rather than by simply prohibiting work. The case of Kerala is a good example.[2]

The alarming increase in some forms of child work - especially those resulting from urbanization processes in the last decade - shows how urgent it is to differentiate between those forms of work which are truly detrimental to child development, and other forms which may contribute to the improvement of children's life conditions. In the cities, children are engaged in activities with widely different character - prostitution, small scale criminality, guarding cars, street-vending - which necessarily have very different effects on children. The urgent question is how to protect children from work which is harmful to their development, rather than to prohibit all forms of work by not taking into account how important that can be for the alleviation of the poor conditions of life which are always at the root of the problem.

A book which certainly illustrates the new strategy is that by two prominent names in child work research, Myers and Bequele.[3] Here an attempt is made to define work that is hazardous to children and to present a plan of action intended to protect children from such work. The essential message is that, because of the complexity and magnitude of child work today, the best way of combating child work is to begin by combating the worst forms of child work.

---

[1]. ILO/IPEC (1995): *Strategies, priorities and lessons for the future: A summary.* Geneva.

[2]. Fyfe, A. (1995): *Government initiatives through child labour legislation and education: the case of India.* IPEC/ILO. Innocenti Occasional Papers. Child Rights Series No. 8.

[3]. Bequele, A. and Myers, W.E. (1995): *First things first in child labour. Eliminating work detrimental to children.* UNICEF. ILO. Geneva.

3.3 From adult- towards child-oriented research?

To try to summarize the major features of child work research from around 1980 up to now is a difficult task at any time, and specifically in the context of this study which focuses specifically on child work in the urban informal sector. The following summary therefore, will perhaps be coloured by this interest in the urban informal sector. It will focus, however, on changes in policies and strategies developed by the organizations which are most heavily involved in child work issues, and how they influence research trends and terminology.

A first characteristic of recent research on child work is that, in spite of the large number of studies presented during the last few years, there is no consensus among scholars about even basic definitions or concepts. A good example of this is the general ambiguousness of the concept of child work. Within UNICEF, as within ILO, one finds differing definitions of what constitutes work, according to the particular programme, author, or subject. In fact, what some consider to be work, others do not. Both individual scholars and organizations have been including and excluding some of the activities performed by children through their definitions of what work is or should be. A dominant approach in defining what work is, has been very much influenced by moral attitudes with respect to which activities should or should not be included. Begging is excluded by UNICEF, but sometimes included in programmes although regarded as illegal work. However, recent studies have shown that this is a well-organized and skill-demanding activity that can provide quite good incomes. Another tendency has been to belittle the economic value of some of the activities performed by children because they are typical for children and no or very few adults are engaged in them. An example of this could be to wash car windscreens at stop lights in the cities. However, there is evidence that younger children engaged in those typical child activities are likely to earn more than older children and adults.

A third approach is that of ILO in which work is defined as any economic activity in terms of its contribution to the Gross Domestic Product, and which therefore has not considered all forms of work performed by the children as work; e.g. work performed at home.

Changes in the definitions and terminology used by UNICEF in official documents and publications are both cause and effect of the lack of consensus about the appropriate conceptual framework for studies of child work. In important ways some of these concepts and definitions are not related to the reality of life of the children at work, and therefore not convincing. An example is the term "working children" that was dropped by UNICEF, precisely because certain activities which children are engaged in were not regarded as "work":

> ... the denomination "working child" excludes an important number of children which are engaged in marginal activities as a way of getting incomes for their survival, but that in any case can be considered as "work" in the broadest sense, for instance, begging, theft, prostitution.[1]

Instead, another concept, "children in survival strategies", was introduced with the aim of further distinguishing between activities which ought to be considered as work and other activities. As a result, "children in survival strategies"[2] was divided into three sub-categories: (i) "working children in the informal sector", (ii) "working children in the formal sector" and, (iii) "children with marginal activities".[3] Another example of an ambiguous concept is the category of "street

---

[1] UNICEF (1989): *Lineamentos para la aplicacion de la guia metodologica para el análisis de situación. Menores en circunstancias especialmente difíciles.* Serie Metodológica No. 8. p. 10–11. (free translation from the Spanish).

[2] "Children in survival strategies" were defined as: - they are children/adolescents up to 18 years old; they have stable bonds with the family or a household; they perform all types of activities which generate income; these activities can be placed in the formal or informal sector of the economy, or are marginal activities; these activities can take place inside the household, in the street or in other places off the street; children work part or full time; they may or may not get payment for their work. The payment can be in the form of money, in kind or in the form of services; the payment can be paid to the children themselves, to their household or to another person.

[3] Having in mind that those classifications primarily had a practical purpose - in the outlining and implementation of programmes directed towards the children in question - some of their shortcomings have to be accepted in view of the general usefulness of the establishment of universal concepts and terminologies in order to build up a methodology for the study of children all over the world. However, there is a risk of perpetuating these definitions by using them uncritically. The *Methodologic Guide for the situational analysis* recognizes to a certain extent these shortcomings by mentioning that in many cases categories overlap each other.

children", which has caused much discord among scholars and confusion about who these children really are. The distinction made between "children on the street" and "children of the street" has been used on the basis of apparently very different perceptions of what these categories represent. No precise criteria exist for defining either of these categories, and as a result, different pieces of research undertaken on these children - which has been one of the most intensively researched groups - can not be compared. These categorizations, imposed upon the study of children in general, affect the study of child work in particular since working children are found across most of the categories. The general tendency of scholars to follow the terminology presented by IGOs has been counter-productive for the development of scientifically sound concepts and definitions, so necessary in the study of child work.

Most recently, the new State of the World's Children report for 1997, shows that UNICEF is changing its overall mission statement, policy stance, and programming priorities in line with its mandate to help facilitate implementation of the Convention on the Rights of the Child.[1] It now claims to base its policy on "child rights" rather than on "needs", as it did previously. This new approach has brought child work into greater prominence than earlier and seems to be affecting the way "work" is defined and thought about. For instance, the report specifically states that UNICEF is against child work which is detrimental to children - as indicated in the Convention on the Rights of the Child - and is not against all child work as earlier.[2] It sees work as a continuum, that ranges from the most intolerable forms of child work at one extreme to purely beneficial types on the other. For the first time it also includes children working at home as workers. Hopefully these substantial changes will lead to more unanimously accepted definitions and positively influence research on child work in the future.

A retrospective view of which trends have influenced studies on child work until recently showed different dominant views of child work. Much research has been influenced by West European concepts

---

[1] UNICEF (1997): *The State of the World's Children 1997*.
[2] Ibid.

of childhood, characterized by a "welfare approach" to child work. This approach tends to focus on the negative effects of work on children´s mental and physical development and on their social integration as adults, and is based upon ideas about "childhood" rather than upon perceptions of the realities of life of working children.

"Moral" approaches have also been used and partly explain the exclusion of certain activities performed by the children from what is defined as work. The study of prostitution is a good example of this attitude, and the children engaged in that activity are not considered as being at work.

"Protectionism", however, is the most common approach and is based upon an adult-centred view of children, which entails ideas about the special subordinate position of children in relation to adults and leads to the exclusion of children from any decision making about their own situation.

The "legalist" approach goes a step further than "protectionism". It focuses on the necessity to create and implement more laws which will make child work come to an end. It tends to see socio-economic problems as purely legal, and its proponents do not really concern themselves with the practical impediments to the implementation of universal conventions and regulations. Such impediments have to do with the variety of legislative systems, the indifference of governments, and many other cultural and social aspects of child work which vary across regions and social systems.

"Abolitionism" is the extreme form of the view that child work is a matter of legislation. No consideration is given to possible positive effects of work on children's living conditions. The goal is to abolish all forms of child work without making any distinction between different types of child work and how they affect children's conditions of life. This approach implies a refusal to acknowledge any kind of positive effect of work on children. However, there is evidence that the application of such legislative measures – without the provision of alternative income sources for the children and their families – may force children into other, much more dangerous activities, aggravate the insecure situation of the children and lead to further deterioration of the household economy.

Recently, a more moderate or cautious attitude has emerged with respect to the positive role of work on children's conditions of life. This approach focuses mainly on the economic importance of work for the children themselves and their families, but also on work as a significant element in building up children's self-esteem, a sort of pride and status that contributes to the formation of self-confidence and independence. Another aspect that has been emphasized is that work discourages children from slipping into illegal or criminal activities, especially in urban environments. This aspect is not yet so much researched but is well illustrated by Valadares study of Favelas, Brazil.[1] The author shows how work might help children to avoid criminality, and even can bring a number of infants back to school. Non-working children living in the same environment were those who formed criminal gangs, survived on robbery, and were unable to break out of the vicious circle of criminality.

It seems as if the methodology used in child work research has not been regarded as a central aspect by very many scholars, since most studies do not even mention what kinds of methods were used. However, judging from those studies in which the methodology is explained, questionnaire surveys seem to be the most common method for collecting information. In general terms, research on child work has slowly developed from an adult-centred perspective to a more child-centred, which means that there is a growing consciousness of the need for studies where children are the subjects rather than the objects of study. However, and in contrast to this trend, "protectionism" is by far the dominant approach in terms of the methodology used. With some exceptions, children are rarely asked about their own situation, opinions or aspirations. Commonly they are not regarded as competent informants about themselves and their work. In the majority of studies the primary informants are still the adults - employers, parents or guardians.

At this stage it is important to say two things. Firstly, research on child work in general has been of a descriptive character. Very little

---

[1]. Valladares, L. (1990): *Family and Child Work in the Favela.* Third World Urbanization: Reappraisals and New Perspectives. Swedish Council for Research in the Humanities and Social Sciences. Stockholm.

analysis has been done of the causes and effects of child work within broader contexts, either locally or globally. Secondly, no research on child work can be classified as independent or objective since most research has been driven by different political, idealistic or cultural ambitions or interests, and many times has been financed by organizations which represent those interests. Research results always have to be interpreted with this in mind. The problems and questions that at a particular moment in time happen to be the foci of policies and programmes designed by IGOs are clearly reflected in the trends found in the literature sponsored by them. Reports and findings of NGOs, on the other hand, often not directly research-based, have not had the same impact on the design of policies and programmes, or on the direction of research. Because of these relationships between the various actors involved in child work issues, the focus of research has often been oriented towards aspects of specific interest to the actors involved. The children, which are after all the principal actors in the world of child work, have had little impact on which aspects should be investigated. In general, they have simply not been asked.

Literature on child work in Nicaragua

During the last few years, reports about the situation of children in Nicaragua have been prepared by some of the national NGOs engaged in children, often in collaboration with international NGOs or UNICEF.[1] These reports have dealt, however, with the situation of children in general, and only partly with the problems of working children. UNICEF has also published reports of its own on the socio-

---

[1.] During the two field work periods in Nicaragua, I established contacts with especially two national NGOs, Centro Nicaraguense de Promoción de la Juventud y la Infancia – Dos Generaciones, Instituto de Promoción Humana (INPRHU), and with the Instituto Nicaraguense de Seguridad Social y Bienestar (INSSBI). These contacts included interviews and visits to projects for homeless and working children in Managua. Contacts were also established with the Swedish Rädda Barnen and UNICEF.

economic situation of children.[1] Research and publications specifically about child work are much more rare, and the work by Mario Chavez on child work in Managua is quite unique. However, it could not be referred to in this study because it came to my attention only just before the publication of this volume.[2]

Child work in the urban informal sector

Although most working children are found in rural areas and agricultural activities, children also make up a great part of the labour force of the urban informal sector, whether their work is visible or hidden.

A review of the literature on the informal sector shows that, in spite of the magnitude of this phenomenon, there has been little critical analysis of the economic activities of children and of their role in socio-economic transformation processes and economic development. In most studies about the urban informal sector in developing countries, the huge number of working children is invisible, often not even mentioned. On the other hand, studies of child work in the urban areas, generally in the streets - which is one of the issues mainly focused in the literature - often do not analyse the work of the children within the context of the urban informal sector. The lack of consensus with respect to the conceptual context of child work studies in general is even more conspicuous in the case of child work studies in the urban informal sector, especially with respect to what kind of activities

---

[1] UNICEF (1991): *Nicaragua: Desafios y opciones en un pais de niños y mujeres. Análisis de situación económica y social*. Managua; Littlejohn, C. (coordinador de equipo) (1991): *Impacto de la Deuda Externa y las Medidas de Ajuste Estructural en la Familia, la Niñez y la Mujer*. CAPRI. Managua; Garcia, N. y Castillo, R. (1991): *Diagnostico participativo de los menores trabajadores del sector informal del Barrio de Acahualinca*. Centro Dos Generaciones. Managua; Coordinadora Nicaraguense de ONGs que trabajan con la ninez (1995): *Segunda Consulta Nacional. Los niños, las niñas, los adolescentes y sus derechos en Nicaragua*. Imprimatur. Managua; Talamante, A. A. and Mercado, M. R (1991): *Análisis de situación de los niños de la calle en la ciudad de Managua*. Instituto de Promoción Humana. Programa de Promoción de la Familia y la Comunidad. Managua.

[2] Chavez, M. (1995): *Entre semaforos y parqueos, el trabajo de los niños, las niñas y adolescentes de Managua*. MILAVF. Managua.

should or should not be included in the sector.

Rodgers and Standing did not use work in the informal sector as a category in their classification of children's activities. Instead, a number of those activities which are performed by children and which are recognized in ILO's definition, as well as by most scholars of the sector, as belonging to the informal sector, were scattered over several categories on their list, with many in the category "Marginal Economic Activities". This was a kind of residual category, defined as,

> In addition to activities which can be clearly interpreted as domestic work, unpaid family labour, bonded labour, and wage employment, there is a set of activities widely undertaken by children which do not fit into such categories. They are typically characterized by their irregularity and short-term nature, though some of the individuals practising the activities may do so on a regular, long term basis. Marginal, semi-economic activities of this type include the selling of news-papers; "looking after" cars; shoe shining; selling of sweets and other items; running of errands; and the sorting of garbage for usable objects...Such work typically does not contribute to capital accumulation and could be described as the activities of the lumpen proletariat...In this marginal category should be included theft, prostitution, and other activities which are typically illegal or semi-legal.[1]

Thus, activities that are included in ILO's definition of the informal sector such as shoe-shining and selling, are classified as marginal and semi-economic activities together with theft and prostitution, and not located to any specific sector of the economy. Another illustration of the lack of concordant terms of reference for the definition of children's work in the informal sector is UNICEF's rather diffuse definition of "working children of the informal sector" in which no activities are mentioned explicitly.

> Working Children of the Informal Sector are: working children and adolescents from the sector of poverty, who work in an independent or dependent way; those who work in conditions of extreme diffi-

---

[1]. Rodgers, G. and Standing, G. (1981): *The economic roles of the children : issues for analysis*. ILO. p. 8-9.

culty, without protection norms, fixed work time, and under salarial discrimination. This sector represents conditions of high risk for the working children who are integrated in it.[1]

Such conceptual and definitional vicissitudes are not unique for child work in the informal sector but apply to studies of this sector in general. The boundaries between "marginal", "beyond the law", "illegal" and "criminal" are constantly revoked in publications on the informal sector, for instance in the Report of the Director-General on The Dilemma of the Informal Sector,

> Their vulnerability (of the activities) is due also to the fact that to a large extent they operate beyond the law, and receive little or no legal protection. This deprives them of the right to appeal to the courts for contracts to be enforced or to claim security of tenure. But the "illegality" of the informal sector with which we are concerned in this Report has nothing to do with criminal activities. If informal sector activities are in any way "illegal", it is because they are unable to comply with existing regulations. Compliance with all regulations would impose an impossible financial burden on the micro-enterprises and the poor households of the informal sector.[2]

And in another document,

> Finally it should perhaps be stated explicitly that the scope of the informal sector covers only gainful economic activities that are considered socially desirable and it thus excludes activities such as criminal, begging, prostitution and drug trafficking - which are considered as anti-social by most governments.

The exclusion of such activities from the sector – and naturally they are not part of the formal sector either – leads to the conclusion that a group of activities virtually "do not exist" in any sector of the urban economy, and that their economic importance therefore is ignored.

[1.] The workshop about the *Analysis of the Situation of the Minors in Specially Difficult Circumstances* which took place in Lima, Peru 1989, was documented in UNICEF's (1989): *Lineamentos para la aplicación de la guia metodológica para el análisis de situación. Menores en circunstancias especialmente difíciles.* Serie Metodológica. No. 8.

[2.] ILO (1991): *The dilemma of the informal sector. Report of the Director-General.* International Labour Conference. 78th session. International Labour Office. Geneva. p. 6.

However, many children are engaged in them, sometimes alongside other more socially accepted activities included by the definition. There is plenty of evidence which shows that children oscillate between several activities, at the same place of work and even during the same day, e.g. selling and stealing, guarding cars and begging. This aspect of child work in the informal sector was first brought out by Rodgers and Standing, but is still ignored by most scholars:

> Clearly these various activities are not mutually incompatible, and various combinations will exist. In some cases, one activity will dominate, as in the case of girls engaged for seven or eight hours a day in domestic work. In other cases, time will be divided – children in the urban slums, for instance, may divide their time between domestic work, marginal and illegitimate activities, schooling and idleness.[1]

Alain Morice (1981) emphasized the complexity of the concepts that need to be developed for studies of child work in the informal sector, and for defining the "informal sector" in general. With respect to "work" he stressed that a definition should be related not only to the activity itself but also to its economic and social context, and he advocated that the question of work should be studied on the basis of whether or not it constituted exploitation. He focused on the exploitation of children in different modes of production and of organization of work in the sector which he classified as "structured" rather than "unstructured". He emphasized the need for new approaches in defining the informal sector, which in turn would contribute to the study of the working children of the sector.

> The consequences of these characteristics (of the sector) for the question which interests us here are clear: cheap and even unpaid labour is an indispensable element in the survival of many petty activities because of the high degree of competition. It is in this sense that a prior scientific and non-empirical definition of the so-called informal sector is necessary for a more profound analysis of the role of the children within it.

---

[1]. Rodgers, G. and Standing, G. (1981): *The economic roles of the children: issues for analysis*. ILO. p. 11.

And he went on to say,

> To conclude this discussion of the obstacles which can not be disregarded when examining the question of children's work in the small-scale production sector, we want to underline the fact that, in our view, these difficulties will not be overcome by initiating vast projects. The urgent and essential tasks are to formulate theoretical systems and to identify research themes; if this is not done there is a risk that the conceptual and definitional problems outlined above will persist.[1]

And in fact they do persist. Though there is far from universal acceptance of the concept informal sector, it has so far not been possible to replace it by another concept that might gain general acceptance.

ILO stresses that children are even more vulnerable than adults as workers and that millions of them work in the most deplorable and hazardous conditions in the informal sector. Apparently ILO makes no clear distinction between activities performed by children and those performed by adults in the informal sector.

> The plight of children in the informal sector is perhaps the most tragic aspect of the problem. Although child work is prohibited in the legislation of most countries, millions of them are working, often in the most deplorable and hazardous conditions, in the informal sector – and sometimes clandestinely in the formal sector as well. They work in small manufacturing establishments, where their docility and dexterity are highly appreciated, but where they can be most severely exploited, often working long hours and in dangerous conditions for a pitifully low wage; or they may work in a family unit; or as 'self-employed' in the streets, shining shoes or selling cigarettes. Children can be subjected to the most extreme and degrading forms of exploitation such as prostitution, or, in some countries tied or bonded labour, where children are hired out by their families in settlement of debts.[2]

---

[1]. Morice, A. (1981): *The exploitation of children in the "informal sector": proposals for research*. ILO. Geneva.

[2]. ILO (1991): *The dilemma of the informal sector*. Report of the Director-General. International Labour Conference. 78th session. ILO. Geneva. p. 8.

However, this statement gives a broader view of the activities of the sector when performed by children.

"Street work" and "activities of the street" are two commonly used terms which often are used synonymously with the informal sector. Some authors use them in ways which suggest that these activities form a kind of island in the urban economic environment, and that the activities are not directly connected with any sector of the economy. Other authors use them instead of the term informal sector, some relate them to the kind of activities that homeless children in the cities do for a living, while others use them only for those activities which are performed in the street, which is looked upon as a huge work place. Alarcón Glasinovich (1991) refers to the work of the children in the informal sector in his study on child work in Lima;[1] he says that it is in production and commerce that children are to be found, but refers specifically to children in the context of small-scale enterprises. Yet he never discusses these matters in terms of the informal sector. On one hand, most of the occupations that he lists correspond to activities which are generally accepted as part of the informal sector, but, on the other hand, activities such as car warding and car washing are labelled as marginal. Furthermore, activities such as ambulatory vending and shoe-shining are labelled "street work", while prostitution and theft are not regarded as work at all.

> In this enumeration we do not incorporate prostitution or theft by child bands, because these are not labour activities, nor can these minors be included, without more precise information, in the category of workers. The often humiliating features of these activities, the noisy "work" milieu, the particular ethic codes associated with them, as well as the background of broken families generally with separated parents, even the personality traits - these are all features that clearly distinguish the children who thieve or are prostitutes from the children who work.[2]

---

[1] Glasinovich, W.A. (1991): *Entre calles y plazas. El trabajo infantil de los niños en Lima.* ADEC/ATC. Instituto de Estudios Peruanos. UNICEF. Lima. p. 72-73.

[2] Ibid. p. 71 (free translation by the author).

These examples are only a few illustrations of how differently the work of the children in the informal sector can be understood. They emphasize that classification of child work outside the urban formal sector is not always a procedure based on the evaluation of objective facts, but that personal values may also influence how work performed by children is classified. One possible way of solving the definition problem would be to simply accept ILO's definition and to focus solely on those activities which are socially and morally accepted as work. However, how should children engaged in other activities, or simultaneously in both "acceptable" and "non-acceptable" activities, be classified? Are they not workers? Are they not seeking and earning their livelihood? If the economic value of those activities in terms of income - in money or in kind - is to be taken into account, then all activities have to be considered as work. In this context, the dualistic view of the urban economy might not be the most relevant for the study of child work in the city. Perhaps other, new approaches have to be developed instead. An alternative could be a child-centred definition of work, where the child's interests should be the point of departure. Obviously the interests of children are not necessarily the same, in different regions and societies, but such an approach should be more sound because it would be related to the living conditions of the child in a much more realistic way. The classification by Myers and Bequele is a promising contribution in that direction.[1] They distinguish between work that is detrimental both physically and psychologically for the children and work that is not, across sectors and segments of the economy, regardless of in which sector of the economy the work is positioned.[2]

After this discussion, I will return to the ILO definition of the informal sector. In my opinion this definition, more than twenty years after its first appearance, and in spite of its deficiencies, still is the definition that is most widely used and accepted by scholars, in many official documents and even in economic policy programmes. It is also the definition that best reflects the complexity of the urban economy,

---

[1.] Bequele, A. and Myers, W.E. (1995): *First things first in child labour. Eliminating work detrimental to children.* UNICEF. ILO. Geneva.
[2.] Ibid.

especially in cities in the developing countries where the "working poor", including the working children, are not part of the recognized and protected labour force, although in many cases they make up its majority. To accept that definition implies that one recognizes the economic role of those workers, including the child workers.

Thus, in the present study the category "working children in the urban informal sector" is defined in accordance with ILO's broad definition of the informal sector, which has also been adopted by the ILO Regional Employment Programme for Latin America (PREALC) and by national institutions and scholars in Nicaragua. In this way, it is believed that the present study will be able to produce information that can be used for comparative purposes.

"Work" is additionally defined on the basis of several criteria, the most important being the children's own evaluation of whether the activity they were engaged in was directly and exclusively related to the production and/or sale of goods and services in the labour market, and irrespective of whether the children could or could not keep an income for themselves. The second criterion implies a focus on those activities which are representative of child work in the informal sector in general, and in particular those which are typical of the informal sector in the city of Managua.[1]

In some contexts it may be difficult to arrive at an objective definition of "child" because of the many criteria that can be taken into account: biological, legal and cultural, and specially if the concept of childhood is to be taken into consideration. In view of the purpose of the present study, other definitions than one based upon chronological age do not seem to be relevant. Thus, the adopted definition is primarily the same as that established in the first article of the Convention on the Rights of the Child: "a child means every human being below the age of 18 years". Even though fourteen is the minimum employment age in Nicaragua, that age was selected as the upper limit. Thus, in the present study, the child workers in the informal sector in Managua are those children, through their 14th year, who work in the informal sector as defined by ILO.

[1.] Part Two includes a discussion about other forms of work as well as of all other activities undertaken by the children of the present study.

Child work activities in the urban informal sector in Central America

A review of statistics and studies on child work shows that it is not possible to speak of typical child occupations, in the sense that there are economic activities exclusively performed by children. The occupations that children engage in are not different from those performed by adult workers. Indeed, and quite often, both categories work at the same place and side by side. However, in spite of the fact that children are engaged in a broad range of jobs, not all activities performed by adults are open to children. Their status as minors and as subordinates to adults in household decision-making as well as in many other respects tends to impose limitations on job access, and because of this children tend to be concentrated in some occupations more than in others.

Although the available information is scarce and relates only to a few cities, and often is based on sample studies, it nevertheless allows one to draw certain conclusions regarding some occupational characteristics of children in the informal sector of the region. Several students of child work in Latin American cities have emphasized the diversity of the activities that children are involved in, and simultaneously the concentration of these activities to a few sectors. In a study of child work in Lima, for example, Alarcón lists the following activities: ambulatory vendors, retail sellers, shoe-shiners, car wards, car cleaners. With only minor modifications, the list provided by Alarcón could be easily extended to cover the activities performed by children in most Latin American cities.[1] Notwithstanding the variety of tasks performed by children, they can conveniently be aggregated into two main sectors - services and trade. Alarcón, for instance, reports that 34 per cent of the working children in Peru were active in services, 28 per cent in trade and only 15 per cent in production. In another study, half of the children declared that they were engaged in activities performed in the streets.[2] Comparative analyses of the urban informal sector in

---

[1] Glasinovich, W.A. (1991): *Entre calles y plazas. El trabajo de los niños en el Perú.* ADEC/ATC. Instituto de Estudios Peruanos. UNICEF. Lima. p. 72.

[2] Glasinovich, W.A. (1986): *Pobreza urbana y trabajo infantil en Lima metropolitana.* Rädda Barnen. Lima. Quoted by Myers (1989).

South America – in Lima (Peru), Asunción (Paraguay), Cochabamba (Bolivia), as well as in several cities in Brazil – enabled Myers to conclude that the range of activities performed by children was limited to a relatively few occupations.[1] He identified three principal occupations which children engaged in: as street vendors, as shoe-shiners, and as car wards and washers. Another survey of urban informal child work in Latin America, by Fyfe and Spinoza, led them to the same conclusion, i.e. that the economic sectors open for working children in Latin America cities were few. The ILO report to the Central American Seminar on Child Work[2] in 1993 provides a more comprehensive account of several aspects related to child work in the region.[3] The report identifies the following sectors:[4]

Industry: Employment of minors in this sector was least important and in part reflects the low level of industrial development in the countries covered by the survey. In Guatemala, Honduras, El Salvador and Costa Rica, children worked in the pharmacological, textile/shoes, chemical and military industries, and in Costa Rica in the seafood industry as well. In Nicaragua, on the other hand, child employment in industry was negligible, save for those working in small family enterprises. In Honduras, children worked as extra hands in informal mechanical workshops, doing painting, foundry, electrical engineering and welding jobs.[5]

Construction: There was no information on Nicaragua regarding child work in the construction industry. The available information indicates that boys were employed as extra hands and as apprentices to

---

[1] Myers, W. (1989): *Urban working children: A comparison of four surveys from South America.* International Labour Review. ILO. Vol. 128. No. 3. Geneva.

[2] Programa Internacional sobre la Abolición del Trabajo Infantil (IPEC) (1993): *El trabajo infantil en América Central.* Documento del Seminario Centroamericano sobre el trabajo infantil. Organización Internacional del Trabajo. (OIT).

[3] The analysis was based upon official statistics, census and household surveys, and official statistical estimations.

[4] The report also describes the situation of child work in agriculture, but for the purpose of the present chapter the inclusion of such information was not relevant.

[5] On this matter the report makes no mention of the situation in the other countries; however, in Nicaragua, there is plenty of evidence on the employment of children in these activities, mainly in car repair and electrical workshops, but the magnitude of the phenomenon is not known.

bricklayers in Costa Rica, Guatemala and Honduras, whereas in El Salvador children worked only in informal construction businesses.

Trade and services: The trade and services sectors include those activities which have the highest incidence of child work. It has been estimated that about 75 per cent of the children working in the urban informal sector in Central America are found in trade and services. Most activities were performed on the streets, the most frequent being: selling, ambulatory vending, car warding and washing, and shoe-shining. In Nicaragua, El Salvador and Guatemala, in particular, the accelerated entry of children into trade has been a major feature of the urban informal sector. To work as a domestic servant, an occupation dominated by girls, is very common throughout Latin America. Costa Rica, Guatemala and Panama are the countries in Central America that have the highest incidence of girls working as domestics.

Miscellaneous activities: a number of additional activities have also been identified by the ILO survey as common to all countries of Latin America. They include prostitution, thievery, beggary, and a host of other activities such as street singing and dancing.

Despite the limited access to reliable statistical information on the occupational structure of child work in Managua, the available information from a few studies and household surveys in general is compatible with the findings of other studies of the informal sector in Latin American cities, specifically studies of urban informal child work in Central America. Although small in terms of sample size and limited with respect to its geographical coverage[1], "Menores en estrategia de sobrevivencia", one of the few investigations on informal child work in Nicaragua, identified a sectorial distribution of child work resembling that found in other Latin American cities.[2] The occupational distribution of children by sector, as reported in that study, is skewed

---

[1]. The sample of the investigation covered three regions: Leon-Chinandega, Matagalpa and Managua, with a total of 90 interviewed children, 53 of them from Managua. The places studied and the percentage of the interviews conducted there were: markets and supermarkets 25 per cent; public gardens 17 per cent; bus stations 17 per cent; traffic lights 13.3 per cent; parking lots 13.3 per cent; amusement centres 12.2 per cent; streets 2.2 per cent.

[2]. Hernandez, V. and Henriquez, S. (1991): *Menores en estrategia de sobrevivencia*. Centro Nicaraguense de Promoción de la Juventud y la Iinfancia – *Dos Generaciones*. Managua.

towards jobs in services and commerce. The proportion of children working in the various categories was as follows: ambulatory vendors 50 per cent, newspaper sellers 16 per cent, car guards and washers 13 per cent, marginal activities 12 per cent, stationary sellers 7 per cent, and other work 2 per cent.[1]

In this chapter, child work in general, and in the informal sector in Central America in particular, has been reviewed. This overview provides the background for the next chapter, in which the situation in Nicaragua will be discussed in greater detail.

---

[1] Marginal activities included e.g. begging and trash collection.

Chapter 4

The case of Nicaragua

The urban informal sector and the living conditions of low income households form the context for this study of child work in Managua. In fact, child work in the city can not be understood independently of the urban informal sector. There are no indications that children work within the formal sector; on the contrary, evidence from several households surveys shows that all working children are to be found in the informal sector.[1]

In this section the purpose is to describe the characteristics and evolution of the urban informal sector in Nicaragua, and—as far as available information allows this—in Managua in particular. The emphasis will be put on the relationship between the state of poverty of the urban low income households and employment in the informal sector, where children make up part of the labour force.

The following account is based primarily upon results from a series of studies and surveys undertaken by Fundación Internacional para el Desafio Económico Global (FIDEG) between 1992 and 1995[2] about the living conditions of the urban population of Managua, León and Granada.[3] To some extent, it also uses results from the Living Standards Measurement survey supported by the World Bank and UNDP in 1995.

[1.] FIDEG (1995): El Observador Económico. No. 48. Managua.
[2.] These investigations are based upon a sample of 870 households of the urbanized area of the three municipalities and were carried out on four occasions: in August and December 1992, August 1993 and August 1994.
[3.] According to the last census (1995) the population of these three cities accounted for 47 per cent of the national urban population.

The living conditions of the urban population

It is difficult to say very much about the evolution of the living conditions of the urban low income households and about poverty patterns in Nicaragua during the last few decades, because of the lack of accurate data. However, in the last few years several studies have been carried out with a focus on the growing poverty that is affecting large segments of the population. In particular, investigations by FIDEG have focused on the behaviour of several indicators of poverty in order to monitor the deterioration in the conditions of life of the urban population[1] and to a lesser extent also of the rural population[2].

Increasing poverty

In 1991, 70 per cent of the population of Managua could not satisfy their basic needs; one fourth of those lived in conditions of extreme poverty and 16 per cent in indigence.[3] Three structural factors have been pointed out as being strongly associated with conditions of poverty, namely, the demographic growth—Nicaragua's annual rate of population growth in 1995 was 2.9 per cent—the lack of employment, and related to that, the lack of regular sources of income. The decline in world prices on export crops, the economic policies during the 1980's which did not stimulate production, the high costs of the war, and a fall in exports by 40 per cent in 1990, caused an increasing external debt and hyper-inflation rates until 1990, and a constant decline in the real value of salaries. All these factors together go a long way to explain the general impoverishment of the population. Investigations from 1991 show that low wage workers used between 80 and 90 per cent of their income to buy food.[4] In general, prices on foodstuff have increased at a higher rate than that of general inflation, and this has affected low income households most severely. The persistence

[1] FIDEG (1996): El Observador Económico. No. 49. Managua.
[2] A survey done by FIDEG in 1993 in rural and urban areas in the regions I, II and IV, including León, Chinandega, Estelí, Madriz, Carazo, Rivas, Masaya and Granada.
[3] Renzi, R. and Agurto, S. (1992): *Pobreza en los hogares de Managua, León y Granada (Urbano)*. Material para Análisis Económico. FIDEG. Managua.
[4] Ibid.

of these factors has led to a constant deterioration in the standard of living for a large part of the population and is reflected in extreme forms in an increasing criminality, prostitution, begging, and drug use in the city.

From 1991, new structural reforms have been introduced at the same time as the liberation of commerce has accelerated and production has declined. The productive resources of the country are in the hands of small and medium-sized entrepreneurs. Their possibilities to save and invest are very limited, and they generate little new employment. During 1992, the rate of inflation finally dropped to international levels—from 865 per cent in 1991 to 3.5 per cent in 1992—but the general economic recession persisted until 1994. From then, a certain reactivation of the economy began to be noticed, based upon renewed growth in a few productive activities. In fact, Nicaragua experienced an economic growth of 4 per cent in 1995, but the growth rate per capita was very close to zero.[1] The GDP grows but poverty grows too. Work opportunities become more scarce, throwing new social groups into poverty.

FIDEG's analysis of poverty is based on the indirect method of measuring poverty which involves the estimation of "poverty lines" related to the income of the household.[2] By this method, a household is considered to be "poor" when the total available income [3] is lower than the cost of two "basic food baskets".[4] Households in "extreme poverty" are those with an income that can pay for one "basic food

---

[1]. Aguilar, R., Stenman, Å. and Aguilar, J. (1995): *A New Door Might Be Opened*. Macroeconomic Report. 1996:1. SIDA. Stockholm.

[2]. Typically, poverty lines are established on the basis of the size of income required for a typical household to buy a food basket with a minimum level of proteins and calories. The composition of the "basic food basket" is not the same across regions, but instead takes into account the local dietary habits of the low income households. In Central America, rice, beans, food oil, and sugar are the main products included.

[3]. The income was calculated as the sum of the monetary income, income in kind and all other types of income such as donations from institutions and contributions from relatives living in the country or abroad.

[4]. An income which only can pay for the cost of two "basic food baskets" allows only the coverage of very basic goods and service needs, and verges upon the limits of survival.

basket" or less, and "non-poor" households are those with incomes which exceed the cost of more than two "basic food baskets".[1]

According to this method, in 1995, 52 per cent of the urban households were "poor", and 27,5 per cent were "extremely poor".[2] Relatively speaking, the increase in the number of "poor" households was faster in Managua, from 36 to 47 per cent between 1992 and 1995, and especially in the case of the female-headed households which were poorer than male-headed households during the period. In fact, the percentage of extremely poor female-headed households increased most markedly in Managua, from 40 per cent of the total female-headed households in the city in 1992 to 55 per cent in 1995.[3]

The purchasing power of the incomes is an important indicator of poverty. Although the average income of the households in 1995 had increased by 31 per cent since 1992, the ratio between the income of the households with high incomes and those with low incomes increased from 27:1 to 53:1 in 1995. During the same period the cost of living rose by 57 per cent, and the purchasing power of average incomes fell by 16 per cent. In 1995, 70 per cent of the population in Managua could only buy one basic food basket, and the number of employed persons who could afford only half of one basic food basket increased from 39 per cent in 1992 to 42 per cent in 1995.

The decentralization and privatization of some public services within the health and school sectors had a negative impact on the general health conditions of the population and led to a higher school drop-out rate—10 per cent in the three cities. Registration fees in school and the cost of school materials were the main reasons given by the surveyed persons for the high drop-out rate. With respect to health, there was a higher incidence of children with bronchitis and

---

[1]. There are other methods of measuring poverty which take into consideration other factors than food. They try to measure to what extent basic needs are met by the household, taking into account access to clean water, adequate housing standards, sewage treatment and disposal, and so forth.

[2]. Correspondent values at the national level, indicate that 74.8 per cent of the households of the country are poor and 43.6 per cent are in "extreme poverty". Source: *Estudio de la pobreza en Nicaragua*. Proyecto NIC/93/016/PNUD/UNICEF. Gabinete Social, Managua. 1994. It was based on a survey made by INEC and the World Bank in all the regions of Nicaragua with a sample size of 4,458 households and 24,566 persons.

[3]. FIDEG (1995): El Observador Económico. No. 43-48. Managua.

diarrhea in 1995 than in 1992. The number of children with bronchitis increased from four to seven in ten children, and the share of children with diarrhea increased from 28 per cent to 38 per cent.

Not surprisingly, there was evidence of a direct relationship between poverty and low educational level of the heads of households; in the poor and extremely poor households the rate of illiteracy was higher and the number of completed school years lower than minimum primary education standards.

The study by UNDP/UNICEF on poverty in Nicaragua gives further insights into general patterns of poverty at the national level.[1] This study was based on the "unsatisfied basic needs" method, housing excluded. It showed that poverty in Nicaragua was regionally differentiated and more intensive in rural areas where 60 per cent of the households were in a condition of extreme poverty. Furthermore, it showed that almost five out of ten households in the country had a low economic carrying capacity in terms of a large number of persons in the household relative to the number of income-earners.

The urban informal sector

As indicated in the section above, there has been a deterioration in the standard of living for a large percentage of the urban population; many households live in conditions of extreme poverty, and the gap between the rich and the poor has widened. However, poverty is not necessarily related just to a lack of employment. In fact, the majority of the poor work, and often work more intensively than the non-poor, long hours but for low pay, and mostly in the informal sector.

In the following section, recent changes in the urban informal sector and the relationship between poverty and employment within the sector will be explored. The primary purpose is to try to show how the informal sector has been transformed in terms of internal structural changes, in response to increasing unemployment and underemploy-

---

[1]. Estudio de la pobreza en Nicaragua. Proyecto NIC/93/016/PNUD/UNICEF. 1994. Gabinete Social. Managua.

ment of the urban population, and what this has meant in terms of the purchasing power of incomes produced within that sector.

Characteristics and changes

A characteristic of the informal sector is its diversity and its ability to constantly adapt to new economic situations. The informal sector operates like a valve, that regulates the changes which occur on the labour market; it colonizes empty spaces in the economy by creating employment, low-cost production, and a supply of low price goods and services of particular importance for the low income sector of the city. In Latin America, during the 1970's, the share of informal sector employment, relative to the total labour force, increased by 3.7 per cent per annum in the region as a whole.[1] During the 1980's, due to the general recession and economic adjustment policies, the sector went through a new period of growth. Between 1980 and 1987, the informal sector is estimated to have grown by 56 per cent, whereas total non-agricultural employment rose by just 30 per cent.

There are no reliable data about growth in the informal sector during the 1970's Nicaragua. However, from the 1980's, the significance of the sector in the economy, at least in terms of employment, has become very obvious and it has thus become a matter of great interest to scholars as well as in politics. Managua early on became the principal focus of attention, largely because the informal sector in Managua went through significant changes during the 1980's. In a study by the School of Sociology at UCA, (Universidad Centro Americana) three periods in the evolution of the informal sector in Managua are distinguished in the period between 1979 and 1989: (i) 1979-1983, the period of expansion, (ii) 1984-1987, the period of diversification and polarization, and (iii) 1987-1989, the period of contraction.

The first period was characterized by politics intended to improve conditions of life for the urban population. They involved large inputs of external resources, subsidies, cooperative production, and several exchange rate adjustments relative to the dollar. The informal sector

---

[1] Tokman, V.E. (1990): *The informal sector in Latin America: Fifteen years later.* Turnham, D. Salomé, B. and Schwartz, A. (eds.): *The informal sector revised.* OECD. Development Centre.

took advantage of the over-evaluation of the Cordoba, and the availability of cheap imported and subsidized products, to expand as a parallel market. During the second period, the enormous costs of the war led to new, more restrictive economic policies, with support limited to certain economic sectors, and severe restrictions on credits and material inputs for production. Inflation accelerated and mass dismissals of workers took place in the formal sector. The informal sector developed new forms and the black market flourished, with negative consequences for the economic policies which had been introduced. The contraction period, finally, was characterized by the application of stability policies in order to control hyper-inflation and reduce public expenditures. The main measures involved the reduction of the public sector, liberalization of prices and markets, the end of subsidization, and persecution of informal activities. This directly affected all levels of the economy, and led to an increase in open unemployment both in the formal and informal sector.[1]

In 1990 the political and economic situation in the country changed dramatically. The civil war ended and with it the USA embargo. The liberalization and privatization of the economy had led to the restructuring of the private sector, to the selling out of state enterprises and reorganization of state institutions, which resulted in both a reduction in state employment and a systematic expulsion of labour from the formal sector of the economy, and thus subsequently to high levels of unemployment and underemployment, as mentioned above. The behaviour of the informal sector from that time up to today has been followed through successive investigations by FIDEG.[2]

[1.] See also: Aburto, R. and Chavarria, J. (1989): *El Empleo: Un Problema de los Sectores de la Economia*. Boletim Socio Económico. May/June. Managua; Aburto, R. (1988): *Impacto de la Reforma Económica en el Sector Informal Urbano-Análisis de Casos*. Boletín Socio Económico. Sept/Oct. Managua; Alemán, M. and others (1986): *La Estrategia de Sobrevivencia de los Sectores Populares de Managua y el Impacto del Mensaje Económico Gubernamental*. Revista Encuentro. No. 29. Managua; CEPAL (1989): *Balance Premilinar de la Economia de América Latina y El Caribe*. Revista No. 485. Santiago de Chile.

[2.] Agurto, S. and Renzi, R. (1992): *Empleo y desempleo en Managua, León y Granada (urbano)*. Material para análisis económico. FIDEG. Friedrich Ebert Stiftung. Managua. Agurto, S. and Renzi, R. (1994): *Mercado de Trabajo: Situación del Sector Informal en las ciudades de Managua, León y Granada*. El Observador Económico. No. 35 and 36. FIDEG. Managua; Agurto, S. and Renzi, R. (1995): *Mercado de Trabajo: Situación del Sector Informal en las ciudades de Managua, León y Granada*. El Observador Económico. No. 47 and 48. FIDEG. Managua.

The definition of the "urban informal sector" used in the investigations by FIDEG is that used by PREALC, which in general corresponds to that of ILO. According to this definition, the informal sector contains those who work in an independent way as unpaid family workers, as employers and employees of small enterprises with up to five workers, and as domestic workers. Thus, the category of workers in the informal sector is not just a matter of ambulatory vendors or sellers at the markets, which have been symbolic of the informal sector in Nicaragua, but also includes producers, technicians, craftsmen and people in many other occupations, who perform a large number of different activities in small-scale establishments, usually based on family labour.[1]

In broad terms, the evolution of the informal sector from the beginning of the 1990's until 1995 has been characterized by a process of new expansion and diversification. At the beginning of the period, society was in a state of social fatigue, as a result of economic stagnation, hyper-inflation and the continuing fall in real incomes. From 1980 to 1992 average income per capita dropped by 50 per cent, and 70 per cent of the population was living in poverty.

From 1992 the economic crisis, that has affected so many urban households, has forced more members of the poor households into the informal sector because this is the only sector of the urban economy which can absorb labour without skills, education or work experience. The lack of jobs in the formal sector in general, both in state institutions and private enterprises, and in particular shrinking employment in the education and health services, because of cutbacks in the public sector, have led to significant changes in the occupational structure within the informal sector. Now, not only unskilled workers are active, but many people with a technical or professional education are also looking for a job in the informal sector. To quote Agurto and Renzi,

> Professional workers have changed to businessmen, primary teachers are offering their services to wash and iron clothes, university

---

[1] Agurto, S. and Renzi, R. (1994): *Mercado de Trabajo: Situación del Sector Informal en las ciudades de Managua, León y Granada.* El Observador Económico. No. 36. p. 18. FIDEG. Managua

students and technicians are ambulatory vendors.[1] Employment in the informal sector in Managua has increased from 54 per cent of total employment in 1992 to 59 per cent in 1995. One of the main characteristics of the informal sector has been its ability to create work in face of the huge open unemployment; in Managua, the open unemployment rate was 19.3 per cent, in 1995. One expression of that characteristic has been growth in the number of small-scale businesses,[2] often in some kind of commerce usually (in approximately 90 per cent of the cases) run by one or two persons of the same household. Often these businesses are short-lived, because of the lack of capital and competition from the large number of these types of businesses. In the last few years, the opening of several supermarkets in the capital has reduced the market of the small-scale businesses, and their numbers have declined. In 1992, 42 per cent of the employed population had a business, in 1994 only 38 per cent, and in 1995, 36 per cent. In 1994 most of those units were not new, but on the average had existed for seven years. This trend illustrates that it has become increasingly difficult to start new successful businesses, and also that apparently only those that were well established –with more experience and no need for new capital –could ride out the general economic crisis.

The closing of many small-scale businesses has led to changes in the occupational structure of the sector as well. Once a business has folded, some members of the household are obliged to start looking for work within the informal sector, and now as wage workers. In fact, the percentage of employees and workers has been increasing, from 22 per cent in 1992 to 32.7 per cent in 1995, whereas the group of employers has declined from 3.6 to 1.5 per cent during the same period of time. The self-employed—which have symbolized this sector of the econ-

---

[1]. FIDEG (1995): El Observador Económico. No. 48. p. 34. Managua. (free translation by the author from the Spanish version).

[2]. The term "business "used here, is the direct translation of the Spanish word "negocio" which is broadly used by the population and by researchers for small-scale units of production or service, mainly of a commercial character; they can be run by one to five persons, which may be employers, employees or self-employed.

omy in Nicaragua and Managua[1]—accounted for 61.7 per cent in 1992, but only 50 per cent in 1995, whereas the category "unpaid family workers" increased from 12.3 per cent in 1992 to 19 per cent in 1994. The changing position of the two basic categories in the sector—self-employed vis-à—vis employees—can partly be explained by the declining trend in commercial activities and a slight increase in the number of family enterprises in construction and manufacturing.[2]

In the cities, the informal sector has been the most important source of employment for women. In 1995, 70 per cent of the working women were in the informal sector (in Managua 63 per cent). Although women traditionally comprised the majority of the informal sector, there have been some changes since 1994 in this respect, particularly in Managua where the men accounted for 54 per cent in 1995. With respect to income levels, the women are much worse off than the men; in 1995 the female average income was 65 per cent of the male.

Working at home is still the only alternative for almost 40 per cent of the active population in the informal sector, and this is particularly true of the women. The production and sale of food products such as tortillas, sweet bread and tacos, the resale of candies and cigarettes, as well as various service activities can provide an income that may seem insignificant in absolute terms, but might be essential for the subsistence of many urban households. Women dominate over men in the manufacturing of products for sale in small businesses—22.7 per cent and 7.8 per cent of total employment respectively in 1995.

The age structure of the sector has also undergone some changes during the early 1990's, with a relative increase in the number of young people in the age bracket 15-25 years, elderly, and children between 10 and 14 years. For varying reasons these groups find it quite difficult to get a job in the formal sector, where adults between 26 and 45 years—with experience, skills and education—is the most sought after segment of the labour force.

---

[1] Agurto and Renzi (1995): El Observador Económico. No. 48. p. 37. FIDEG. Managua.

[2] Agurto and Renzi (1995): El Observador Económico. Several issues in 1995. FIDEG. Managua.

One characteristic of the informal sector, as previously mentioned, is that its labour force in general has limited formal education or none at all. In Nicaragua, this characteristic is very evident. Recent statistics show that in 1995, the share of those working in the informal sector with none or only primary education was as high as 61 per cent.

Expansion at what price?

Agurto and Renzi frequently alert the reader to significant changes which have begun to affect the informal sector. They regard the falling rate of self-employment, the increasing number of "unpaid family workers" and the declining percentage of new recruits to the sector, as the major indicators of the barriers against entry into the sector that are becoming increasingly visible. A slight decline in the number of elderly workers during 1995 is also seen as a further sign of the saturation of the sector. The growth of the category of unpaid family workers, which is replacing the "typical" self-employed category in the informal sector in Managua, is seen as an indicator of the increasing difficulties that the urban population is facing. Indeed, the "unpaid family worker" often does not earn a salary or any other monetary income but perhaps works in exchange for a meal. For the self-employed, who need at least a minimal surplus capital to keep their activities going, it is apparently becoming more and more difficult to maintain the necessary surplus capital.

Other factors, according to Agurto and Renzi, which contribute to the emergence of entrance barriers through stiffer competition within the informal sector in Managua, are the decline in demand for various domestic chores due to the low and declining purchasing power of the population in general. Activities such as gardening, electricity work, and washing and ironing of clothes, for instance, had increased for some time but dropped from 17 per cent of all informal activities in 1992 to 12.5 per cent in 1995. For the same reasons, activities performed in the street [1] have also dropped from 16 per cent in 1992 to 9 per cent in 1995. It seems as if the fixed places of work in the streets

---

[1] "Street activities" mainly referred to activities performed in the streets—commerce and services around traffic lights on the major streets in the city where there is heavy traffic. The markets are not included.

are no longer as accessible as they used to be. Instead, ambulatory vending, mainly in Managua, has become an alternative for many workers, who are now selling products and services *door to door*. This type of activities increased from 10 per cent in 1993 to 18 per cent in 1994.

At this stage one may wonder where this expansion of the informal sector is leading. For how long will the informal sector be the principal form in which new labour and old labour expelled from the formal sector is absorbed. For how long will it be able to support, as the major source of urban employment, the increasing number of poor households in the city?

Poverty and the urban informal sector

Employment in the informal sector is not always synonymous with low income.[1] In the case of Nicaragua, however, FIDEG's findings provide plenty of evidence that incomes in the informal sector now generally are lower than in the formal sector.

Renzi states that there is a relationship between poverty and employment in the informal sector.[2] Among the households in a state of poverty or extreme poverty there was a higher incidence of employment in the informal sector than among the non-poor households.

Very significant differences were also found with respect to the salaries. In 1994, the salaries in the formal sector on the average were 40 per cent higher than those in the informal sector and in 1995 that difference had increased to 45 per cent. In terms of the purchasing power of the salaries, 84 per cent of those employed in the informal sector in 1995 could not afford the cost of one "basic basket", to compare with

---

[1.] In fact, in many cases the salaries in the informal sector can be higher than those in the formal sector. Even in Managua, the income of a "self-employed" in the informal sector in the late eighties could be twice as high as that of a state employee and the income of an owner of a small-scale informal enterprise on the average was higher than the highest income of owners of businesses in the formal sector.

[2.] Renzi, M. R. (1996): *Condiciones de vida de los hogares urbanos de León, Granada y Managua (1992-1995)*. El Observador Económico. No. 49. FIDEG. Managua.

the 53 per cent in the formal sector.[1]

In sum, the informal sector in Managua, as well as in the other cities surveyed by FIDEG, continues to be the expanding part of the economy where many of those who can not find a job in the shrinking formal sector, in one way or another try to find work. However, job opportunities in the informal sector have dwindled. The street no longer offers so many fixed places of work as it used to; instead, workers have to look for business by ambulating through the city, or around the markets. Stiffer competition in commerce and services has forced many of the self-employed business operators to instead work as unpaid family workers or employees. Greater competition has reduced incomes and the general economic crisis has caused a decline in some of the activities which used to be typical of the sector, such as street sales. The number of teenagers and children in the informal sector has been increasing through the nineties, and this tendency must be considered as a warning signal that indicates the deteriorating situation of an even greater number of households in Managua.

Strategies of the households

Given the present situation in the informal sector, and the widespread poverty, it is not surprising that in 1995 as many as 93 per cent of the surveyed urban households declared that they were looking for ways to improve their economic situation.[2]

Renzi identified three important and common survival strategies that urban households develop in order to improve their situation: (i) to set up a business,[3] (ii) to rely more on economic support from outside the household (contributions) and (iii) to increase work intensity.[4]

---

[1]. Agurto and Renzi (1995): El Observador Económico. No. 48. pp. 42-43. FIDEG. Managua.

[2]. Renzi, M. R. (1996): *Condiciones de vida de los hogares urbanos de León, Granada y Managua (1992-1995)*. El Observador Económico. No. 49. FIDEG. Managua.

[3]. See earlier note on the term bussiness.

[4]. Ibid.

To start a business has been a significant and very common strategy (as mentioned above) but its significance has been decreasing in recent years, especially in the case of female-headed households; the state of poverty has become so severe that the capital needed to set up even the most insignificant business usually is not available. In Managua, for instance, the percentage of new started businesses decreased from six to three between 1992 and 1995.

In contrast to this, *contributions* have become more and more important. In 1995, every second household depended on contributions from different sources and of different kinds for their survival. Worst off were the female-headed households of which 62 per cent were dependent on such contributions (43 per cent of male-headed households). Economic support from relatives has been a widely used and accepted practice for a long time, and the fact that over a few years the percentage of all households that receive such contributions has dropped from 55 to 35 per cent is another indicator of deteriorating living conditions. On the other hand, institutional support from state institutions and NGOs has risen from 4 per cent in 1992 to 25 per cent in 1995. The importance of monetary contributions has increased, while contributions in the form of food, medicine and housing has declined.

The third strategy, to increase work intensity, is, however, not so easy to practice in the informal sector which, to start with, is characterized by long working days. According to FIDEG, attempts to put in more working hours per day does not significantly increase the income of already poor households. Households in the "extreme poverty" category on the average managed to increase their income in this way by just 9 per cent, whereas the "non-poor households" could raise incomes by 14.5 per cent.[1]

Child work—the last resort?

Another way of increasing work intensity is to send more members of the household to work. Generally, it is when it becomes necessary that children begin to work.

---

[1]. FIDEG (1995): El Observador Económico. No. 37. p. 26. Managua.

In Nicaragua this strategy has become increasingly important during the last five years. Although there is no accurate statistical information on the number of children at work, it is known that more than half of the country's four million inhabitants are below the age of eighteen and that more than one million is younger than ten years (INEC 1994). If we take into account that 60 per cent of the total number of children below the age of fourteen, is estimated to live in poverty, and around one fourth in extreme poverty, we are entitled to assume that a large number of those children do work, either in agriculture, in the formal sector or in the urban informal sector.

In Managua, the opportunities for children to work seem to be limited exclusively to the informal sector. According to FIDEG, all the children who worked, did so in the informal sector.[1] The number of working children in Managua is not known; the official figure of about 8,300 working children between 10 and 14 years in 1994 (MITRAB), and UNICEF's statement that there were 13,000 working children in the city in 1992, illustrate the incompatibility of information in different surveys.[2] However, more important than these estimations are the findings of FIDEG. Even though household surveys may not be the most appropriate method to use in research on child work, their surveys clearly show that the number of children at work has increased significantly in the first half of the 1990's and in 1995 accounted for 5 per cent of those employed in the informal sector. It is significant that girls accounted for an increasing part of this growth. FIDEG's surveys only concern children between ten and fourteen years, and the participation of children of lower ages in the labour market is not known; however, it is assumed to follow a similar pattern.

The increasing participation of children in work is a matter of major concern, especially because so little is known about the conditions under which they work. However, there is no doubt that, on one hand, child work reflects the deteriorating living conditions of the low income households in Managua, and on the other hand that it will affect, in different ways, the situation of these children and of the labour market in the city in the future. To quote an article by FIDEG:

---

[1] FIDEG (1995): El Oservador Económico. No. 48. p.36. Managua.
[2] Household survey of the Ministerio de Trabajo (MITRAB) 1994. Managua.

Even though these are strategies for survival which have to be used by many households, they imply a regression in terms of the social and economic situation in the long run, and a severe situation of physical risks for the children who work because of the high incidence of violence in the country.[1]

---

[1] FIDEG (1994): El Observador Económico. No. 35. p. 20. Managua. (Free translation by the author from the Spanish version).

Chapter 5

Methodology

Rationale for the selection of a research methodology

To do research about child work is a delicate undertaking since it touches upon a quite complex set of moral, cultural and social aspects which are not easy to approach through formal and standardized methods. The general tendency that child work is hidden—by parents as well as employers and even by official institutions and authorities—calls for the use of more exploratory methods that enable the researcher to approach this subject with sensitivity and prudence. The choice of methods for data collection, from the use of official statistics as secondary sources to open-ended interviews and observation methods as primary sources of information, depends of course on the objectives of the study in question.

The selection of methods for my investigation was based on an extensive review of the literature on child work in the informal sector, on literature about the urban informal sector in developing countries, especially focusing on Latin America, and to a certain extent also on my own professional experience of the production of official statistics in Managua, related to a broad programme of large-scale household surveys.[1]

A review of the literature on child work showed that the great majority of the authors did not say very much about the selection and implementation of the methods used in their studies. A good deal of

---

[1] UNDP assignment at INEC, Managua, 1988-1990.

the literature thus did not provide any real guidance in methodological questions. This lack of transparency in most studies was, however, compensated by the work of some of the leading scholars in the field, who paid special attention to the question of methods.[1] The main message emerging from their studies, even if they did not agree on all methodological issues, was that there is no single method which can be applied in a universal way. In the words of Hull, a combination of interviews with other techniques is an essential ingredient in this type of investigations:

> Several techniques are discussed (below), starting with the most directly observational, and proceeding along a continuum of increasingly structured mass-interview methods to national censuses. This sequence is arbitrary, but is not without importance. Good censuses are grounded in knowledge of the nature of socio-economic conditions, derived from observational studies and surveys. However, it is also true that the researcher is likely to interpret observations more accurately if informed about the general patterns revealed in surveys and censuses. Thus the order of exposition does not seek to suggest a temporal pattern when it comes to applying the techniques: they should be regarded as interactive, with research methods evolving as broader understanding of the nature of the research problems is achieved. No one technique should necessarily be used first: but the researcher's initial step should be to review the experience of others in applying a variety of methods.[2]

The message, then, was that the best way to do research on child work is to use both secondary and primary sources in such a combination that they complement each other. This multiple method approach should also include methods of validation and cross-checking.

---

[1]. See the works, referred to earlier by Guy Standing, Gerry Rodgers, Jo Boyden, Alec Fyfe, Terence Hull, and Bill Myers. Some authors did make a few references to the method they had used, but generally no reference at all was made; at best, the word "interview" or "survey" was simply mentioned in the text. The authors mentioned above, on the other hand, included discussions about methodology and presented guidelines and advice. My apologies to other authors that I may have overlooked.

[2]. Hull, T (1981): *Perspectives and data requirements for the study of children's work*. Rodgers, G. and Standing, G. (eds.): *Child work, Poverty and Underdevelopment*. ILO. Geneva.

Though it is not my intention to explore the pros and cons of all possible methods, I want to argue for the choice of methods for this study, by focusing firstly on the disadvantages of some of the most generally used methods. One of these is the large-scale household survey, a method which I have had the opportunity to use myself in other studies. It is my opinion that it is not well suited for research on child work. Several factors contribute to information loss in surveys— whether labour force surveys, household surveys or socio-demographic surveys. First of all, they are designed and conceived to analyse adult labour force participation and not that of children. If they are also used for collecting information about child work, usually no special questions about children are included; the minors are simply included as other members of the household. In other cases, a sub-set of questions about child work have been included in the questionnaire, but the interviewer is the same person and the questions are usually the same as those that are put to the adults. Secondly, only persons older than 18 are usually interviewed in person. All information concerning the minors of the household, including the child workers, is given by the head of the household and/or the spouse; the children themselves are not questioned.

Because of such procedures, and also because of the structure of the questionnaires, that usually follows international recommendations with respect to contents and layout, the answer to the introductory question about children and work, can, once it has been put in a certain way, jeopardize all the information about the working children which may be part of the household. This introductory question is usually formulated as "Name all persons of the age of ten/twelve or older, who work", or "Are there any children of ten/twelve years or older, working inside or outside the household?".[1] Since sending one's own child out to work involves many quite complex moral, cultural and social aspects, which people cannot do justice to in such a standardized way, the general tendency is to keep quiet about children's participation in work. In many cases the easiest way to avoid to give any

---

[1]. In large-scale household surveys, the minimum age for the economically active population is usually 15, since this is the legal age for working in most countries. However, in order to calculate the number of children in work, that age is sometimes lowered to 10 or 12 years.

information about child workers is simply to answer "no" to that first question. In my opinion that is the main reason why the results of such surveys always show an extremely low rate of participation in work by children, both inside and outside the household.

Another aspect to take into consideration is the interview situation itself; for example, the general atmosphere of the interview session, the frequent use of long questionnaires, the inclusion of all members of a household, as well as the manner in which the questions are presented. The questionnaires often include different types of questions—either closed or open-ended—the majority usually falling in the first category. In that case, the answers are already prepared in the form of alternatives, and the respondent has to choose one among them; thus, there is no room for qualifications or personal opinions. Even if this type of questions were free from prejudices on the part of questionnaire designer, they reflect what in his/her opinion is relevant. Open-ended questions on the other hand, give the respondent a chance to express his or her opinions freely, within certain limits. The main limit here is time; these questions are very time-consuming, and in one way or another the limited time and money available for the field work is likely to have an impact upon the study. Sometimes the questions have to be adjusted so that more standardized answers can be given, and time limitations all too often leave little or no room for dialogue and exchange of ideas.[1]

In the case of Managua, efforts have been made during the last few years to obtain information about child work through this type of surveys, earlier at the INEC[2], and later at FIDEG.[3] For that purpose, the minimum age for the members of the household to be considered as potentially economically active, was reduced to six years, instead of

---

[1]. These comments are based upon my own experience of work in household surveys in Managua, mentioned above. From my own observations of numerous interview situations, I can affirm that the inquiry was, almost without exception, experienced as a solemn occasion in the lives of the persons being interviewed. There was often a great deal of nervousness and fear of giving "the wrong answers", which led to constant double-checking by the interviewer and thus very long interview sessions.

[2]. INEC (1988–1990): Household Surveys: *Encuesta de Conyuntura y de Impacto*. Managua.

[3]. FIDEG: Household surveys from 1990 to 1995 included a special section about children's participation in work.

the usual fifteen. But the attempt to capture the percentage of working children by these means gave no significant results, since the highest value obtained was far below the lowest estimations based on a combination of several other sources. It was clearly not an adequate method for studying child work.

Rodgers and Standing commented upon the use of large-scale surveys and instead recommended the use of small-scale surveys, complemented with other methods:

> Small-scale surveys designed to clarify concepts and analytical approaches should be strongly encouraged, including actual observation of the behaviour patterns of children by means of participant observer techniques and other anthropological data-collection methods. Large-scale surveys of time allocation also have a role, especially as they permit the application of econometric techniques, but they risk hiding more than they reveal if used alone, without complementary data permitting the estimation of misreporting, the assessment of work intensity and productivity, and the depiction of the structural context within which the child work occurs.[1]

Apart from large-scale official surveys, other official statistics offer secondary data about children and work, e.g. national censuses, sociodemographic surveys, health statistics, educational statistics and others. These types of secondary sources have been used especially when the purpose has been to quantify child work at the national or regional level. Such studies have usually been sponsored and performed by governments in collaboration with international organizations such as UNICEF, the World Bank, WHO or ILO. Since they are extremely expensive to run, individual researchers cannot undertake investigations of such a magnitude on their own, but the results can be used to supplement data collected in other ways. There are examples of research that has been based solely on this sort of secondary data; it must of course be used with caution, particularly because the information to a large extent is based upon estimations, the accuracy of which can vary greatly from country to country. This can be illustrated by the

---

[1]. Rodgers, G. and Standing, G. (eds.) (1981): *Child work, Poverty and underdevelopment.* p. 41. ILO. Geneva.

enormous variations in the number of working children at national, regional and even local levels, that have been reported by different institutions.

In general, however, researchers in this field have recommended, and have themselves used, small-scale surveys and/or interviews (semi-structured or unstructured interviews) as the principal and most appropriate method in research on child work. The main argument for this approach is that it provides the best possibility to get unexpected information which is very difficult to acquire with structured and standardized questionnaires. Other methods which have been used primarily by social anthropologists have the disadvantages that they usually are very time demanding. One example is the various forms of direct observation techniques which require that the researcher resides in the study area for long periods of time, and participates, more or less, in the daily activities of the population under study. This approach also presents problems with respect to the validity of the observed facts, which requires the use of other complementary techniques. Life stories and daily activity diaries are other techniques that may be used as well as community-level investigations and periodical investigations.

A question of exceptional importance in any survey that attempts to collect primary data from informants is how they are to be selected. The selection of informants must be related to the type of investigation as well as to its objectives. As was pointed out above, a major reason for the lack of information about child work in large-scale surveys is in fact the selection of informants: usually the parents or other relatives of the children, or even their employers. The majority of studies on child work has thus been based on information supplied not by the children themselves but by other persons. The prevailing attitude among researchers, whether explicitly stated or not, has been a lack of faith in the capacity of the children to serve as informants. This is surprising and certainly would never be acceptable from an ethical point of view in research on any other human population. On the other hand, it reflects what some authors express as a problem in this type of research and which essentially has to do with the relationship between adult and child or between authority and subordination. To some people, children are incomprehensible to adults since "they live in their own world". Others believe that children are not capable of expressing their opinions and feelings. In my opinion, to avoid contact with the child is to accept and in fact to perpetuate a relationship based on the authority of adults over children; it might even emanate from a fear of confronting the children's own version of their own lives as children and as integral parts of the labour force. Terence Hull is one among a number of researchers who strongly advocate that information should be collected directly from the children.[1]

The Methodology of the Study

Drawing upon results and suggestions in previous research, presented above, and considering the nature and the aims of this study, a combination of different but complementary methods have been used. The central method was, however, of an exploratory character since this was the only way in which it seemed possible to collect the kind of information needed for the purposes of the study. Therefore, the major source of information was a series of semi-structured interviews with working children in the urban informal sector of Managua. Those interviews, which together can be described as a small-scale survey with a common guide, were then followed up by more extensive interviews, more in the form of free conversation, with some of the children. The choice of semi-structured interviews as the main source of information was also related to the fact that I wanted to collect information that in certain ways would allow me to make comparisons between children at different places of work in the city. In fact, on one hand semi-structured interviews seemed to offer a possibility of collecting information which would allow a certain quantification of some variables of interest for the comparative analysis and also would make possible cross-checking of this information with available official statistics. On the other hand, they offered opportunities for free conversations with the children, and a chance for them to express their

---

[1.] Hull, T (1981): *Perspectives and data requirements for the study of children's work*. Rodgers, G. and Standing, G. (eds.): *Child work, Poverty and Underdevelopment*. ILO. Geneva.

own opinions about different topics. Later on, during the conversations, some of those topics were brought up to discussion but then in a completely informal format. The contents of the interview form were partly inspired by Fyfe's guide for project design[1] and by UNICEF's methodological guide.[2]

One of the aims of this work is to study the everyday life of the working children. Whether they succeed or not in organizing the activities they have planned to perform depends, among other things, on the constraints that their plans meet. Among a variety of restrictions, time is a very central one, as well as the distance between the locations where different activities can, or must, take place. These basic principles, which rule all our lives, have been the focus of many studies. In geography, Torsten Hägerstrand has developed an approach—time geography—which, among other aspects, is characterized by a mode of graphic description that can visualize the time-space paths of individuals in different temporal contexts.[3] This study is not, however, an application of the time geography methodology. The type of information required, e.g. in the form of diaries, was certainly not possible to collect when the purpose was to study the everyday life of children who in many cases could not yet write. Thus, the interviews and conversations with the children will give the necessary information for the study of their everyday life. However, I have certainly been inspired by time geography and, besides the writings of Hägerstrand, especially the work by Friberg on the different life forms of women and Åquist's review of the development and methodology of time geography have been sources of inspiration.[4]

From the very first beginning of the study, I was firmly convinced that the main informants should be the working children themselves.

---

[1]. Fyfe, A. (1993): *Child Labour: A guide to project design*. International Labour Office. Geneva.

[2]. UNICEF (1989): *Lineamentos para la aplicación de la guia metodológica para el análisis de situación. Menores en circunstancias especialmente difíciles*. Serie Metodológica. No. 8.

[3]. Hägerstrand, T. (1974): *Tidsgeografisk beskrivning. Syfte och postulat*. Svensk Geografisk Årsbok, årg 50. Lund; Hägerstrand, T. (1974): Studier i samverkans tids- och platsberoende. Svensk Geografisk Årsbok. 50.Lund.

[4]. Friberg, T. (1990): *Kvinnors vardag. Om kvinnors arbete och liv. Anpassningsstrategier i tid och rum*. Lund University Press. Lund. Åquist, A. (1992): *Tidsgeografi i samspel med samhällsteori*. Lund University Press. Lund.

I could see no reason why individuals, who have enough responsibility to engage in activities side by side with adults, would not be capable of telling me about their work and their situation as workers. They, better than anyone else, should be able to describe their life situation, and, furthermore, there is no evidence at all to suggest that working children should hide or distort information more than adults might do in an interview situation.

Research strategy

Two alternative procedures for selecting a sample of children for the present study were considered. One alternative would have been to identify and select a sample of working children on the basis of data from the household surveys carried out in Managua. This would have been a time-demanding process, but more importantly, such a procedure probably would have made it quite difficult to interview the children alone, apart from their parents or other relatives with which they lived. It would also have resulted in a very fragmented view of the spatial variations in child work in the city. The other alternative was to select the sample of individuals in the field, at a set of places which could be characterized as foci of child work in Managua. I chose this second alternative for two reasons. Firstly, because this approach allowed a careful choice of different types of places of work in the city, it seemed more likely that this procedure would bring to light variations in the spatial characteristics of the working situation of the children. Secondly, this strategy seemed to be a more child-oriented approach since it would provide greater opportunities for the children—as the main informants in the study—to speak freely and more openly away from their households.

The field work was carried out at two different times in Managua, the first in 1993, lasting for about four weeks, the second in the 1994 lasting for about six weeks.[1] A more detailed description of the field work, the selection of the places of work, and of the sample of children will be presented later on in the study.

Other Sources

In addition to the information collected through the interviews, data from secondary sources have been used as well. Among those sources, the most useful have been the household surveys performed by FIDEG in Managua, partly published in the magazine El Observador Económico, as well as other reports from that institution. Published and unpublished reports by several NGOs in Nicaragua on children and publications by different agencies of the United Nations on Nicaragua or on the larger region of Central America and the Caribbean have also provided useful information.

---

[1] The fact that I had lived in Managua during a period of four years until the end of 1990, and had been engaged in a household survey programme in the city, had given me quite a detailed knowledge of the city, as well as good command of the language. This knowledge of the city explains why the first period of field work did not have to be longer. The interviews were mostly carried out by myself. However, I was assisted by a Nicaraguan colleague with vast professional experience in interview techniques, who helped me during all the interview period.

Part Two

Figure 2   The boy who sold used newspapers, with a friend

I met Terner one morning at the Roberto Huembes market, when he was selling used newspapers that he wheeled around in a small wooden barrow along the passages of the market. He was properly dressed, cheerful, and seemed younger than the eight years he told me that he was. He said that he was seven years old when he began to work; at that time his parents separated and, together with a sister, he moved in with his grandparents, who lived in a district nearby the market.

He said that he enjoyed his job very much because he earned good money. In fact he had two jobs. Every day, at seven in the morning, he went to a nearby district, Altamira, and knocked on doors offering his services—to throw trash away. He had a certain number of regular customers who paid him mostly by giving him used newspapers, but sometimes with some small change. He said, however, that he preferred the used newspapers because selling newspapers was his best job. He stacked the newspapers into small bundles, tied them up with a piece of string and took them in the small wheel-barrow to the market where he sold them. Usually he sold them in the course of a couple of hours before going to school; otherwise he sold them in the afternoon, when he had finished school.

He usually worked every day of the week, including the weekends. School began at half past twelve, so first he went home, gave the money he had earned to his grandmother, took a bath and had something to eat. Then he went to school. He began to go to school when he was seven years old. With his earnings he paid for his school uniform and his shoes. Sometimes he himself bought some food at the market before going home, such as beans or rice or whatever his grandmother asked him to buy, but usually he gave her all the money.

He said that he did not need any money—he had all he needed. In his opinion he had plenty of time to play with his friends, either at school during recesses, or in the afternoon after school. That is, if he had any time for that, because at home he had to do his homework, and he used to sweep the backyard for his grandmother as well. He said that if he had not been working, he would do more homework and play more with his friends. On the other hand, he said, he thought that it was a good thing that children worked, so that they could pay for their own food. He never thought about what he wanted to be when he grew up.

Chapter 6

The case study

Part Two of this work is a case study of the working children in the informal sector in Managua. My ambition was that children should be the leading actors in this study, and therefore must be given the opportunity to speak out themselves about their life situation, without any interference from adults. From a methodological point of view this represents a somewhat innovative approach, in contrast to the many studies in which, information about the children and their households has been obtained not from the children but from other members of households. The selection of the sample of the children was made "in the field", as it were, at places where the children actually worked, in an attempt to bring to light place characteristics which might influence the organization of the everyday life of the children.

The field work

The two field work periods had different character and objectives. During the first one, the purpose was to identify the main foci of child work in the informal sector of the city and to select the places of work where the study should be conducted. Also, some interviews with working children were carried out in order to check certain aspects related to the communication with the children, such as the contact with them, and the interview environment. During that first visit, contact was established with several organizations that worked directly, in one way or another, with the children, in order to get acquainted with place-specific aspects which might not have been mentioned in the literature or acquired from other sources.

The main objectives during the second field work period were, firstly, to make the final decision with respect to the sample of places of work, to decide upon the size of the sample of working children at each work place and finally to interview the children. In the process of this final phase I made a large number of visits to each place of work, not only to do the interviews, but also to observe the general features of these work environment, and specifically to observe the working children as they performed their activities. Additional short interviews with some adults—and a few parents—working at the investigated places of work, were also made in order to complete the information especially regarding the places of work.

The interviews with the children

At this stage it is important to describe the interview situations in order to enable the reader to get some idea about the kind of milieu in which they took place.

I have to confess that the interviews turned out very differently from what I had originally expected, for several reasons. My original intention was to give a free rein to the children during the interviews; the main topics of the study would be presented to the children and they would talk spontaneously about them. Very soon, however, after some pilot interviews, I realized that information collected in this way would be very disparate in terms of quality and coverage, and consequently would be difficult to analyse in a comparative context. It was obvious that the children were quite willing to talk about their life situation, both with respect to their family life and to their life as child workers and students. But it was also obvious that it was necessary to structure this flow of information more strictly, at least in some respects. The children were obviously expecting to be asked questions, and as a result, the open discussion format was abandoned in favour of semi-structured interviews. Since the children were the only informants used in the study, the information that they provided about the socio-economic characteristics of their households ought to be collected in such a way that a comparative analysis between the individual cases would be facilitated. As a result, the interviews followed a schedule of questions which was used as a kind of frame for the conversations with the children. The questions were open-ended. Although the interviews followed the format of the interview form, the open questions often led to impromptu discussions in which the children talked spontaneously about their lives.[1]

Since I made many visits to the different places of work, I became a familiar sight there, and the children often came up to me and asked to be interviewed. The major difficulty encountered was to say "no" when a child wanted to be interviewed rather than to get the children to accept to be interviewed. Each day more children wanted to be included in the study, particularly at the largest places of work.

The interview situation varied from one place of work to another, but all the children were first introduced to the aims of the study and then asked if they wanted to participate. Before the interview began, they were asked if they wanted to speak in the presence of the other children or alone. With very few exceptions the children chose to speak in the presence of the other children. Often the children sat down inside my car so that, as they said, they really could concentrate on the questions. The windows were open because of the heat and the car was surrounded by the other children who were curious about the interview. The fact that the interviews were made in the presence of other children was in fact very positive because I early on realized that, because many of the children knew each other very well, their presence became a way of double-checking the information given. In fact, it happened that older children corrected some of the answers that the younger children gave with respect to transportation times and addresses. It is important to note that the children looked upon the interview situation as a very solemn occasion, and they really enjoyed to speak to a recorder, and later to listen to their own voice and statements.

[1.] The interview guide is presented in Appendix.

The interview form was meant to serve as a guideline for the interviews rather than as a fixed format that the children were supposed to follow rigorously. However, most children put themselves in the situation of answering the questions they were asked, rather than to speak freely about the subjects that were brought up, for instance about their household and family. Therefore, my decision was to follow the questionnaire in all the interviews but always to give the children an opportunity to add whatever information they thought was relevant, if they wished to do so.

The length of each interview varied, mostly depending on the children, but also on the character of the place of work. The children had no difficulty in understanding the questions, but some questions were of an exploratory type and required that the children's answers were checked carefully by phrasing the same question in different ways; in some cases this led to relatively long interviews. The length of the interviews also depended on the age of the children and on their ability to express themselves. Some children followed up each question with a lot of additional information, whereas other kept very close to what the question was focusing upon. The interviews at the smaller places of work took very little time, between thirty and forty minutes; because of the character of those places—less traffic in the surroundings, and not so many people moving around—the children were calm and the interviews were seldom interrupted. It was also easier to speak with the children afterwards, when the interview had been completed. In the largest places of work, the situation was quite different. The high level of noise from the traffic, and the presence of people who were curious about what was going on, led to many interruptions of the interviews, and made it difficult for the children to concentrate on the conversation with me. Some of the interviews took almost one hour, and some had to be completed later on the same day. The general conversations after the interviews were often very lively and the other children who had not been interviewed usually took part in them as well. These conversations were not recorded.

After having interviewed sixty working children in the informal sector of Managua, I can honestly say that these children were the most cooperative and forthcoming informants one could wish for. Although in some respects their life experiences are limited because of their young age, on the other hand they have acquired incomparable experience from their engagement in work in the labour market, where they work side by side with adults. These children were very much aware of their living conditions, often tough and burdensome, but still willing to share their thoughts about how they live in the present and what they wish that their future should look like.

Finally, I would like to note that although all the children who participated in this investigation provided me with a good deal of personal data, they will only be referred to by their first name and their age, in accordance with normal ethical rules of research, and in order to safeguard their right to anonymity.

Chapter 7

The study area

The selection of the working places

The street is one of the principal working places of the children who are active in the urban informal sector. The concept of the "street", however, may mean different things to different people and can be perceived in very different ways. The physical dimension is perhaps the one that comes directly to mind, in the sense that the most common perception of "street" is a physical structure with a certain layout and form. A less common perception of the "street" concept posits the "street" in more abstract and nuanced ways. Here, the "street" may be a symbol for or a relatively vague catch-all term for all places and spaces outside of the home. Thus conceived, the "street" would, for example, represent or include even the institutions and structures often associated with formal activities as well.

In Managua, most working children congregate around easily identified "foci", often in the streets and around places with well defined economic functions such as the markets. In this study, I chose to focus my attention on two of the most frequent "foci" for children working in the urban informal sector, namely markets and parking areas. The final sample of the study areas consists of two parking areas and three markets. The purpose of selecting several working places was to bring out those place characteristics which could explain certain variations, if any, in the organization of work, activities and mode of employment. The five places which were selected are described below.

The sample of parking areas

Managua is a fast-growing city, with relatively many cars. The polycentric spatial and economic structure of the city has meant that there are several centres of commerce spread like islands throughout the city, ranging from traditional markets to supermarkets and small-scale malls. Many of the parking areas which function as foci for urban child work in the city's informal sector evolved as necessary and supplementary structures to the supermarkets and malls. The exceptions are the parking lots at the airport, international hotels and the universities, where car guarding is prohibited since these places have their own parking lot guards or are fenced in. Until recently, car guarding and washing was one of the most common activities and children could be seen in almost all parking areas in Managua. Of late, however, the situation has changed dramatically, reflecting the high adult unemployment rates in the city, and to a large extent these activities have been taken over by adults, mostly men who deny or restrict children access to work as parking lot guards.

Repeated visits to the major parking lots in the city, conducted at different times of the day, enabled me to identify the parking areas where children were still working. Two of these were selected, namely, the Galeria Internacional parking area, and the parking area at the Market Roberto Huembes. Beyond the fact that these two places have distinct characteristics, several other criteria were employed in the selection, such as the location, the size, the organization of work and the number of active persons.

The sample of markets

Numerous markets are found all over the city of Managua. The markets have different functions, offer various services and concentrate on a wide variety of activities. The degree of functional differentiation among the markets is considerable. They vary in size, physical structure, types of services provided, activities performed, and with respect to their relative location vis-à-vis other non-market related activities and centres, such as public institutions, as well as government and private offices. Some of the markets are large and located next to central

Figure 3   The location of the selected places of work in Managua

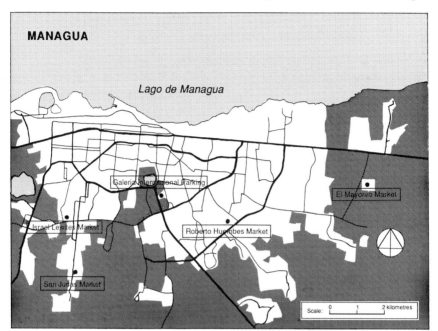

bus stations, while some are small and only serve the immediate neighbourhoods. Some markets run wholesale businesses, others serve as centres for different handicraft workshops and products. The objective behind the selection of markets to be studied was to capture some of the variations in their location, functional specialization and differentiation, in order to have a relatively broad spectrum of market types in Managua. Put differently, the objective behind the selection strategy employed was to search for specific characteristics in child work and whether these reflect market types. The markets selected for this study were: (i) San Judas; (ii) El Mayoreo; (iii) Israel Lewites, and (iv) Roberto Huembes.

Portrayals of the places of work: spatial activity patterns, organization of work and work milieu

In order to make clear the variations which exist between the different places of work in terms of economic and spatial aspects and the organization of work, as well as to present an overall picture of these places to the reader, a relatively detailed description of the work places will be presented below. These portrayals will be supplemented by discussions of the work milieu as well.

There is a close relationship between types of activities and places. In spite of the mobility and dynamism which characterize some of the activities of the urban informal sector, the nature of the tasks involved is such that certain activities become more or less confined to certain places. Warding cars, for instance, is an activity that is restricted to a certain type of place, in contrast to other informal sector activities that are footloose, i. e. not necessarily located at a specific place, such as vending or shoe shining.

The available information is not sufficiently extensive to make possible a comprehensive account of the spatial patterns of child work in Managua. This is in part due to the fact that some of the activities performed by children are hidden to the public eye, as in the case of work in small family enterprises, apprenticeships in various workshops and domestic work. For the visible activities, those that are discussed in this study, on the other hand, some rather well defined patterns of association between places and activities could be discerned.

What follows is an attempt to identify, describe and analyse variations between as well as within the work places investigated, in terms of the spatial distribution and types of activities at these places. A more specific objective has been to analyse the situation of these work places from a gender perspective. The investigation is based mainly on information collected through direct observation, supplemented by information collected through conversations with the children who were working at the selected work places, as well as with some adults.[1]

---

[1]. Partly through the interviews, partly through spontaneous conversations.

The Galeria Internacional parking lot

The Galeria Internacional is an exclusive shopping centre that has replaced the former Diplomatic Shop. It is a huge one-storey building that occupies a whole block, and is located in a nice area surrounded by greenery and a splatter of small buildings with shops. Just a block away from the Galeria Internacional there is another big department store with a fenced parking lot and a guard on duty.

Just in front of the main entrance to the Galeria, there are two paved parking lots. The smaller of the two had parking space for six cars, whereas the larger could accommodate up to 20 cars. There was an even larger unpaved parking space for approximately 50 cars on the northern side of the store. There was some parking space available along two sides of the building as well. During the economic embargo of Nicaragua that was instigated by the US in the late 1980's, this was the only store in Managua where one could buy imported goods for foreign currency (US $). Initially, this was only possible for foreigners and diplomats, but later on wealthy Nicaraguans could also shop here. The Galeria became a very popular place to visit and the parking lots here were always full. When the Sandinista era came to an end and a new right wing government came to power in 1990, the reintroduction of a market economy meant heightened competition from other newly established shops, or from shopping centres already in existence in the city, and this led to a drastic decline in the popularity of the Galeria Internacional and in the number of customers. These changes have had an impact in several far-reaching and visible ways on child work in general and on the situation of the working children at this foci in particular, in terms of the organization of work, activity type, earnings and relocation of activities.

As of 1992, the opportunities for informal activities around the Galeria Internacional had deteriorated substantially. The income earned from informal sector employment in the streets alongside the places of formal economic activity—the shops—has been steadily diminishing and it was no longer sufficient to support the same number of people. The daily struggle for income, and the hardened climate of competition, became a constant source of disputes for a period of time. Some gave up their work and moved out. Others have

Figure 4   The parking lot at Galeria Internacional

had to make adjustments and compromises in the form of a new organization of work because of these changes in the local situation.

One such adjustment is the evolution of an allocation system for parking lots, i.e. assigning or distributing the parking lots and places surrounding the parking areas to a limited number of persons. The main criterion for the system of allocation was a sort of graduated seniority system whereby those who had been working longer obtained priority to the best places and parking lots. In practice, the new arrangements were neither smoothly arrived at nor easy to implement since they implied the exclusion of some people who previously had been working here. It appears that threats and even violence have been resorted to in this process. In any case, those who became entitled to the parking lots and places apportioned these amongst themselves. Some of the consequences are seen in the evolution of various forms of territorialization of the places and parking lots and the emergence of a sense of boundary consciousness, the institutionalization of formal and quasi-formal codes of respect for borders and working spaces. In spite of the absence of fences, this informal work place had well defined symbolic boundaries that barred others from gaining access, and demarcated the spaces of different activities. The place of work at the Galeria Internacional was almost the exclusive domain of two related families, which allocated space for different activities among the family members. The parking lot was run by children from both families, whereas the fruit-selling stand and the canteen were operated by the adults.

The parking lot at the Galeria Internacional was characterized by a calm working atmosphere. The children knew each other very well and some of them were relatives. A twelve year old boy was in charge of organizing work at the parking lots and maintaining order among the children. He succeeded his father in this job. He used to accompany his father who worked as the official security guard at the Galeria parking lot before he died. After the death of his father, the security guard of the Galeria decided to give the boy an informal and non-salaried position in honour of his father. Vested with the responsibility of overseeing and organizing work at the parking lot, the child assumed the role of the leader, and the identification badge that he wore enhanced this function. He assigned work to the children on a rotational basis which ensured a fair distribution of work in the sense that at the end of the day the children had warded the same number of cars. In his position he was empowered to intervene in and solve conflicts, if and when they arose, as well. In the conversations I had with some of the children, they informed me that his status was not negotiable and they understood that this was necessary. Furthermore, his role was necessary for maintaining an orderly work place and to avoid the intrusions of newcomers. Judging from the quiet and orderly work atmosphere at the Galeria Internacional, which I noticed during my visits, and the approval of the security guard of the shops surrounding the parking lot, the boy must have been doing a good job.

This place of work was dominated by one activity of the children alone, namely guarding cars. Although the summary data presented on the distribution of activities between girls and boys suggests that guarding cars is on the whole an activity performed by boys, at the Galeria Internacional this task was performed both by boys and girls. Here, the activities of children were under strict supervision of the security guard of the parking lot, who banned other activities in the park besides car warding. Car warding was thus organized in such a way that it did not allow children to perform other activities. The children's own organization, a trade union of sorts, also required all children to be permanently at disposal for car guarding. It thus functioned as a complementary factor in the regulation/supervision of the activities of the children working at the Galeria Internacional. This preempted the possibility of many children running other activities in addition to car warding. It thereby minimized the risk that a situation would arise where, as described by the boy "head" or "leader" of the parking lot, "if someone drops out, the whole 'system' would come to a halt". To all intents and purposes, the system appeared to function, since only the interviewed girls admitted that they helped their relatives in selling their products (fruits and food) when work slackened in the parking lot. In contrast, all the interviewed boys stated that they were not involved in any other activity while working as car guards in the parking lot.

Although the girls to some extent were engaged in selling food products for their relatives besides guarding cars at the parking lot, it is not really appropriate to speak of an occupational differentiation on the basis of gender at the Galeria Internacional, since both boys and girls performed the same basic activity, car warding.

San Judas market

San Judas market is quite unique in its character compared to the other work places in the sample. It is located in the San Judas district, in southwest Managua, alongside the main street with the same name. This market is a typical district market which primarily serves the population that lives in the surroundings. It consists of just one single building, inside which there are lines of stalls where different products are sold: vegetables, fruits, meat, cheese and so forth. In one part of the market there are also bars and food-serving stalls. There is a small parking lot at the back of the building and some of the bus lines have

Figure 5   The San Judas market

their stops there. Along the outside walls of the market there were also stands with clothes, shoes and many other articles for sale. Movement was intense inside the market, but very slow on the outside. Activities on the sidewalks were almost non-existent and apart from the traffic in the main street in front of the market, and at the bus stops on the backside, the first impression, if one visits the place in the afternoon, is that the market area is very quiet.

A characteristic feature of this market, however, is that it is very active in the morning, since most people come here mainly to buy products for their daily use, but is extremely lethargic in the afternoon, when it is almost empty of customers. There were not so many children working there, and those who did knew each other quite well. They worked mainly inside the market, but also at the entrance to the market. They said they did not work next to the bus stop area. In this environment, the children seemed calm and apparently there was no competition among them. Most adult sellers at this market had permanent selling stalls, there did not seem to be any competition between the child sellers and the adult sellers. The difference between this market and the other markets of the sample was so striking that one could almost imagine that this market was somewhere else but in the city.

The occupational distribution by gender at the San Judas market stands in stark contrast to that at the other places of work. Here, the proportion of boys and girls was the opposite, and the dominance of girl workers was substantial. This was in part a reflection of the limited range of activities that were conducted at the San Judas market place. In fact, only two types of occupations were found here: sellers and helpers or extra hands. No gender differentiation by activity could be found; boys and girls engaged in the same occupations.

Israel Lewites market

The official name of this market is Boer market, but it is known as Israel Lewites market, and that is the name that will be used in this study. Contrary to San Judas market, Israel Lewites is a very big market and has a very central location. It is situated in the middle of the city quite close to one of the principal roads—Pista Juan Pablo, to the Ministry of Education, and to the City Hall. This market occupies a large area and consists of different open buildings, each one with its specific activities. There are several parking lots around the market. On the north side of the market there is a big bus terminal and a taxi stand, which gives to the market that atmosphere so common in other big cities, but less usual in Managua, of intensive movement from early morning to late evening. The very diversified character of the market, its size and its spatial openness can give one a feeling of not quite being able to control the place in its entirety. At the same time and precisely because of this diversity, however, this is an extremely attractive place of work for vendors of all kinds.

The work environment was quite stressful because of the very high noise level that all the people, the buses and the cars produced. There were many children working here, most of them did not seem to

Figure 6   Israel Lewites market

know each other. From the conversations I had with the children, it became clear, however, that some of the children were related to each other, but still worked individually. Because of the large area of this market, the children had to work separately from each other and thus were not directly competing with each other for the clients. In fact they mostly circulated, often on their own. The bars serving food and drinks, as well as ambulatory sellers of food and beverages, had a large clientele here, and the presence of children selling all possible items or products was a distinct feature of this work place. There was no marked difference in child work in terms of gender. Both boys and girls engaged in guarding cars at the parking lot of the market or in selling. As in the previous market places, shoe-shining was totally dominated by boys. Another, but less significant occupation, and one that was also dominated by boys, was that of bearer, carrying the luggage of bus passengers from buses to taxies or private cars. They did not receive any threats from adults or from other children, they said, although, many adults were engaged in selling the same type of products as the children.

El Mayoreo market

This market is quite unique in Managua because of its character as a wholesale market. To this market come all kinds of merchandise from other regions, which are then bought by retailers from other markets. For most of the 1980's, this was the only type of sales, but during the 1990's the market has been open to all kinds of commerce—wholesale, sales to retailers and direct selling to customers. Earlier, the market's activity was more or less regulated by the state, but with the introduction of a free market economy in the country in the last few years the market's character has been changing and the informal vendors have invaded the market area. In fact, large areas of informal sales activities, primarily of vegetables and fruits—are now spread all along the fringes of the market but still inside a restricted area, which is delimited by a fence.

This market is located in the extreme east of Managua, near the Carretera Norte road and quite isolated from the residential districts of the city. It is a very large market composed of several very huge buildings—some closed, others open—where the various products are sold. Besides the usual types of market commerce, at the entrance to the market there are some areas with very different activities, such as a bank office. In spite of the size of the area, the market is spatially well demarcated and is subject to some guard surveillance.
Although in principle open all day, the intensive period at the market was in the very early hours of the morning, when the lorries arrive from the countryside and the products are unloaded. The working atmosphere of this place was one of great bustle and movement in the mornings and almost of sluggishness in the afternoons.

Here, as at Israel Lewites market, it was difficult at first sight to form an idea about the number of children working there. However, after a few visits to the place, it became clear that actually quite a number of children worked here. They were very dispersed over the

Figure 7   El Mayoreo market

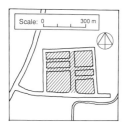

huge area of the place; they were not working in groups, but alone or in the company of a relative who was also working there. In spite of the calm atmosphere of the place and the presence of guards, the children confessed that they were often afraid to be there alone. They referred to an act of crime a few days before my visits, that had made a great impression upon them. Otherwise, they were not really afraid inside the market area, more so on their way home, since the market was very isolated.

In addition to all of the occupations mentioned earlier, new types of activities were found at the El Mayoreo market place. It was immediately easy to observe that there were as many girls as boys moving around. Some children were engaged in picking up vegetables and fruit from waste dumps both for consumption and selling. Some of the activities at the El Mayoreo market place were tied to a specific day of the week or even time of the day. Since the El Mayoreo is mainly a wholesale market, there is plenty of work available for the children during supply days, unloading lorries in the early hours of the morning. No girls worked as loaders and bearers, whereas this activity engaged a relatively large number of boys of varying ages. Later on during the day and on other days most of them moved in and around the market offering their services as bearers to customers. Many children worked as extra hands for the sellers with permanent stands, washed vegetables and fruit, and cleaned the selling stands.

An interesting and peculiar feature of this market was the absence of car warding, despite the fact that there were several parking lots at the market. However, the location and distance of the parking lots in relation to the different buildings in the market was such that people could easily keep an eye on the cars from the market itself.[1] Consequently, the activity of guarding cars was a marginal or sporadic one and not the main activity of any of the children. Compared to the boys, the girls engaged in a more limited scope of occupations, mainly confined to selling. Another unique feature for this market was the fact that boys tended to combine several activities, on different days of the week and even during the same day. For instance a boy seller might help unload a lorry early in the morning, guard a couple of cars later on when some richer customers came to shop, and sell razor blades in between.

Roberto Huembes market: the parking lots and the market

Roberto Huembes is one of the biggest markets in the city. It has several parking lots, the main one very large with parking space for about 200 cars. It is located within the market area, on one side of the market, in front of the main building where fruits, vegetables and groceries are sold, and where most of the bars are located. The parking lot is not fenced in, but the area is well defined because it is surrounded by

---

[1]. The parking places were located in front of and along the buildings, making it possible for the visitor to observe them from inside the buildings without any great effort. Some of the buildings were quite far from each other and therefore it was more practical for the visitors to move from place to place by car; as a result, the parking time at one place was not so long as to justify the car ward.

Figure 8   The Roberto Huembes market: the smaller parking lot

buildings along two of its sides, and is bounded by ditches and uncultivated terrain along the other sides. A smaller parking lot for about 50 cars is enclosed by two buildings (the main building along its frontside, and another building running along the main entrance with several shops facing the parking lot), and the road. Neither of the parking lots is asphalted. In the upper and lower parts of the largest parking lot, a few trees, rather than painted lines, mark the area where cars should be parked.

For a long time this parking area was an important working place for children of both sexes, with no adults guarding and washing cars. The situation was quite different at the time when I visited the area for the purposes of this study. At that time more than half the work force was made up of adults and younger men. Some of these men stated that they were not interested in sharing work with children, but were obliged to do so in order to avoid the possible disapproval of some organizations that advocate the interests of working children at the market. At the same time they claimed that customers tended to prefer to be served by them rather than by the children.

The children had a very different perception of the situation. It was evident to them that the men controlled the place and used their status as adults to exercise authority; at times they even resorted to sheer force. To force the children to move to less attractive, remote parts of the market, where there was no shade, was one expression of the authority exercised by the men. At times when business was slow, however, the children challenged the spatial and economic marginalization enforced upon them by the adults by invading "their" area to get more cars to guard and thereby earn more money, which often led to violent incidents. The smaller parking lot was dominated by a group of younger men sharing a part of it with some children who were protected by relatives working at the market. On what was called the good days[1], i.e. Fridays, Saturdays and Sundays, the territories of dominance were much less clearly defined and the children succeeded in transgressing them. The most disputed and conflict-ridden zone ran along the invisible line drawn to separate the areas of the adults and the children, respectively. Each time a car approached the contested zone, many of the children tried to woo the drivers to park on "their" side by calling, screaming or whistling. The adults, used identical tactics on their part.

There were no small children working in the parking lot at this market. The children were poorly organized and for the most part worked on their own, save in the few cases where children bonded together to form very small groups of two or three and collaborated in trying to attract drivers to their area. These bondings were informal, were formed spontaneously and varied from day to day depending on variations in the work load. Still, the children did not practice income sharing. On the other hand, as has been shown to be the case among child labour in the urban informal sector in other cities in Latin

---

[1]. The children informed me about the "good" and the "bad" days of work, which they defined in terms of the opportunities for earning money. These days were not the same at the different working places, but depended on the characteristics of the places.

America, no organized economic exploitation of the children by the adults was found here, with children being "employed" by adults who collect their income and pay them a fixed salary on a daily basis.

The work environment at the Roberto Huembes market was rough and characterized by a constant competitive atmosphere among children and adults over guarding cars in the parking area. Some children confessed that they were afraid of the adults and the group of younger men in the smaller parking area, because some of them were armed, used drugs, and could become very aggressive. Children often complained about the absence of security guards in the parking lots, which left them unprotected. They named several children who had had to quit work because they were too afraid. The adults established their superiority and power through threats and even by means of physical violence. Moreover, the adults frustrated attempts by the children to organize, either through preferential treatment of some children, for instance by allowing them to guard cars in the "best" parking lot spots, or by provoking conflict among the children. On the whole, however, the children expressed positive opinions about the working place, not least because it was a good source of income. One reason for this was the handicraft section of this market, which tended to attract many foreigners and tourists who usually paid more for car guarding.

In comparison to the Galeria Internacional and San Judas market, the division of work by sex and the spatial distribution of activities performed by children at the Roberto Huembes market was much more clearly demarcated. On the whole, boys were more prominent and outnumbered girls in all activities. Due to the almost complete division of activities by sex, the physical structure of the area, as well as the organization of work at the Roberto Huembes market, child work patterns were easily discernible. The market was divided into three main areas: the parking lot, the market for food, and separate buildings for different purposes—handicraft, services such as hairdressing and manicure, workshops such as shoemakers, and clothes and shoe stalls. In the parking lot, the tasks of guarding and washing cars were performed by boys, and no girls worked there. If one takes the rough work milieu at this place into account, the fact that girls were in a minority is not really surprising.

Figure 9   Another view of the Roberto Huembes market

Selling in the parking lot was a sporadic and risky activity. If children were caught in the act by the adults guarding the cars they risked being thrown out from the parking lot. The children thus preferred to offer such services as carrying shopping baskets for the customers at the market. Again this activity was performed exclusively by boys. Another typical boy's activity was shoe shining. This activity was not confined to a specific place in the market. Yet, it tended to be performed mainly in the vicinity of the parking lot area and the bars, since many of the clients, i. e. men, who come to the market with their wives, tend to hang around the buildings surrounding the parking lot or in the bars.

Even though selling was an activity that was common to both boys and girls, it was nevertheless dominated by boys. It was not a place-specific activity, but was rather undertaken anywhere in the market place, except in the parking lot, inside the malls as well as in the open. In addition to working as sellers, girls also worked as extra hands doing miscellaneous work for the owners of various businesses in the market, but most typically as extra hands in the hairdressing business. Boys, on the other hand, often worked as helpers to vegetable and fruit sellers, as cleaners and in loading or unloading various types of merchandise.

The small number of girl workers can be attributed to a set of factors (not dealt with in detail here), which partly reflect the overall characteristics of the Roberto Huembes market. One of those factors concerns aspects which have to do with the control of place or space. The parking lot was a place that was controlled and run by boys and adult males. A second factor behind the very low participation of girls in activities related to selling things, is simply that the majority of children engaged in the activities under study were boys. Thirdly, many homeless children were drawn to the market place during the day, because free food and school facilities were available, provided through aid programs and located at the market. The combination of strict control over space, overrepresentation of boys and the considerable concentration of children at the market, accounted for the fact that most girls felt insecure. They expressed their fear in the interviews by describing the Roberto Huembes market as a dangerous place and in general perceived as one not safe for girls.

Concluding remarks: the struggle over urban economic space

The urban informal sector has different kinds of "barriers" which restrict access to it by outsiders. Some of these barriers have a spatial expression. The struggle for urban economic space observed in the work places discussed above are examples or expressions of the variety in the organization of economic space within the informal sector in the city of Managua. The type of organization of economic space that prevailed at the Galeria Internacional was based on binding or contractual, though unwritten, agreements within a group of persons that divided up, or rationed, the economic rights, i.e. access to and use of public space (the streets and the sidewalks) and private space in and around the parking area. These contracts provided for sole or exclusive rights in the use and exploitation of the public and private resources and spaces. Within the framework of the contract, the rights of access to work in these spaces covered the younger members of the family, i.e. the children, as well. At Galeria Internacional the children were accepted as full-fledged contractual partners, in contrast to the situation at the Roberto Huembes market where similar contractual arrangements were absent. At the Galeria Internacional, children were entitled to apportion and dispose of the places or spaces allocated to them as they deemed fit. The contractual principle at work here is similar to usufructual rights, that is, the rights of access to and use of resources such as land are conditional upon exercising these rights.

One consequence of the contractual arrangements at the Galeria Internacional was that the entitlements or rights became spatially entrenched, thus making access for newcomers and outsiders practically impossible. These rights and arrangements, however, are not necessarily permanent. Rather they are subject to renegotiation, with excluded persons contesting and challenging such arrangements and those already established at a place trying to defend their rights and to deny access to others. As a consequence, the struggles over the control of and access to economic space go on continuously. Newcomers or outsiders have been known to resort to force in an attempt to gain access to and use of streets, sidewalks and parking lots. The incident when an outsider group of adults invaded the area and took over the rights of economic exploitation of the private parking lot from children at the Roberto Huembes market serves as an apt illustration. However, it is not always that invaders succeed in establishing exclusive rights over working places, as what happened in the informal parking lot at the same market shows. The intervention by the relatives working at the same market meant that the children could keep a share of the parking lot. The situation at the parking lots at the Roberto Huembes market can be interpreted as an expression of the exercise of power by one group (the adults) over another (the children). In the struggles over economic space children often end up as losers and some have been forced to give up altogether. The absence of informal arrangements or contracts between the adults and the children over the use of the parking lots accounts for the continuous struggle over control of space at the Roberto Huembes market place.

I believe that the ease or difficulty of entry of working children into the urban informal sector in Managua is primarily governed by the type or nature of the activity in question, but also, to a great extent, by links to social networks of which also adults are part. Guarding and washing cars are very attractive activities, not least because there is no need for capital investment. Although these activities are performed in open places, both private and public, the worker must get access to and obtain location rights to the parking lots through the contractual systems described earlier. Social networks and investments in social capital loom larger in this respect than economic ones as determinants of access to activities and work places. Working children are no exception. Indeed, due to their status as minors, they are disadvantaged because the social networks and capital that they can muster or summon on their own are very modest. The different systems of organization of economic space at the Galeria Internacional and the Roberto Huembes market places are a direct consequence of the existence or non-existence of adult support.

At the Galeria Internacional children could count on the support of adults in organizing their work and in making it possible for them to maximize their income. At the large Roberto Huembes parking lot, on the other hand, adult support for the organization of the children's work was nonexistent or weak. Consequently, the children who worked here lacked the sort of work organization that existed at the Galeria Internacional. The absence of contracts or agreements, such as those at the Galeria Internacional, implied that at the Roberto Huembes market the interests of individuals came first, rather than group interests, which contributed to the already tense and stressed work environment. On the other hand, at the smaller parking lot just next to the bigger one, the children were allowed to compete with the adults, simply because they had the indirect support of their relatives which worked in other activities, but at the same market. These situations illustrate that the children, if left to themselves, have great difficulties in competing with adults which engage in the same activity in the urban informal sector. Even though the activity in question was a very typical activity of working children, the children alone were not able to win the struggle for economic space, when it became attractive for the adults.

Chapter 8

Selection of the sample of working children

Child work activities investigated in this study

The ILO report, the findings of previous studies of child work in the region, discussed in Part One, and the representativeness of the activities at the selected places of work, formed the basis for the selection of activities to be investigated in this study. It is consequently highly representative of the occupations of the children in the urban informal sector in Managua: vendors, car wards and washers, shoe-shiners, helpers of adult vendors, and a final category which lumps several activities together, under the heading *diverse tasks*. The decision to include this last category was based upon the fact that many children were performing several of these tasks during a single working day and almost every day, as one occupation.

Patterns of gender differentiation

As has been discussed above, working children are mainly found in the urban informal sector, because of a combination of several factors, such as low capital demand, no need for skills, access to family resources as a means of entry, to mention some of the more important ones.

When the occupational structure at various work places was examined, it was observed that there also is a gender component in these structures. In part, this observation is compatible with the findings of other studies of the urban informal sector in the region. As the results of the surveys of the five working places studied in Managua indicate, only two occupational categories were the exclusive domains of boys—shoe-shiners and bearers. In the other occupations one could find both boys and girls. Hence, it is difficult to speak of an overall and clear-cut pattern of gender differentiation in child work in the urban informal sector of Managua.

It is, in fact, not that easy to identify any simple explanatory factors behind gender segmentation of work, such as the greater physical capacity of boys or the greater sense of responsibility that is perhaps characteristic of girls. Rather, the reasons have to be sought in the complex interplay of economic, socio-cultural and place-specific aspects and structures, and how these impact on the urban informal sector and the size and sex distribution of child work. Thus, one need not be physically strong in order to work as a shoe-shiner, still this is an occupation that is completely dominated by boys. On the other hand, loading and unloading is an activity that requires muscular strength; but then how is one to explain that very young and small boys did this kind of work at the markets? Conversely, why is it that the older and relatively stronger girls are not engaged in the activity of loading and unloading?

With regard to shoe-shining in Lima, Alarcón has suggested an explanation for the predominance of boys in the urban informal sector, one that relates gender differentiation to aspects of distance, mobility, family and social attitudes.[1] In Lima, shoe-shining was performed within a wide spatial range and hence far from the place of residence or the home of the worker. Because of the distance and type of mobility involved, families perceived shoe-shining to be an activity that is inappropriate for girls. In Managua, on the other hand, shoe-shining took place at fixed locations, the markets, which were generally located in the neighbourhood of the childrens' residences. Nevertheless, girls were not engaged in this activity. The gendered occupational distribution of child work in the informal sector, it would seem, is likely to be a reflection of broader gendered social rela-

---

[1]. Glasinovich, W.A. (1991): *Entre calles y plazas. El trabajo de los niños en Lima.* p. 74. Instituto de Estudios Peruanos. UNICEF. Lima.

tions and mores which directly or indirectly impact on the division of child labour between girls and boys.

In his comparative analysis of child work in Latin America, Meyers notes that in Lima only 14 per cent of all the children surveyed were employed in household and domestic services; 42 per cent of the girls were found in that occupation, but a mere three per cent of the boys.[1] The explanations for the high incidence of girls in this typically female occupation clearly had to be sought in the realms of cultural and gendered social relations. The division of labour and child work in the household and domestic sector by sex is a reflection of traditional gendered social relations, and contributes to the continued reproduction of gendered relations of work.

The role of place-specific factors in the gendered distribution of child work in the informal sector in Managua can be illustrated by the activity of guarding cars. Car guarding was exclusively performed by boys at the Roberto Huembes market, whereas at the Galeria Internacional and the Israel Lewites parking lots it was also performed by girls. Place-specific characteristics impact on the evolution or emergence of contrasting distributions of activity by sex, through their role as factors restricting or facilitating the levels of access to activities which are open to both sexes.

Aspects of spatial closure and access are influenced not only by gender and gender roles but by age as well. In his study of Lima, Alarcón found a clear pattern of occupational distribution arising from limited access to activities as conditioned by the age and sex of children. He noted that age-specific differences in the occupational distribution of working children tended to be very tenuous up to that age of nine. Both girls and boys performed the same activities up to that age but gendered patterns became more pronounced with increasing age. No such clear-cut relationship between occupation and age could be established for child work in Managua in the present study. Indeed, and contrary to the findings of Alarcón, age did not loom large as a factor governing activity or occupational access or closure. Save for shoe-shining, children of all ages performed the same activities in

---

[1] Myers, W. (1989): *Urban working children: A comparasion of four surveys from South America.* International Labour Review. p. 326. ILO. Geneva.

Managua. In other words, the age of children did not play a significant role for the division of child labour by sex.

In sum, there was no pronounced differentiation in the occupations by gender and age at the working places in Managua covered by this study. With the exception of two activities, bearing and shoe-shining, the children engaged in similar tasks irrespective of their sex and age. On the other hand, the characteristics of the places of work, with respect to above all work organization and milieu were instrumental in facilitating or restricting the access of children to certain occupations. Indeed, it can be argued that place-specific features was one of the main factors behind the regulation of activity types and the gendered variations in occupations found at the work places covered by this study.

The sample of working children

The selection of the sample of children to be interviewed was based upon the analysis of the places of work, and the types of activities which have been presented above. The intention behind the selection of the sample was to capture (i) the main occupations of children in the urban informal sector in Managua, (ii) the range and variations of occupations, and (iii) the distribution of occupations by sex and place of work.

Several other criteria were also considered in the selection of the working children, such as the age of the children and their willingness to be interviewed, i. e. to be included in the sample. Inducing the children to participate in the study did not present a problem. Indeed, the problem was how to exclude all the children who were willing to be interviewed but were not included in the sample

In the selection of individual children two variables in particular were considered, age and sex. With respect to age there were some specific difficulties. Initially I had decided that the sample should include children between the ages of six and fourteen years, and be distributed proportionately by the places of work. The lower age limit was chosen in order to make sure that the sample would have as broad a representation of ages as possible, so that age-specific and gender-related variations regarding different aspects of working conditions and characteristics of work could be brought out. However, after several interviews with the children, it became clear that it would be difficult to obtain detailed and reliable information from the group of six year olds in the sample. Consequently, these children were not included in the study. The age limit for the final sample was thus revised upwards, and the sample only includes those between the ages of seven and fourteen.

Because of the fact that the total number of working children in each place of work was impossible to determine, (with the exception of the Galeria Internacional parking lot), that number was simply not known, the ambition that the final sample should have a representative size, in pure statistical terms, came second in the decision about the number of children to interview. The priority in the selection of the sample was instead given to the type of activities which the children were engaged in at the different places of work and their representativeness in the regional and economic sectorial context. Thus, in the only place where the number of working children was known, Galeria Internacional, out of a total of 12 children, seven were interviewed. In the largest markets, the information about the total number of working children was so disparate that a judgment of its validity was impossible to make. For instance, it could vary between 50 and 150 at the Israel Lewites market, between 100 and 300 at El Mayoreo, between 20 and 50 at San Judas, and between 100 and 400 at Roberto Huembes.[1]

The final sample consisted of sixty children, aged between 7 and 14 years old, with 43 (72 per cent) boys and 17 (28 per cent) girls. The distribution of the children in the sample by place of work is given in figure 10.

[1.] The information about the number of working children at the different places of work was given by adults working in the same places, some NGOs and in a few cases officials of social programmes for children.

Figure 10 The sample of working children by age, sex, and place of work.

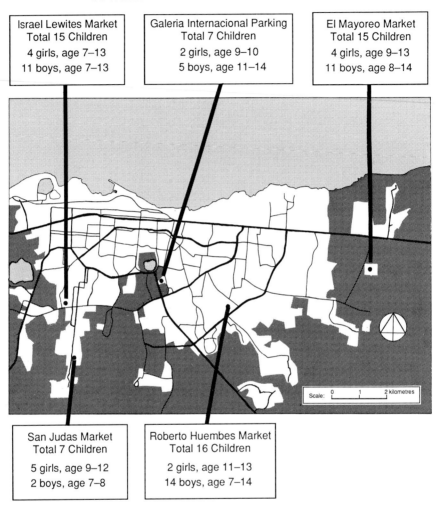

Chapter 9

Living conditions of the children

Housing

Managua is a city with quite a mixed and dispersed urban structure. Low income districts are found side by side with middle and upper class districts, forming a mosaic of slums blending with the more exclusive districts or residential areas. The slums and squatter settlements in Managua are from different epochs and differ from each other in various ways. In some cases the slums lie hidden behind houses built long before the earthquake of 1972. Initially they were quite nice old districts made up of traditionally built houses of stone and adobe.[1] However, the houses were neglected for a long time, badly maintained and thus fell into disrepair so that they now must be classified as slum areas.

After the earthquake of 1972, the growth of squatter settlements has been a permanent feature of urban sprawl in Managua. The city has experienced tremendous expansion, especially after 1989. The rapid urban growth can be explained by several factors, mainly tied to the end of the war in 1990. The two most important factors are mass migration into the city following the end of the war, which also coincided with the second factor, drastic changes in housing policy implemented during the period after the 1990 elections. The policy changes led to large sections of the inner city being leased or sold for symbolic prices and at more than favourable terms. In order to ensure or guarantee ownership of lots, people built shelters rather hastily using low

---

[1.] Adobe is a traditional construction material which consists of a mixture of stones and mud.

quality building materials. On the other hand, those who did not get lots resorted to uncontrolled squatting over large vacant areas in the inner city alongside the main roads, thereby initiating a new cycle of squatter settlements. Many of the squatters were not in-migrants but inhabitants of the city, who lived in overcrowded conditions and who took the opportunity to escape from these areas and get a new house. This is still an ongoing process, with new squatter settlements springing up all over the city, driven by the ever worsening conditions of life in the countryside, which cause heavy flows of migrants to the city as well as deficient urban planning. For the most part, Managua is made up of a number of older housing districts of similar standards and in varying states of maintenance, and lacking access to basic services and infrastructure, particularly water supply. Only a minority of the population lives in exclusive areas with very high residential standard. As in other cities in Latin America, houses in Managua can vary from sumptuous mansions to simple shelters constructed with recycled materials like cardboards, plastic sheets, wooden boxes and car tyres. Many of Managua's inhabitants live in such dilapidated houses.

A typology of the districts of Managua based on housing standard ranked the districts into 12 types.[1] The variables used for this classification included the physical appearance of houses, materials used for construction, the structure, and whether or not the houses were incorporated within an urban planning zone. On the basis of this typology and a number of criteria related to the social and economic structure of the district population, the city was classified into six strata of housing quality: very low, low, middle-low, middle-high, residential, and high residential.[2]

[1.] 1: inferior, in ruins; 2: inferior, in bad condition; 3: inferior, being improved; 4: wood, uninhabitable; 5: wood, in bad condition; 6: wood, in acceptable condition; 7: wood, in good condition; 8: bricks, in good condition; 9: traditional; 10: residential, standardized production; 11: residential, higher quality; 12: residential, sumptuous. Source: Instituto Nicaraguense de Estadisticas y Census (INEC) (1985). Managua. (Free translation from the Spanish).

[2.] Instituto Nicaraguense de Estadisticas y Census. (Free translation of the Spanish terminology of the strata).

Where do the working children live?

It is a widely held view that the children working in the streets or other open places are either homeless or inhabitants of slums and squatter settlements. It is commonly assumed that children working in the streets of cities in Latin America have partially or totally cut their family bonds. Images of abandoned children spending the night in the open, in bus stations, markets or other desolate places in cities, are widespread. This is one of the many myths about working children, deeply ingrained in the popular imagination. Since their activities are seen as marginal, and even illegal, many find it difficult to accept or tend to forget that the children working in the streets may well live in a house and be part of a family. Thus, although by no means all children who work in the streets live in such imagined deplorable circumstances, the impression is not so easy to alter.

Many studies of child work are based upon samples of working children extracted from larger household surveys. With this method, the answer to the question of whether working children live in a house and belong to a household or not, is given a priori.[1] It has been argued that this sampling method (large household surveys) captures only an insignificant proportion of all working children and an even lower percentage of children working in the activities investigated in the present study. In the present case, because of the random method used to select a sample of children, no a priori information about the housing conditions of the children was available. As noted above, the children were selected directly in the field at different places of work in the city. Consequently two central issues regarding the living conditions of the children remained unknown; (i) did the children belong to a household or did they for the most part live in the street, (ii) to what extend did they live with their own families?

Not only will answers to these two questions provide important information on the housing situation of the children as well as on their family ties, but housing standard and place of residence are also useful

---

[1] The most common housing type in Managua is the single family house; the housing standard is of course highly variable depending on which socio-economic stratum the family that owns it belongs to. Apartments or flats are few in the city, as i.e. the case of Barrio San Antonio with apartment buildings. One main reason for the favoured type of construction in Managua is its location on an active seismic zone.

indicators of the general socio-economic characteristics of the children and their families. Finally, knowledge about where in the city the working children lived and worked was regarded as a first step towards building up a picture of the spatial structure of child work in Managua.

Place of residence and housing situation

Because of the structure of the city, as briefly described above, the name of the district or place of residence by itself was not a sufficient basis for classifying the housing situation of the children and their families. Consequently, the children were asked not only about the place of residence (districts of Managua, another city, or other place), but also about the characteristics of their houses (housing standard). Initially, information provided by the children about where they lived was used to establish the proportion of children commuting to the city and to map residences and flow patterns into the city as well. Only 12 per cent of the children resided in a village or city outside Managua, all the others lived in the city of Managua. With the exception of those living in very new squatter areas, some of which had no name at the time of the interviews, the children had no difficulty in naming their residential districts, and it was possible to conclude that many children lived nearby their places of work.

Supplementary information about house types, intended to capture the socio-economic conditions of the life of the children and their families more accurately, was obtained by asking the children to specify three characteristics of their houses: the type of construction material used, the number of divisions or rooms, and whether water and electricity was available or not. The information collected showed that, save for the houses in the newer settlements, all houses had access to electricity. In almost all cases, however, electricity services were not provided by utility companies, rather it was "diverted from the power lines of neighbours".[1] The majority of the houses had no direct access to water and the inhabitants had to bring water either from municipal

---

[1] It is a very common practice in low income districts that people make their own connection to the nearest electric cable and thus get electricity at home without having to pay for it.

water pipes and wells in the neighbourhood or had to buy it from mobile water wagons.

Regarding the size of the house (number of rooms/divisions), all children stated that they lived in very crowded conditions and expressed their dissatisfaction with the situation. Considering the fact that more than half of the children shared single room dwellings and that the remaining lived in two room dwellings with their families, it is not difficult to understand their complaints. In Managua, single room tenements dominate low income housing districts and the impression of an overcrowded living milieu obtained from this sample survey captures the overall living conditions in the city rather well. The scarce living space impacts on the daily lives of individuals in critical ways. Congested living conditions render domestic tasks difficult, make it difficult to maintain a healthy and clean environment and to take care of one's personal hygiene, and leaves little room for privacy. For children, congested conditions reduce their possibilities to play, and encumber educational development. In the case of the children living outside Managua, the small size and congested internal space of their homes were compensated for by plenty of space outside the home, as the houses are often surrounded by courtyards. In the city, on the other hand, the space outside the home remains very restricted or confined, especially in low income districts.

The characteristics of the houses described by the children fit quite well the types of houses in the districts where they said that they lived, and in general their descriptions conformed to the official classification of the districts of Managua. The results showed that almost half of the children lived in houses which judging by their characteristics belonged to the three lower classes of districts, ranging from districts with bad and very bad houses built of inferior construction materials, such as pieces of scrap wood, plastic sheets, cardboards and other materials (categories 1, 2 and 3), to districts with older houses built of wood and in a bad state of repair, pertaining to the district category 5. These children, hence, lived in the very poorest and poor districts of the city. Quite unexpected, however, was the fact that almost the same number of children, 40 per cent, lived in houses considered to be of average or good standard and characteristic of districts belonging to categories 6 and 7 of the official typology. In some cases, the children lived in

Figure 11   The place of residence of the sample of children by district type and place of work

Place of Work	District Type	Place of Residence
Israel Lewites	2,3,6,8,9	New squatter, Monte Fresco, El Recreo, Alta Gracia, Camillo Ortega, San Judas, Batahola, Batahola Norte, La Subasta
	Other municip./city	Villa El Carmen
El Mayoreo	2,7,9	New squatter, América I, Villa Venezuela, Anexo Villa Venezuela, Waspan Norte, La Subasta, Santa Ana
	Other municip./city	Tipitapa, La Concha, Masaya
Roberto Huembes	1,2,5,6,7	New Squatter, Acahulinca, La Fuente, Isaias Gomez, Jayali, Reparto Schick, Waspan,
	Other municip./city	Masaya, S. Juan de la Concepción, Ticuantepe
Galeria Internacional	3	Jorge Dimitrov, Cristo Rey
San Judas	6	Jorge Casaly, Marvin Marin, San Judas

houses built of bricks, typical of districts classified as belonging to categories 8 and 9 of the same typology. It was not possible, however, to determine the level of maintenance of these houses.

In sum, the working children interviewed for this study lived in houses of varying quality, ranging from the very bad to houses of average standard and infrastructure, and in districts that ranged from slums and new squatter settlements to traditional districts with a much better housing standard. If these findings are used for a preliminary attempt to describe the socio-economic characteristics of the working children and their families, it is possible to conclude that they did not belong entirely to the poorest strata of the city; in fact, these children were found within a wide range of districts and social strata, from the very-low to the low stratum and, to a considerable extent, in the middle-low stratum, in accordance with the typology named above. This suggests that child work is not a phenomenon restricted to the poorest groups in the city. It is more widespread. This can be seen as a sign of an extension of the process of pauperization of the city.

The household and the family

To recapitulate, the children of this study did not live in the street; they lived in houses on a permanent basis. Furthermore, the children did not all live in similar districts, but rather represent several socio-economic strata in the city. This was confirmed by the description of their homes made by the children themselves, which indicated that the houses were quite typical of the districts where they lived. Thus, some children lived in houses in very bad condition in poor districts, whereas other children lived in houses of a better standard, in districts belonging to the low-middle stratum.

Another question that was regarded as essential concerns the household, i.e. with whom the children lived; if they lived in small or large households, and if they lived with their natural families, with other relatives, or with other persons. The aim was to search for possible relationships, if any, between the number of working children per household and household size and family type.

A review of the literature on urban child work in Latin America indicates that three major hypotheses have figured predominantly in the discussions of the family and the household as determinant factors for child work. The hypotheses postulate that (a) the fewer the adult members of a household, the more likely that children would be obliged to work; (b) the probability that children which belong to extended families are engaged in child work is low, and, conversely, that the probability that children coming from nuclear families are engaged in child work is high; and, finally, that it is more likely that (c) children belonging to single parent-headed families work than that those living with both parents do so.

Household size and family type have been considered to be determinant factors of children's participation in work both inside and outside the household.[1] Both variables have often been studied in a demographic perspective, where the fertility rate is regarded as the causal factor influencing the number of working children in a family or household. The underlying reasoning behind this demographic perspective is that as long as families consider children to be economic

---

[1.] By household is meant a group of persons, related or not related to each other by family links, who live and eat under the same roof.

assets, they will continue to have as many children as possible. Only when children become liabilities rather than assets, entailing income losses or higher costs of upbringing for the families, will fertility rates decline.[1]

However, the links between fertility, family or household size, poverty and child work are much more complex than is suggested by the simplistic demographic equation. Family fertility levels are not fixed in space or time, but vary regionally, over time, by type of society, between urban and rural areas, etc. Moreover, fertility by itself cannot be the causal factor, since whether children engage in child work or not is affected by or dependent upon many other factors including income, education, wages and employment, landholding, child mortality, nutrition and health, as well as access to means of fertility control.[2] Analyses of the determinants of child labour in cities in Latin America must consider, in a broad approach, the role of overarching structures and processes, such as poverty, corruption, the debt trap and global inequality.

Even if it is a contributive factor, population pressure in the developing countries can hardly be the main cause of poverty and, by extension, of child participation rates in the informal labour market. Although the relationship is not always so clear, the fact that in most developing countries the population is very young, in some cases the age group below 18 years makes up almost 50 per cent of the population, implies that the dependence of poor households on income from child work is not negligible. Rodgers and Standing point out two crucial elements that affect the relationship between fertility and child work, namely, (i) the work of children and the costs and benefits of childbearing, and (ii) the compatibility of female labour force participation and childbearing.[3] Research by Rosemweig on Colombia from 1981, and by Levy on India in 1982 and for Egypt on 1983, shows that fertility tends to be higher where opportunities for child

---

[1.] Dahl, G. (1984): *Det nyttiga barnet*. Aronsson, K., Cederblad, M., Dahl, G., Olsson, L. and Sandin, B.(eds.): *Barn i tid och rum*. Liber Förlag. Kristianstad.

[2.] Rodgers, G. and Standing, G. (1981): *The Economic Roles of Children: Issues for analysis*. Rodgers, G. and Standing, G. (eds.): *Child work, Poverty and Underdevelopment*. International Labour Office. Geneva.

[3.] Ibid.

work are greater, and lower where possibilities for school enrollment are better.[1] Empirical evidence from other studies, however, suggests that the actual or potential economic benefits derived from having children do not figure as primary factors in household's fertility decisions, because consumption costs are higher than the economic profits in raising children. Musgrove's study of per capita household consumption in ten Latin American cities shows that there is a direct relationship between large household size and lower per capita consumption.[2]

In rural areas the relationship between child work, household size and fertility depends primarily on the type and extent of landholding. Some studies argue that landholding reduces fertility, while others argue that it increases fertility. The contrasting arguments are based on empirical evidence and analyses of the relationship between household and landholding sizes on the one hand and the contribution of child work to household income on the other. From a review of the literature on this subject, Sharif draws the conclusion that the contradictory results are due to the authors' formulations of the problem as a unidirectional "negative only" or "positive only" relationship.[3] In the first case the problem is stated such that the number of children stands as proxy measures of landholding size, whereas in the second formulation they supplement landholding. In contrast, Sharif followed a different approach, by constructing a theoretical model, which enabled him to conduct analyses of the different factor combinations across households with variable landholding sizes. The farm size, extent of landholding and mode of production influence fertility, household size and

---

[1] Levy, V. (1985): *Cropping Patterns. Mechanization, Child Labor, and Fertility Behavior in a Farming Economy: Rural Egypt.* Economic Development and Cultural Change. Vol. 33. Chicago; Rozenzweig, M. (1982): *Household and Non-household Activities of Youths: Issues of Modelling.* Rodgers and Standing (eds.):*Child Work, Poverty and Underdevelopment.* ILO. Geneva.

[2] Musgrove, P. (1978): *Consumer behavior in Latin America.* Estudios conjuntos sobre integración económica Latinoamericana. (ECIEL). Washington.

[3] Sharif, M. (1993): *Child participation, Nature of work, and Fertility Demand: A Theoretical Analysis.* The Indian Economic Journal. Vol. 40. No. 4.

participation of children in work outside the household, but not in a linear, unidirectional way. The results led Sharif to conclude that:

> In a landless or near landless household, children participate in wage work; but in a self sufficient small farm household, prestige cost forces the children out of wage labour even if their marginal family farm income is lower. Thus the latter is expected to have a lower demand for fertility. However, as farm size increases, the marginal child productivity on the family farm goes up; this raises the demand for fertility. On the other hand, raising the prestige cost reduces the gain from marginal child income; this curtails the increasing fertility demand at some level of landholding; and beyond that fertility demand declines. Thus it appears that landholding reduces fertility initially, increases it at the intermediate levels, and then decreases it when the household becomes a non-cultivating rental income earner.[1]

Sharif's study indicates that the determinants of child work are multiple, interact in complex and dynamic ways not only with economic factors, but with social and cultural factors as well. The use of linear regression analysis has been the dominant approach in the analyses of the determinants of child work. In consequence the conclusions drawn, though not totally misleading, convey only part of the truth regarding the society, community or case under study, and the results can hardly be generalized. Quite often, household size has been seen as one factor determining child work and, in spite of the inherent problems, the assumption that the larger the household the more likely that children participate in economic activities outside the household in order to raise household income, is thus still widespread. The work of Sharif, however, shows how complex the role of household size for the number of working children in a household is.

Structure and size of the households

The working children of this study belonged to households of all sizes, ranging from a low of four to a high of sixteen persons per house-

---

[1] Ibid.

hold.[1] The average size of households was seven persons. This average size is slightly higher than the average size of low income households in Managua, which is 5,8 persons. More interesting, however, is that the majority of the children's households (77 per cent) had no more than five members, which means that the largest households were under-represented.

The households were dominated by the young; almost 80 per cent of the household members were less than 15 years old. Of that group almost half were working children; of the others, many were too young to go out to work.

Regarding household size, no clear-cut relationship could be established between the total number of household members—adults, youth and children—and the number of children at work. In fact the highest incidence of working children was found in the smallest households, where on the average 50 per cent of the children worked. The smaller and medium-sized households overall had the highest number of working children. The largest households, those with more than 10 members per household, had the lowest share of working children (25 per cent). From these findings, however, it is not possible to draw the conclusion that the smaller the household, the greater the number of children at work and vice versa, since there was no continuity in the distribution of the values. Other variables, such as the exact age of all children in the household, would have to be included in order to conduct in-depth or conclusive analyses. In the present study, however, it turned out that such information could not be extracted from the children. On the other hand, the preliminary results can contribute to the discussion in the sense that yet again they confirm that there is no linear relationship between household size and the number of working children per household. With regard to the importance of the structure or composition of the household, the underlying reasoning behind has rested on the supposition that the fewer the adult members in a household, the more likely that the children are impelled to work. This study found that in the households

---

[1] The children were asked about the number of persons living with them, including any co-resident brothers and sisters, infants and seniors. Because there apparently was a certain tendency to omit the babies and the older household members, this question was explored in detail.

with a larger number of adults there was a smaller percentage of working children. This was most evident in the single parent-headed households which had, relatively speaking, more working children. Furthermore, in households with older brothers or sisters, there were lower work participation rates for the youngest children. These results give an indication of the complex relationship that exists between household structure and number of children at work, in some contrast to the simple or straight relationship between household size and number of children at work suggested by other studies.

Family type

Since the household is the unit of analysis used in most surveys, the significance of the family as a determining factor for child work has not been fully explored. Studies of the role of the family have been largely confined to an examination of other issues than child work, such as child abuse, the exploitation of children, child abandonment and the like. A review of the relevant literature indicates that the linkages between family type and the participation of children in work show broad regional variations and in some cases are even place-specific. Assumptions to the effect that the probability of children entering the labour market, to a certain degree depends on the type of the family of the child have been difficult to substantiate, and it has been difficult therefore to draw general conclusions.

It has been observed that within the extended family, the incidence of abuse and exploitation of children in work is rare. Extended family households are made up of more than two generations living together (parents, grandparents and often uncles and aunts, cousins and other relatives). The presence of many adults in such families, means that children are released from certain tasks at home, such as taking care of infants and working outside the home. Such family types were common primarily in rural areas, but are also quite common among the urban low income families. The extended family is, on the whole, considered to be a family type that offers protection for children and one in which children work less.

In their study on child work in Colombia, Rodgers and Standing also found that children from extended families were less likely to work than those from nuclear families.[1] However, the results of correlation analyses do not always show a one-way relationship. In his research on child work in Lima, Glasinovich looked at the proportion of working and non-working children in different family types in urban Lima, and found that nuclear families indeed had the highest percentage of working children.[2] At the same time, however, the highest percentage of non-working children also came from nuclear families, leading him to concur with what Rotondo found, i.e. that the nuclear family was the most common type of family in Lima, and thus "belonging to a nuclear family does not make minors more vulnerable to be workers.[3] The majority of the children (59 per cent), whether working or not belonged to nuclear families".[4] The other family type with many working children was the extended one. These households had a slightly higher percentage of working than non-working children. Since the proportions of working and non-working children were not substantially different, Glasinovich concluded that belonging to an extended family does not prevent children from entering the informal work force. In sum, it is difficult to establish an unequivocal relationship between family type and incidence of child work.

Another aspect considered by Glasinovich is discussed by Rodgers and Standing, who maintain that children from single parent families were more liable to work than those from complete ones. Having tested this hypothesis in the case of Lima, Glasinovich did not find any corroborating evidence. Indeed, he cites the works of Dejo, Van Oort, and Engelhart, which show that most working children lived with double parent families.[5] Another investigation of working children in the streets in Asunción showed that a high percentage of working chil-

---

[1.] Rodger and Standing (1981).
[2.] Glasinovich, W.A. (1991).
[3.] Rotondo, H. (1980): *Situación de la familia y del niño en el Perú*. Problemas poblacionales peruanos. AMIDEP. Lima.
[4.] Glasinovich, W.A. (1991).
[5.] Dejo, F. (1989): *Los hijos de la pobreza*. CISE. Rädda Barnen. Lima; Van Oort, A., C. (1983): *Niños que trabajan*. Tesis de Licenciatura. PUCP. Lima; Engelhardt, S. (1982): *Diagnóstico sobre el menor trabajador en Comas*. OIT. Lima. (not published).

Figure 12   The sample of children by family type

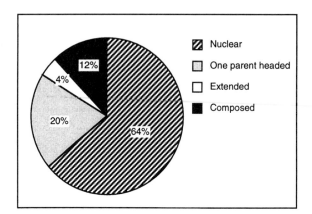

dren (51 per cent) lived with both parents, a fact that supports the conclusions of Glasinovich and Dejo et al.[1]

In the present study, the majority of the children (64 per cent), came from nuclear families, and only one in five belonged to families headed by single parents.

Thus, the working children mostly came from nuclear families and the findings from Managua lend additional support to the findings of Glasinovich mentioned above. As in Lima, the nuclear family is the most common type also in Managua. At the same time, it is interesting to observe that the proportion of working children living in extended families was the lowest.

The composed family type rarely figures in the studies under review here.[2] In Managua, however, this type of family is much more common. The war seems to be one of the factors behind the emergence of this type of family. Often, the death of the father left the mother in a precarious economic situation. She found it difficult to sustain a household on her own and consequently moved in with relatives. Secondly, the worsening economic conditions of families in rural areas have often compelled parents to send their children to live with relatives in the city in search of employment in order to help the rest of the family. In the present study it was found that the children

[1]. Espínola, B., Ortiz, R. (1989).
[2]. In Glasinovich's study, only 2.2 per cent of the families in Lima were in the category "composed" and of them only 1.6 per cent included working children.

in that situation lived in composed families, either with their grandparents or with their uncles or aunts and their families in large households. Most of the children had emigrated to Managua alone, sent by their parents in order to work; in some cases they moved in the company of other brothers or sisters. The narrative of Ramón, an 11 year old boy from Boaco, can serve as a concrete example.

> I used to live with my family in Esquipulas, Boaco, but now I live in Managua with my aunt, uncle and cousins. We were too many at home in Esquipulas and we worked with my father in the fields with a machete. It was hard because we had to walk two hours to the field. Sometimes we did not have enough food for all of us. So they sent me and two of my brothers to Managua to work. We moved two years ago. I miss my mother very much. I send all my money to her. I am glad I can help my family. There is no money in Boaco. I came with two brothers; one of them does the same work as I do. The youngest stays at home and helps my aunt with her "venta" (selling stand at home).

Scarce household resources was the basic reason that made children leave their families. However, it is important to point out that all those children lived with relatives. Because of drastic changes in their lives, either upon the death of one parent or through divorce, the relatives took the children into their care and functioned as a link in a series of strategic actions that involved the children, the children´s natural families and the composed families.

With the exception of the children who lived in composed families far from their parents, the majority of the children had contact with their natural families on a daily basis. In fact, more than half of them lived with both natural parents, 15 per cent with one natural parent in a new marriage, and 20 per cent with a single parent, almost always the mother.

In sum, it has been shown that all the children in this study belonged to households where they lived with their families or relatives on a permanent basis. For them, "home" had an obvious and central place in their lives. Irrespective of whether they lived with their natural families or not, the household was a place to return to and a

Figure 13   Presence of parents in the households of the children

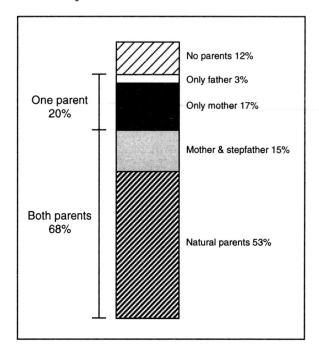

place of security, in contrast to the street that was identified with drugs and criminality, and looked upon as a space of fear.

Most of the children lived not very far from their places of work; in fact, in many cases the districts of residence were located nearby or bordering upon the markets and the parking lots. The other children lived in another city or village or in other remote districts of Managua, and travelled to their places of work regularly. The information that was gathered about the children's housing conditions—standard of houses and district characteristics—indicates that a significant number of the children obviously did not belong to the lowest socio-economic stratum of households in the city. This finding underscores one of my central research hypothesis, namely that child work in Managua is not restricted to the households most affected by poverty, of the city and gives a first indication about the incidence of child work in other types of household than the poorest in the city.

With respect to their family situation, it was found that almost all the children lived with one or both of their parents, regardless of which type of family they lived in—nuclear, one parent-headed or extended. Only the children which lived in composed families had only sporadic or casual contacts with their parents, not because they were abandoned, but because circumstances made it extremely difficult for them to keep in touch on a regular basis. This contradicts the common assumption or myth about the marginalized nature of the life of working children and that they have weak contacts with their parents or none at all. Barring unseen, unknown or undivulged circumstance, my information gives no cause to assume that the living conditions of the children at home indicated neglect or abandonment. Living with their families or relatives was considered by the children, to be the norm or really only acceptable form of living and the idea of living in the streets was quite alien and unreal. Asked about their ideal type of family, most children mentioned first the nuclear family, but with a preference for one that included both their natural parents. As some of them put it, the best for every child is to live together with his or her father and mother.

Chapter 10

The economic role of the children

Against the background of the previous general discussion about child work, this chapter will analyse children's economic role as participants in the open labour force and as contributors to the household economy. It will focus on all the activities performed by the children that have an economic component or purpose, i.e. are related to patterns of production, services or commerce and that directly or indirectly contribute to the household's and the child's own economy. It will concentrate initially on the activities performed at the places of work outside the children's households, in order to explore the characteristics of children as members of the economically active population of Managua. The occupations of the children, their occupational categories, income, and their use and allocation of time will be reviewed in the context of a general discussion about child work in the urban informal economic sector.

The occupations

As mentioned earlier, the selection of the children aimed to reflect both the dominant occupations of the working children in the urban informal sector, and the gender characteristics of the activities which took place in the different work places. Consequently, the final sample of children reflects the distribution of child work activity types in the urban informal sector of Managua which is dominated by services and trade. Figure 14 presents the final sample.

In addition to the previous analysis of the factors influencing the number of working children in specific activities and sectors, one must not forget the broader context within which child work has to be considered—poverty. The occupations chosen often reflect the degree of poverty of the children and the lack of surplus capital of their households. Among the activities presented here, selling what most children are engaged in and perhaps the one that best illustrates their situation, and therefore deserves to be looked at more closely.

Selling: a sign of poverty

Selling remains one of the principal employment opportunities for a major group of the work force in the urban informal sector of developing countries, and it is certainly one of the activities where working children are well represented. In as much as selling is an activity which requires a product to be sold, and presumes capital that can be invested in that product, it may seem paradoxical that so many from low income households engage in selling.

When considering the types of products offered for sale in the informal sector, however, it appears that they usually do not require much capital investment and in some cases no advance outlay at all. It is precisely the small amount of capital needed that makes informal sector activities so attractive to children. This also implies that the goods are mainly meant for final consumption, mostly foodstuffs, such as tortillas, fruits, refreshments, vegetables and water; lottery tickets is another example. The amount of capital needed to set up shop can also serve as a proxy indicator of household poverty levels; the more severe the poverty level, the smaller is the capital that can be invested. The market value of the goods children sell tends to reflect the amount of capital that a child or the family can acquire. Children which sell soda, for instance, may have surplus capital tied up in bottles, but given the very low profit margins, this surplus can easily disappear during periods of low sales, when the children may be forced to pawn the bottles to remain solvent. Once the surplus has gone, they have to resort to selling water for a time until sufficient capital has

Figure 14   Distribution of the sample of children by occupation, gender and place of work

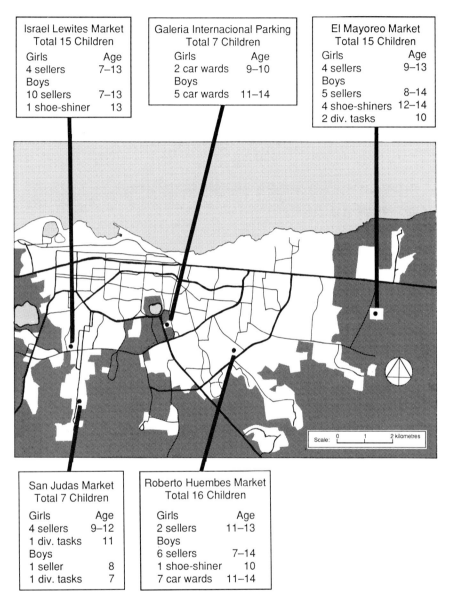

been saved so as to enable investment in soda bottles. As an informal sector activity, selling is characterized by the fact that it is relatively easy to adjust to fluctuations in the market or in the economic situation of the sellers. It is precisely these features that partly explain the ubiquity of selling as an activity as well as the large number of sellers in the urban informal sector in Third World cities, and by extension the relatively greater concentration of children in selling than in any other activity.

The previous argument can be illustrated by taking the case of Marisa, a ten year old girl working as a seller at the San Judas market at the time of the interview. Marisa told me that her mother made and sold tortillas at home, while she herself used to sell tortillas at the San Judas market. Now, however, she was selling mangos for her aunts and lemons that she received from another woman:

> I used to sell tortillas that my mother made at home, but nowadays, because the price of the flour has increased so much, she (the mother) can not afford to buy it; therefore I am selling whatever I get from my aunt and other ladies.

Another girl, Lucia, nine years old and a seller at the San Judas market, said that she used to sell home-made cookies, but since sugar and butter had become too expensive, her mother could no longer afford to bake cookies. The adjustments made to the fluctuations in market and capital resources mentioned above, can be surmised from the fact that, at the time of the interview, the mother was selling lime, Lucia was selling water and the father was unemployed. Some water sellers declared that when sales were good, they bought plastic bags, fruit and sugar, and made refreshments and fruit drinks for selling; others said that sometimes they had to sell water only, because they could not afford the ice. These examples are representative of the general trend towards rising levels of poverty, which gradually force households and children to sell goods that generate successively smaller returns and hence lower incomes.

Another important factor which facilitates entry into the occupation of selling is the spatial flexibility inherent in this activity, that is the fact that selling need not necessarily be undertaken at fixed locations. This is a key feature that maintains the threshold of entry into the occupation of selling at low levels and accounts for the fact that even the groups with the smallest resources can engage in this activity. Also, it reduces the risk for conflicts with stronger competitors and the risk of being ruined because of intense competition with other

Figure 15   Lemon sellers at the San Judas market

activities in gaining access to economic space. Moreover, the quality of spatial flexibility gives ambulatory sellers greater leverage in choosing places of selling and thereby increase the possibility of maximizing incomes as well. The activity of peddling can serve as a good example of benefits derived from "locational floating". Thus, an ambulatory vendor can move around all day within the same place of work, a market for example, or along the streets between several places or markets during a day. In this way he can adjust his activity to variations in customer shopping habits, by taking advantage of the higher influx of customers during certain hours of the day, or even move around all day in search of customers. The combined effects of the spatially flexible nature of this activity, the low levels of investments in capital required to set up business, the variety in products that can be offered for sale, and the fact that most items on sale are final consumption goods, account for the concentration of children in this activity. The survey data collected in this study suggest that ambulatory vending is undertaken as a secondary occupation, whereas selling as a principal activity tends to be locationally more fixed.

The status of sellers as self-employed or as dependent sellers is largely a reflection of differences in access to capital. The majority of the children were not self-employed. Rather they worked for family members or others engaged in informal sector activities. Although a major factor behind the low proportion of self-employed children is their status as minors, other factors contribute to this situation. Self-employment is primarily a function of whether the necessary capital to invest in and to run an activity can be acquired. Given that most children enter the urban informal sector in order to contribute to family income and/or to support themselves, the meagre income derived from engaging in activities with low levels of return reduces the possibility of building up sufficient reserves of capital to start a business of their own. Consequently children have no choice but to work as dependent workers for middlemen who usually retain the bulk of the child's income, making saving even more difficult. In informal sector parlance, the vendor "lends" the product to the child worker, and more often than not a greater part of the profit goes to the intermediary. In some cases the children stated that they were forced to hand over up to 75 per cent of the profits. Complaints regarding unfair practices are not uncommon, although few cases were reported during the interviews for this study. Children selling newspapers, for instance, have been known to have made complaints about the rules and controls they were subjected to when working for adult distributors who demanded monetary deposits as guarantees for the newspapers handed over to the children. Failure to meet the demands of the middlemen could mean cuts in the profits made by the children.

The products most frequently obtained by children through an intermediary for sale included soda, lotteries, and newspapers. In most of the cases, however, the children worked with a member of the household, often the mother, the father or an elder sister or brother, usually in the same occupation but not always selling the same product at the same place. In many cases a household member made the products for sale, such as refreshments or food, at home, and sent the child to sell these in the market. In some cases, both the children and their relatives worked at the same location and at the same times. Yet another type of partnership involved the child and the intermediary selling different products. What is common to all these cases, however, is that children need not invest capital to undertake such activities.

When the child was self-employed, he or she had to reserve a share of the surplus from sales as extra capital in order keep the business running. The various day to day needs that have to be met, coupled with the meagre earnings derived from informal sector activities, however, severely limit the opportunities for building up sufficient reserves of capital, and thus making the chances of a child keeping its own business going for long even more dim.

The independent sellers sold candies, chicklets, or the like, which they bought from a deliverer and sold at low margins of profit. The margin was about 25 per cent for a packet of cookies, but could reach 100 per cent in the case of chewing gum. Given the very low product prices, the unit resale price also had to be low which kept the profit margin at low levels. These prices were much lower than the prices for the same products at the supermarket, but nevertheless the sale generated significant incomes for the children.

The products sold in the three sub-categories of selling were similar in kind, but there were some differences related to the type of product and the occupational category of the children. Self-employed children and those working in family "partnerships" usually sold products of very low value, such as ice water, refreshments, fruits, used newspapers, candies, chicklets, cookies and home-made food, whereas children working for middlemen (sellers, distributors) were usually engaged in selling other kinds of products such as lotteries, soda, and newspapers.

One may get the impression that the sellers are a relatively homogeneous group. However, within this group significant differences were found, in terms mainly related to the occupational category of the sellers. The proportion of self-employed sellers, only 14 per cent, was much lower than in other occupations. The largest category (56 per cent) of dependent sellers worked with a member of the household and 30 per cent as employees of another person.

The main reason for these differences was the lack of investment capital on the part of the children and of their households which meant that they had to work for an intermediary, selling someone else's products in exchange for nominal "wages". However, dependent children were not necessarily better off working as sellers in household or family partnerships, since more often than not such arrangements were

Figure 16   Sellers by occupational category and type of products

Occupational category	Type of product
Self-employed (14%, n=5)	water, ice water, candies, vegetables, used newspapers
Dependent on relative (56%, n=20)	manufactured food, soda, fruits, vegetables, ice
Dependent on other person (30%, n=11)	lotteries, newspapers, soda, ice-cream

a reflection of the very strained economic conditions of the family or household, which meant that the children received little or no payment at all.

Differences in the level of earnings in the three categories, were however relatively insignificant. The self-employed obtained the largest earnings among the sellers, whereas those working for intermediaries had the lowest income. The data on the earnings of children working in partnerships with household or family members are incomplete, but it became quite clear that they had the lowest income of all the children. The results indicate that product value and income are not necessarily related, suggesting that the type of employment was a much more significant factor behind income levels, justifying the wish of "running my own business" expressed by many children. Lastly, the products sold by the children could serve as indirect measures of household poverty levels and the lengths to which children might go in order to earn an income every day by engaging in almost any activity.

Occupational categories

The position of children in the labour force derives, on the one hand, from the set of social and economic relations between individuals performing an activity, i. e. the workers, and the persons or institutions for whom that person works, i. e. the employer. It is of course not always the case that the employer and the worker are different people; the self-employed comprise a separate category. How the two basic categories of employer and employee relate to each other forms the basis for the classification of occupational categories used in censuses and household surveys. Employer or patron, employee, independent worker or self-employed and unpaid family worker, are the most frequently used classifications or categories employed in censuses and surveys. These categories, however, are not always relevant or applicable in the case of working children since the distinctions tend to become quite diffuse, mainly due to the nature of the social relations of work that exist between the actors involved. Many children work together with a parent or other members of the household, and the relations of work outside the household are an extension or reproduction of relations between adults and children within the family or household. Consequently, the employee-employer relationship is not always as clear-cut as in the formal economic sector and this tends to affect both the payment and type of income of children. An extreme situation is that of children working together with a parent or parents where obviously neither the children view their parents as patrons, nor the parents regard their children as employees in a contractual or formal meaning. The information obtained from the interviews illustrates this quite well. The uncertain or ambivalent perception that family workers have about their own situation is indicated by responses such as "my work", "I work" etc, when they refer to the activities that they performed, whereas in situations where they worked "together" with parents or other relatives, the responds was "I help". This shows the children's awareness of their subordinate situation as unpaid workers which also was expressed when they said that they wanted to work on their own.

Nevertheless, and in spite of the inherent ambiguities, the criteria for the classification of the occupational categories of children in the urban informal sector resemble the criteria of the established classifications for the adult labour force in this sector.

The children were firstly classified into two main categories: dependent workers and independent workers. The former includes those requiring the economic support or participation of other persons to perform an economic activity, either in the role as suppliers of products or as employers. In turn, these are classified into children who worked together with a parent, relative or another member of the same household, and those who worked for a person who did not belong to the child's household.[1] The category of "independent

Figure 17 Sellers in front of the bus station area at Israel Lewites market

worker" includes those children who had the necessary capital for an activity and were self-employed, or were engaged in activities which did not require capital investment.

Studies by Alarcón and other authors (which will be presented later) show a broad variation in the incidence of working children in the different occupational categories across the region. The findings from Managua provide additional confirmation of significant place-specific variations. Here the dependent and independent child workers were almost evenly distributed between the two categories, 55 per cent and 45 per cent, respectively. An even more significant aspect, however, is the clear gendered pattern in the distribution of working children by category of dependent and independent workers. Indeed, as many as 82 per cent of the working girls were dependent on an adult in their work, whereas the proportion for boys was 44 per cent.

The over-representation of girls among the children who worked together with one of the parents, or with another member of the same household, can be interpreted as a sign of a protective attitude by the

---

[1.] In no case did a child work for a relative who did not belong to the same household as the child.

Figure 18   Occupational category of the children by sex

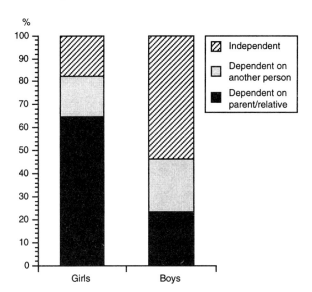

parents or relatives towards girls working outside the household. In fact, the large number of children working with a relative is explained by several authors, not surprisingly, as a way of protecting children from the harsh working and social environment in cities.

In fact, when asked about dangers in the street, many girls acknowledged that they were aware of them, yet they were not so afraid as they knew that parents or other relatives were near. Declarations such as "My mother does not want me to work alone", and "I am not afraid because my mother works at this market too", demonstrate the existence of a certain extra security net woven around girls in particular, reflecting among other things the relations of work between the girls and their parents or relatives. This is also indicated by the fact that whereas 63 per cent of the girls worked together with a member of their household, only 23 per cent of the boys did. But to be a dependent worker does not mean that a parent or another relative is at the same work place as the child. Many times the relation of dependence exists only in economic terms and the children may be working in the city on their own, as in the case of children selling food prepared at home by their mothers.

With regard to the age distribution of children, it would appear that there is a modest relationship between age and occupational category. The mean age in the two groups differed by two years, from 10 years old for the dependent children to 12 years old for the independent. But when looking at the age distribution in each group it became clear that most of the young children, those between 7 and 9 years, were found in the group of dependent workers, while there was an over-representation of older children, between 12 and 14 years, in the self-employed category. The age distribution was not gender-related, however, as all ages were represented for boys as well as girls in both categories.

In sum, there was a clear-cut relationship between gender and age of the children and their occupational category. The large majority of the girls were dependent workers, in most cases working with a parent or relative, while the boys either were independent workers, or dependent workers, working together with a parent or relative or for another person outside their household. It is also clear that there was a tendency for children to become self-employed workers with increasing age.

Occupational categories and activities

As has been demonstrated earlier, the spectrum of visible activities in the urban informal sector which are performed by children is not very broad. Children are restricted to a limited number of activities. The question is, therefore, which factors determine why a child engages in one activity rather than another. In this context, I believe that two factors are of major importance; first, the occupational category of the children—whether they work as dependent or independent workers—and secondly the activity of parents or other relatives who head the children's household.

In this study there is no doubt about the existence of these relationships. The children who were dependent workers were almost all sellers (91 per cent), followed by the "diverse tasks" activity category (9 per cent). In this group of dependent workers, the children in diverse tasks were all employees of individuals outside the household, whereas all the children in selling worked for a parent or a relative of their household.

In contrast, all the investigated activity types were found in the category of independent child workers. However, half of those children worked in activities, such as guarding and washing cars, which require very little or no capital accumulation at all.

Principal and secondary activities

It is not known what proportion of the children in the urban informal sector are engaged in more than one economic activity at the same time. An overview of current research suggests that very little attention has been given to this issue and hence the available information is too patchy to allow for any calculations of reliable indices of the magnitude and significance of secondary activities. Usually the research focus has been on activity types performed by children without any attempt to distinguish between principal and secondary activities. Alarcón is one of the few researchers who has paid attention to secondary activities in the urban informal sector in his study of Lima. He reports that 15 per cent of the working children had a secondary activity, of which selling was the most frequent one. However, Alarcón does not delve any further in his analysis of the topic, beyond mentioning another study by Buse of the urban informal sector in the city of Cajamarca, Peru, where a third of the children had a secondary occupation.[1]

The study of secondary activities, however, can give valuable insights into the conditions of life and work of children working in the urban informal sector in cities of the Third World and should be able to contribute to our knowledge of the magnitude, nature and intensity of child work.

When an attempt is made here to examine the extent and importance of children's secondary activities in Managua, some conceptual

---

[1] Buse, N., Torre, A. and Lopéz. N. (1986): *Para reflexionar sobre los niños que trabajan.* Publicaciones del episcopado. Cajamara.

and methodological problems have to be considered. A principal activity is, by definition, that activity on which the worker spends most of his or her working time or the one through which the bulk of the income is earned. A secondary activity can be performed at either the same place as the principal activity or at a different place, but it will be performed at different times and will differ in character from the primary activity.[1] To distinguish between the two types of activities is no easy task, and even the children could not easily make this distinction, since for them, all tasks they performed were simply "work". Even if some of them could use the category of "other activity" with respect to other children, and especially those who did the same kind of work but at different places and times, the distinction was not important to themselves. Bearing in mind these difficulties, in the interviews the children therefore were first asked if they had another "job" at the same place or at another place, from which they received any kind of payment, besides the activity they were performing at the time of the interview. If the answer was affirmative, they were further asked to specify this other type of activity and rank it in order of importance, more specifically in terms of both monetary value and time spent on the activity. The common criterion used here for the classification of activities was income. Without exception secondary earnings were much smaller than income from the principal activity and in some cases even non-existent. The results suggest that as many as 25 per cent of the interviewed children had a secondary activity.

The claim is often made that boys engage more frequently in secondary activities since the burden of household work falls on girls and hence they cannot engage in secondary activities to the same extent as boys. The data collected in this study, however, does not suggest that this is the case. Almost the same proportion of boys and girls was found to be engaged in secondary activities—24 per cent and 26 per cent, respectively—which suggests that there is no direct relationship between gender and children's participation in secondary activities. With respect to the distribution of this group of children by age, no clear pattern was found. In fact, children of all ages, from seven to

---

[1.] ILO's definitions.

Figure 19   Principal and secondary activities

```
Activity:

Principal            Secondary
selling       ──▶ selling, car warding, loading/unloading, garbage collecting
shoe-shining  ──▶ apprenticeship, selling
Car warding   ──▶ selling, loading/unloading, gardening, shoe-shining
```

fourteen, were involved in secondary activities. Selling was the most common secondary activity and engaged almost half of the children, but shoe-shining, car-warding, loading and unloading as well as various forms of apprenticeship, gardening, working in the manufacturing of food and collecting garbage were also represented. One might ask whether or not principal and secondary activities are related in any meaningful way. An attempt was therefore made to examine whether some sort of correspondence between type of principal and secondary activity existed. However, any direct or clear-cut relationship or correspondence in that respect did not exist. With the possible exception of selling, it is difficult to derive the type of secondary activity that children would engage in from their primary occupation. The absence of such a correspondence between primary and secondary activities is also brought out by figure 19.

A comparison of the primary and secondary activities with regard to their locational characteristics, i. e. whether they were performed at the same place or not, showed that 60 per cent of the secondary activities were performed at some place other than the location of the principal activity. Furthermore, only 13 per cent of the children had a secondary activity that was identical to the principal occupation performed at the same location. In those cases, the children did the same work but as part of different occupational categories: in the principal activity they worked as employees of a seller, whereas in the secondary activity they were self-employed. As one of the children put it, as a secondary activity they were "running their own business".[1]

---

[1] Some boys said that they bought plastic bags and ice at the market and sold ice water on the weekends.

With one exception, all those who had selling as both the primary and secondary occupation, engaged in the secondary activity upon returning home, usually in the neighbourhood, at home, or in what is known as "venta", i. e. a sales stand at home. This group of children undertook unpaid work, varying in time from one to three hours per day, every day after regular working times and often after school.

In the case of secondary activities other than selling, there were considerable variations in the types of locations. Most commonly, these activities were undertaken in the streets and in other markets, sometimes in the parking lots of the markets where the principal activities took place, while others were undertaken in private houses or through door to door ambulation. Figure 20 summarizes the distribution of primary and secondary activities by location.

In most of the cases the children's secondary occupations were different from the principal one, and in more than half of the cases they were performed at other locations than where the principal activity took place. It is interesting to notice that almost all of the children which engaged in secondary activities came from two places of work: the Roberto Huembes (47 per cent), and El Mayoreo (33 per cent) markets. The concentration of children with two occupations to the two largest places of work may be an indicator of the poor earning opportunities available at these locations and/or the level of poverty of the families, an issue which will be explored more in detail later on.

This study thus has shown that occupational diversification of child work in the informal sector is not so significant, and that the variety of tasks performed by the children were concentrated to the services and trade sectors. On the one hand, this lack of any great diversity of activities may reflect strategies of maximizing household income which are pursued by the children and their relatives. At the same time, the concentration of many of the activities undertaken by children to a narrow range of relatively simple tasks or types, confirms the low economic returns to and value of child work, and the limited access that children have to other types of activities. From this point of view, the frequency of involvement in secondary occupations can be interpreted as an important proxy indicator of poverty levels of the children and their families. With the long hours of work implied by multiple activities, children have less time for leisure and rest, and are

Figure 20   Location of principal and secondary activities

PRINCIPAL ACTIVITY		SECONDARY ACTIVITY	
ACTIVITY I	PLACE OF WORK	ACTIVITY II	PLACE OF WORK
Selling shoe-shining	El Mayoreo market	Selling Apprenticeship Selling	Home Workshop Neighbourhood
Car-warding selling	Roberto Huembes market	Shoe-shining Car-warding	In the street Parking lot at the same market
Car-warding	Galeria Internacional	Selling Gardening	Fixed place in the street Private house
Selling	Israel Lewites market	Selling	Home/neighbour-hood

of course also more exposed to risks at work. With the exception of apprentice occupations, this conclusion holds for all activity types.

If one attempts to summarize the characteristics of the children with two occupations the following general features stand out. Engagement in a secondary activity was not gender or age related. In fact, the proportion of boys and girls with a secondary activity was similar and they were of all ages. The main activity was selling and in most of the cases, children worked after school and after their principal activity had ended. In contrast to the principal activity that took place at specific places of work—parking lots and markets—the secondary activity took place at the children's home or in the neighbourhood of the home. The households of most of these children were single-parent households headed by the mother, who in almost all the cases made food at home for selling. This finding clearly indicates that the children with two occupations came from the poorest households which badly needed the children's economic contribution. Finally, children with secondary activities made up 25 per cent of the sample, but they accounted for almost half of the children in the sample who had moved into the city. This suggests that children belonging to migrant families, headed by the mother, were those who worked most.

Occupational mobility

This section has two aims. First, to establish the extent of occupational mobility experienced by working children for the activity types under study, and, secondly, to examine to what extent changes in type of activity are the result of decisions by the children themselves or by parents or other adult relatives. The term occupational mobility is used here synonymously with changes in occupation. The frequency of changes and duration of "employment" in one and same activity are used as indicators of occupational mobility, which is a little explored issue in child work research. In fact it is rarely mentioned in the literature. This is ironic since one of the myths regarding child work in the urban informal sector is that it is highly erratic. The prevalent notion is that children lack job commitment and thus shift from one activity to another in a casual manner. An analysis of four surveys on child work in Latin America, conducted by Myers, cites Alarcon's sample study from Lima, where 42 per cent of the boys and 14 per cent of the girls reported that they never had changed their activity.[1] Another study is that from Asunción by Espínola, who found that half of the interviewed children had changed occupation once, 8 per cent twice and 7 per cent three or more times.[2] Close to 40 per cent of the children in that survey indicated that they had worked in the present occupation for a period that varied from three to six years.

Neither of these studies provide age-specific information on the children that changed occupations. Nor is information supplied on the type of activities the children were involved in before and after changes in occupation. Nonetheless, both authors venture to interpret occupational mobility as a means of improvement used by the children. Alarcón found that 34 per cent of the children had changed activity with increasing age and noticed that there was a tendency to shift from less stable towards more stable activities as children become older. Espínola, on the other hand, went further in the analysis and identified three main reasons behind changes in activity: (i) economic, (ii) external non-economic, and (iii) the children' s own desire to change to what they considered to be better activities. With respect to

---

[1] Myers, W. (1989). Only two of the surveys brought the subject up for discussion.
[2] Espínola, B. et al. (1989).

the third point, she arrived at this conclusion by relating mobility to the aspirations of the children to "ascend" occupationally. Her reasoning was that children aspire to change to activities which are regarded as "better" by society in general, towards more formal and stable work with fixed jobs and salaries, as this was regarded as "real work" by the children. It is not clear whether the conclusions are based on her interview material or derived from theoretical assumptions or combinations thereof. Nevertheless, that study is the only one that attempts to provide analytical interpretations of occupational mobility in child work in the urban informal sector.

I found that 22 per cent of the interviewed children had changed their occupation, but in all cases only once. By itself, the low proportion of children—all boys—who had changed activity, was a strong indicator of low mobility, especially when one takes the relatively high age of the children—10 to 14 years—into account. In order to understand the factors behind mobility, however, other indicators have to be considered, such as the type of activities between which the children moved, reasons for changing, age at which the changes took place, duration in each activity, and place of residence when they engaged in the former activity.

In view of the restrictions on entry into the informal sector, in terms of location rights and access to contact networks, and keeping in mind the age of the children, it seems highly unlikely that, having once secured a position in an occupation, children would venture to change occupation on their own. Consequently, mobility has to be analysed within the context of the child's family or household which may have a greater say than the child in such decisions. The responses of the children regarding this question indicated that this was indeed the case. The economic factor was the decisive aspect behind occupational change. Over half of the interviewed children (54 per cent), stated that they changed to another activity because of poor earnings in the former occupation, whereas in 23 per cent of the cases the change occurred because the mother wanted that. In no case did a child attribute the occupation change to personal decision. The responses remind us of the subordinate position children have in decision-making in relation to adults in general and parents in particular. These findings suggest that there is little reason to expect that working

Figure 21   Car wards at the Roberto Huembes market

children have any great say in decision-making as long as they live as members of a household. Other reasons given by the children for changes in occupation were maltreatment by the employer, the need to work for the family as extra hands, that the employer had disappeared, and finally because they moved to the city.

The occupational mobility of children in the urban informal sector is thus influenced by a complex set of factors, although many of these could be subsumed under "economy" as the overarching factor. An examination of the factors behind occupational mobility among children in the urban informal sector suggests that there are two dominant and interrelated set of causes. Firstly, the economic, expressed through the children's wish to maximize earnings and their aspirations to be able to enter higher profit activities. The second set of factors relate to the broader social context, as expressed in the subordinate position of children in decision-making regarding both the family and their own future. The subordinate position of children with respect to the decision to change occupation implies that occupational mobility is not always governed by an ambition to move up the social ladder.

It seems that there is some co-variation between occupational and spatial mobility, since for most of the children occupational change

Figure 22   Occupational mobility

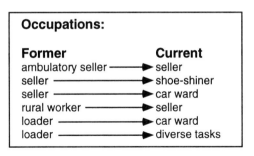

was accompanied by a change of residence either within Managua or between places outside Managua and the city itself. On the other hand, when reviewing the type of activities in the former and current occupation, it appears that the sectors open for shifts in occupation are few, reinforcing the conclusion that occupational change is often circular, confined to movement within the same activities. Moreover, the concentration of children in but a few activities in the urban informal sector reduces the opportunities for occupational mobility even further, and indirectly highlights the constraints on entry into other activities in the urban informal sector.

The duration of engagement in an occupation is a key indicator of mobility, yet it cannot be analysed on its own as it is highly conditioned by the factors mentioned above. The duration of engagement in an occupation for the children under study varied from less than six months to up to six years. The average duration in the former occupation was 17 months and in the current one 30 months. If one excludes the children aged 12 and above, the average duration in the first activity was just over 19 months. An examination of the age when children began to work and the age at the time of a change in occupation indicates that the earlier a child starts working, the longer the duration before a change to another occupation takes place. Conversely, the older a child is when he or she enters the urban informal sector, the shorter the time it takes to change to another occupation.

When asked about the main reason for changing occupation, in all cases the children who had worked for short periods (up to one year) in their first occupation mentioned low income. On the other hand, children who worked longer in the first occupation (from over a year

Figure 23 Age and work career of children who had changed occupation

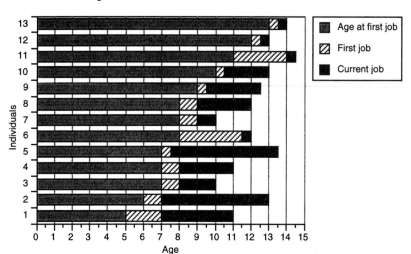

up to six years), mentioned "decision by the mother" and "change of residence" as the main reasons for shifting to another activity. However, since all the children who stated that it was their mothers who wanted them to change occupations also had changed place of residence, it appears that occupational shift followed upon change of residence. It can thus be concluded that for the children who had worked long in the first occupation, occupational change was imposed or compulsory since it was conditioned by the decisions of others. Whereas the factor of "low income" as the reason for occupational mobility is primarily a reflection of economic conditions, that of change in place of residence need not necessarily be conditional on the economic situation.

In sum, to speak about occupational mobility of the children in this study in the conventional or purely economic terms, is misleading, since what is characteristic is that occupational change was limited to a very narrow range of alternative activities. Occupational change was induced by a combination of the subordinate position of the children in decision-making and economic factors. The small number of children who had changed occupation, the length or duration of engagement in one and the same activity, the reasons for occupational changes, as well as the narrow range of activity types open for occupational mobility—all these facts support the conclusion that occupational mobility is low. The conclusions of Myers, in his analysis of child work surveys in the urban informal sector in Latin America, capture the situation with regard to occupational mobility of these children in Managua quite well. Myers provides a picture that is different from the predominant notion that " most urban working children shift nonchalantly between unrelated economic activities according to whim or sudden opportunity. On the contrary, the evidence of these surveys suggests a certain degree of structure and commitment within these occupations which encourages continuity."[1] This seems to be true of the children who have been studied in the present work.

The income

There is a general consensus about the impossibility of accurately calculating the income of working children in general and of those working in the urban informal sector in particular. This is partly due to the difficulties in obtaining accurate information about how much the children earn, from employers, parents and the children themselves, and partly because of the sensitivity of that information, since it often reveals patterns of exploitation of the children as workers. Also, the forms of employment and of payment are factors which make such estimations difficult. However, and in spite of such difficulties, there is enough evidence to permit us to outline some common features of the income situation of most working children. It is generally assumed that,

(i) the income of the children is highly variable
(ii) it is always lower than that of adults performing the same work
(iii) it is seldom anywhere near the minimum wage levels for the country in question
(iv) a large number of children receive a combined income, in money and in kind

---

[1] Myers, W. (1989). p. 326.

(v) many children work without remuneration
(vi) there is a lack of written employment contracts

However, there are significant variations by country, region, type of economy (rural/urban) and type of activities. Variations in forms of employment in the urban informal sector, relations of work, and forms of payment, as well as certain temporal aspects of the informal sector in general and child work in particular, present additional difficulties when one tries to go beyond the general aspects mentioned earlier and to explore more fully the income situation of working children.

From the methodological point of view, it has sometimes been easier to determine the income earned by children in the cases where their work involves tasks confined to specific and well defined places of work and activities. These include, for instance, cases where children work in hazardous occupations, small workshops or family enterprises in the formal or informal economic sector. A large number of case studies that focus on the working situation of children have attested to the widespread occurrence of hazardous working conditions. Reviewing research on children's income in the informal sector, Bequele and Boyden provided a summary that is worth quoting at length. Thus:

> ...in the wood industry in the Filipinas, the rates of renumeration varied broadly depending on the size of the produced items and other factors. In a large number of industries the payment was made after the accomplishment of a task or of a specific work period and often discounts were made because of defaults in production, delay in delivery, absence because of health problems and other reasons. The conditions and the amount of the discounts were of course fixed by the employer. Oosterhout describes a certain system of payment in the fishery of Muro Ami (Filipinas), not based on a salary but instead on a system through which each fisherman´s income was depending on the total value of the fishery. .....this form of payment builds up a feeling of extreme insecurity, because the workers have to wait until the fishery is over to know the amount of their earning. Both in the fisheries of Muro Ami and in the gold minery in Peru, the discounts for medication, complementary food

and lost working days can be so high that at the end of the work period the worker finds himself in debt to the employer. ...According to this scheme, the children can be obliged to work for the same employer for the rest of their life.[1]

In the same work, in a study of the tannery industry in Cairo, Egypt, it was found that 60 per cent of the working children were paid on a daily basis, whereas only 36 per cent were salaried apprentices.[2] The children stated that they received payment regularly, save during periods of low production, when they received only a fraction of their normal salaries. The earnings of child workers were low compared to that of the adults, between one fourth and one third of the income earned by adults. The study of child work in brick kilns and stone cutting in India, by Salazar, found that the most common form of payment was in kind, with about half of the children in both activities receiving their principal payment in kind.[3] However, Salazar also found that children worked without remuneration as well. Thus, 22 per cent of the children working in stone cutting and 31 per cent at the brick kilns received no money at al.

In the description of the situation of working children in his study of the informal carpet manufacturing sector in India, Kanbargi also stressed the difficulties involved in trying to calculate real income.[4] Although he obtained information about the minimum wage, Kangari had no means of establishing the exact size or nature of the various deductions made by employers for a variety of reasons, such as claims of flaws in manufacturing, delays in delivery, and the like. Nevertheless, he was able to establish that employers systematically withheld and made arbitrary deductions of 8 to 10 per cent of children's earnings. As a general rule, a child's salary was collected by the parents, whereas in

---

[1.] Bequele, A. and Boyden, J. (1990): *La lucha contra el trabajo infantil*. OIT. Ginebra. (Free translation from the Spanish by the author).

[2.] Ahmed, A. (1990): *El trabajo infantil en Egipto: las curtiembres de El Cairo*. Bequele, A. and Boyden, J. (eds.): *La lucha contra el trabajo infantil*. OIT. Ginebra.

[3.] Salazar, M.C. (1990): *El trabajo infantil en Colombia. Las canteras y hornos de ladrillos de Bogotá*. Bequele, A. and Boyden, J. (eds.): *La lucha contra el trabajo infantil*. OIT. Ginebra.

[4.] Kanbargi, R. (1990): *El trabajo infantil en la India: la fabricación de alfombras en Benares*. Bequele, A. and Boyden, J. (eds.): *La lucha contra el trabajo infantil*. OIT. Ginebra.

the case of migrant children the money was mailed to the parents. The children had no rights to leisure time, free food or other facilities at the place of work. Indeed, the children cooked their own food, and in the case of the youngest children they had to pay for a rather poor diet that the employer offered to them.

The list of examples of these kinds of studies is long and the documentation in this respect is quite good, perhaps due to the appalling situations of working children in work places which have drawn the widespread attention of the media and thereby extensive research response.

An overview of the findings of numerous studies of child work in the informal sector leaves no doubt about the pervasive nature of the economic exploitation of children. The difficulties encountered in establishing the income earned by children working in the urban informal sector still remain, however, and hence much less is known about their income situation. The problems met in calculating the income of children in the informal sector are not unique, but arise with respect to the income of adults as well. Yet, in the case of children, the difficulties are compounded by other factors which, directly or otherwise, are related to the status of children as both minors and workers.

First of all, many of the children are not workers in the legal sense, given the national labour regulations in many countries, which define 15 years as the most common minimum age for admittance to employment. This renders the status of the children in this study, for example, de facto illegal. Ironically, the illegality of child work makes the children as workers particularly vulnerable. The social attitudes, mores and adult conceptions of what is or is not work and what children should or should not be doing, belittle the real economic worth or value of child work. The absence of legal rights regarding child work together with such social attitudes imply that many times working children come to be regarded as a nuisance and no better than beggars or vagabonds. The combined effect of this is to make children economically vulnerable, since the economic activities of children are often not interpreted as such by adults, which in turn justifies not to pay children, or to pay them only a pittance, not much better than alms. In sum, the income of the children is subject not only to general constraints arising from the nature of the urban informal sector, but also tend to be deflated because of attitudes on the part of adults and society at large which specifically undervalue the work of children.

Income determinants

In this section, the focus of the analysis will be on those factors that I regard as having a major determining effect on the type and size of the income earned by the children of this study, namely, the places of work and types of activities, and the relationships between work and the occupational categories of the children, with respect to (i) modes of payment and (ii) destination of income.

Places of work and activity types

Most of the informal sector activities have certain spatial and temporal characteristics which influence the working conditions and earning levels of the children. Conditions of work, and by extension income, are highly sensitive to external factors. Not least important is the weather, a factor which affects many of the activities conducted in the open in a negative or a positive manner. Open air activities in markets, streets or parking lots which lack shades and/or roof cover, are very sensitive to fluctuations in the weather, and particularly to weather conditions during rainy, windy, dusty and hot periods. Consequently, such activities as car-washing, selling, shoe-shining and the like are extremely dependent on the weather in Managua. In the rainy season, for instance, which lasts for six months, downpours and even torrential rains occur almost everyday. When it is raining, people are obviously not particularly interested in having their cars washed. And who would want to have his or her shoes shined when it is raining? Likewise, an activity such as selling ice water is highly dependent on weather conditions.

The temporal character of the activities is also a factor that influences the income of children. The temporal aspects reflect the characteristics of working places as well. In general, the income of children is highly variable, by season, month, week, day of the week and even during the day. For instance, during the last week of the month or the last week before payday, the income of a car ward drops because people are short of money and do not use their car. Every market has its own *strong* and *weak* days. For instance, for a vendor at the El Mayoreo, which is a wholesale market, such activities as selling and bearing are more profitable during days when products are delivered. A vendor's income is related to *good* and *bad* days at the markets, with Saturdays, Sundays, and the first days of the month after payday being good days. Conversely, the bad days are characterized by low customer inflow and usually coincide with weekdays and the last week of the month. Activities and incomes are also very much affected by the periodicity of the school year and special occasions such as religious, national, and other holidays and celebrations.

Changes in the general price level is another factor that also affects the income of working children. Price increases are rarely compensated for by corresponding increases in income for those engaged in the informal sector. If the prices of the products used in the manufacturing of food items rise, for instance, this does not necessarily result in higher earnings for vendors. Indeed, it may sometimes have the opposite effect, as when children or their families cannot afford to buy these products and the vendor instead will have to sell a substitute and cheaper product, with a consequent drop in income. Many of the informal sector activities involve the provision of services, and increases in the prices of inputs often result in lower profit margins. This is so partly because of the strong competition in such activities, and the child is left with no choice but to accept a lower income level, at least for the short term, and to make adjustments accordingly. Increases in the price of bus tickets, for example, have meant that some of the children could no more afford to pay for a bus trip to and from the place of work, but instead had to travel on foot. The time spent in walking to and from the working place shortens the time available for work and consequently reduces the incomes of these children.

Furthermore, there are a host of other factors of a personal nature which impact on the earnings of children engaged in the informal sector. Individual skills and abilities, and the physical and mental con-

Figure 24   A boy who sold vegetables at El Mayoreo market

dition of the children cause differences in income among the children involved in similar activities and within the same working places. Different activities require different abilities and the effort that can be exerted depends on the strength or endurance of the children, which in turn implies that their daily earnings can vary significantly. Guarding cars, for example, is an activity that demands a lot of effort from the children and the income gained depends on the child's capacity to run, quite often and as rapidly as possible, after incoming cars. A lot of energy is also expended in trying to persuade the client that the child is the right car ward. Asked about the income of his last working day, Roger, one of the children in this study, said:

> Yesterday I was not in good shape; I was too tired to run after the cars, so I did not earn as much as I use to.

There are other activities which depend as much or even more on individual skills and abilities, such as selling. As in the case of car guarding, vendors have to be able to convince clients to buy just their products, often by pursuing the clients for a while. This is not an easy task, since competition among vendors is tough and may involve contending with three or more vendors at the same time for the attention of the same client. Scenes of altercations, as when irritated customers insult vendors, are quite common. The story of Lucil, the girl who sold refreshments at the Roberto Huembes market, illustrates this rather well. She confessed,

> I really do not like to be here selling. I am too shy, but I have to help my mother selling.

The testimonies of the children about the skills required to maximize the earnings in their occupations were many and clearly showed how aware they were of the difficulties they faced, but at the same time also testified to their commitment and the pride they felt in their work.

Nevertheless, most factors affecting the income do not depend on the attitude of the children, but on factors such as their general health and current physical condition. The activities they are engaged in require a lot of energy; a child who is sick, malnourished or too tired obviously does not have enough strength to run after cars or customers. In spite of sometimes heroic efforts, the outcome of a sick child's work is obviously lower than that of a healthy one.

Be that as it may, most of the interviewed children were very active and showed no signs of undernourishment, at least as a first impression. However, many of them were complaining about fatigue and that they were sleepy during the day, which can be a sign of a certain degree of malnutrition combined with long hours of work and too little sleep.

Occupational categories and modes of payment

One aspect, which to a certain extent reflects the position of children in the labour force, is the mode of payment. Due to the sometimes diffuse forms of payment and the small monetary gains that children get from their work, there has been a certain reluctance to look upon certain kinds of earnings as income by working children. Of course it is not easy to find an appropriate term for all forms of payment usual in child work, since they do not fit the common economic terms and concepts used in studies of the "adult labour force", but it is my belief that this difficulty depends mainly on adults' perception of the role of children as economically active individuals. The unwillingness to perceive children as full-fledged workers in their own right also has to do with deeply rooted beliefs and norms, grounded in Western market economy concepts, relating to the nature of work, who is entitled to work and what work is worth. There is a tendency to view the act of paying a child for a product or for a service as no more than an act of charity, and such payments as alms or a tip.

Indeed, "tip" is one of the terms most commonly used to denote "non-formal" modes of payment to children in the urban informal sector and it is indiscriminately used across occupational categories, forms of employment and activity types. The same term is rarely found in studies of the adult labour force, even when adults perform the same type of activities as children. During the interviews, the children never used the word tip when talking about the way they were paid in their jobs, and it is my opinion, therefore, that as long as children do not conceive of their earnings as simply a tip, the term should not be used.

Those children who worked together with a parent or another relative as dependent workers were those whose incomes were most uncertain or irregular and in some cases even non-existent. Those who had an income were paid in one of two ways. A more or less regular payment, where the child received a variable lump sum of money at the end of the week, and a second highly irregular one, both in terms of periodicity and amount of money. When asked about what they thought of being paid sporadically and whether they thought that such payments represented earnings for their work or simply was pocket money, the children expressed no doubts about it being their income. They argued that the other non-working siblings in the family did not receive any money at all from the parents and that they knew for sure that what they received was payment for their work. A considerable number of children, however, declared that they never received any money for their work. Those children, then, are by definition "unpaid family workers".

Despite the varying modes and irregularity of the payments, some of the children spoke very proudly and enthusiastically about the sig-

Figure 25   A boy who wards and washes cars at the Roberto Huembes market

nificance of their earnings.[1] Some declared that they saved their earnings in order to buy a pair of shoes, materials for school, or other things that the household's tight economy could not otherwise afford. The significance of such income is generally belittled in conventional economic studies, maybe because it seems to be very marginal in the context of established ways of defining waged labour. However, it certainly is not negligible since it was of great importance to the children themselves, and also contributed to the income of the household, if only indirectly.

The situation of the dependent workers was quite different. Those working for a person outside the child's household were all paid on a daily basis, but in two different ways; either a fixed sum based on the "agreement" between the child and the employer, or alternatively by unit or per piece. The latter was the usual form of payment for those selling lottery tickets or soda. In the opinion of the children, daily payments were preferable to payments on a weekly basis, since the former meant that they could come home every day with money that

---

[1]. This issue was discussed at lenght with the children working together with a relative or one parent.

they could give to their parents or that would allow them to buy the items they needed. The children's preferences for receiving payment on a daily basis highlight the conditions of constant and urgent needs under which the children's households live; in order to make ends meet a poor household requires the immediate input of the income of the children as well as that of other members of the household. Under such circumstances, there is often no room for the accumulation of capital.

No children received a "salary", which is not surprising. With the exception of wage workers employed in small workshops or small service enterprises, this is not a common mode of payment in the informal sector. In fact, one of the major and ever present problems in studies of the labour force in the informal sector is to calculate with any accuracy the incomes of working children and adults alike. In general, though, both adults and children are paid on a very variable daily basis.

Due to the difficulties and the methodological complications outlined in the discussion above, most analyses of modes of payment and type of income employ a descriptive approach. One such is the study by Mendelievich, in which he reviewed the modes of payment for child work in very general terms and without differentiating between occupational categories or considering other significant factors.[1] Mendelievich enumerated all known forms of payment: salaries, tips, payments in kind, and payments by piece, and underscored the fact that a large number of children work without any kind of renumeration, which is best exemplified by the children who work as apprentices. Other authors prefer to focus their analysis on the group of children who work as dependents for an employer who might be a relative or another person outside the family. Even this approach, however, excludes the large number of children that work in the urban informal sector as independent or self-employed workers.

Alarcón's study of Lima shows that as many as 89 per cent of the children were dependent workers, of which 72 per cent worked with a parent or another relative.[2] Only 11 per cent were independent

---

[1] Mendelievich, E. (1979): *Children at work.* p. 39-40. ILO. Geneva.
[2] Alarcón (1989). p. 69 and 86.

workers. He focused his analysis of the modes of payment on just those children working as dependents for a parent, relative or another person, and found that 29 per cent were unpaid workers, 54 per cent received tips, whereas only 3 per cent received payment in kind and 9 per cent a salary. On the other hand, he could observe a clear relationship between the age of children and the mode of payment; 75 per cent of the children in the lower age group (up to 10 years old), did not receive any payment but only tips. Only when the children reached the age of 12 did they begin to receive a "salary". He also found that the form of payment was gendered, such that payments in kind and non-remunerated work were by far more common among girls than boys. Espínola's study on the other hand, showed that in Asunción the group of children who worked as independents (65 per cent) far exceeded that in Lima, and that dependent workers made up 35 per cent of the working children, of which more than half worked together with a member of their family.[1]

Income types

Starting from the findings regarding the distribution of children in different occupational categories, I will now proceed to examine the kind of income they received and search for possible relationships between type of income, occupational category and activity type. As José , car ward at Roberto Huembes, said:

> If one does not earn money, it feels like one has not been working at all; besides, my mother does not like me to come home without money. A mango or a sweetbread I will eat at once because I am always hungry. With money we can buy whatever we want.

This statement sums up the opinion of the children in general about the type of income they expect to receive in exchange for their work. But income does not necessarily mean cash. Even in terms of the type of income they receive, children occupy a subordinate position in

---

[1.] Espínola, B. et al. (1989).

relation to adults. In fact, they are dependent on the "good will" of adult customers as well as on the decisions of adult employers. The dependent child worker in the service sector, for instance, can neither request a certain type of payment nor specify the amount she or he should be paid for the services offered to customers. The same thing can be said of the child vendor: she or he might decide on the kind of payment in exchange for the sold product and yet can not set "a fixed price", since as a rule prices are almost always negotiable. In general, the children talked with interest and enthusiasm about the types of income they received, and they had very pronounced opinions about what they preferred. With few exceptions, they regarded the income in kind as a diminution of their total daily income.

The children interviewed for this study thus had two types of income: a monetary one and one in kind. The money they received most often was payments in the national currency, the *cordobas*, in rare cases in foreign currency, particularly US dollars, but also in Guatemalan *quetzales*. Income in kind was very varied in type, consisting mainly of candies, sweetbreads, fruits and vegetables. In no case did a child work solely in exchange for a meal, even though some received meals as a complement to their earnings.

The children's perception of the two different types of income was very clear, and without exception monetary income was considered to be the principal or "real" income while that in kind was seen as supplementary, and something which the children did not include in their calculation of daily earnings. For them, the purpose of working was to earn money and there was widespread disapproval of being paid in kind. Some of the children felt cheated when they did not receive money in exchange for their work, as when they guarded cars. They told about the different tricks they deployed, and which sometimes were successful, in order to avoid payment in kind. As the 10 year old car ward Roland put it:

> I want to earn money; that is why I am working out in the street. When I see that the person is not the kind of person willing to pay in money, and I do recognise them at once, I use to tell them that if I come home without money, my father will beat me and I will not get my dinner; often they believe me and pay me in money.

Figure 26 Type of income by occupational category

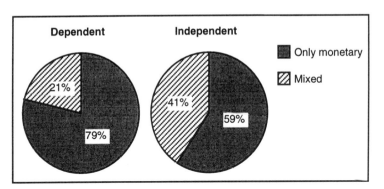

All the children in fact stated that they earned money, while some said that they received payment in kind as well. In other words, they had a mixed income. A review of the type of income by occupational category shows that, irrespective of the occupational category, most children received the bulk of their income in money.

In terms of the two types of income, it was more common among the dependent child workers to receive cash income. The income of the independent child workers differed from the dependent ones in that the former more often received a mixed income. Total income therefore tended to be more variable in their case than for the dependent child workers. There is an element of gender differences as well in the distribution of types of income. In fact, 72 per cent of the children who had mixed incomes were boys. This is not surprising as boys were more engaged in activities that were mostly paid in kind.

In sum, there is an obvious relationship between the occupational category of the children and the types of income they receive but this conclusion per se is not surprising. A factor that might affect this relationship could be the type of activity. The hypothesis would be that certain activities were more prone to provide income in kind than others. A first interpretation of figure 27 might lead to the conclusion that all activities could provide income in kind. Still, for the category of independent child workers, there was a clear concentration of this income type to the activities of car warding and washing.

The high proportion of sellers with mixed incomes in the dependent group can be explained mainly by the fact that it is the major

Figure 27   Mixed income by activity type and occupational category

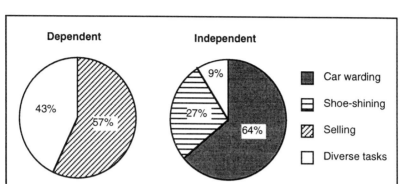

activity for that group. It might also be interpreted in terms of the value of the products sold. Figure 28 shows the distribution of the two income types by occupational category and type of activity.

Undoubtedly, selling was the activity which most often generated monetary income. No independent seller declared that she or he had received payment in kind. A closer look at the information for sellers in the dependent group shows that more than half of those employed by an established vendor received food, fruits, sweetbread, tortillas, a meal, and sometimes a soda.

The few sellers who worked together with a member of the household and received payment in kind from the customers without exception came from the poorest families. The products they sold, such as lemons, mangos or other seasonal fruits, had very low value and without exception they worked with their mothers who sold the same products. Contrary to the majority of the children, they indicated that they were happy to receive payment in kind, as their earnings were very low and for them it provided one means of obtaining food during the day.

Another group of children that did not dislike receiving income in kind were those who worked in the type of activities labelled "diverse tasks". They could work for a retailer or a wholesale vendor as employees, or were self-employed. They said that they had an agreement with the vendor about their payment which was partly in kind, often vegetables but sometimes also fruits. They seemed satisfied with this form

Figure 28   Type of income by activity and occupational category in per cent

Type of Income	Dependent		Independent
	Family	Employed	Self-employed
Mixed	14	8	41
- car ward	-	-	26
- seller	14	8	-
- shoe-shiner	-	-	11
- diverse	-	-	4
Monetary	86	67	59
- car ward	-	-	26
- seller	86	67	22
- shoe-shiner	-	-	11
Total	100	100	100

of payment because they could later sell the vegetables at the market and believed that they earned more this way than if they would get all their income in money. One of the boys, for instance, said that he brought the products he received as payment home, and gave them to his mother who in turn sold them. What initially was an income in kind, was subsequently transformed into monetary income.

In sum, it is possible to find a relationship between income type and occupational category in the sense that children working independently received a higher proportion of their income in kind than those working as dependent workers. However, if one analyses the activity types in both occupational categories, it becomes evident that activity types influenced the type of income that children received even more than the occupational category. In general, service activities, where children had no product to sell but their own labour, were those which led to a "worse" payment situation, to use the children's own expression, while selling was the activity which, with a few exceptions, primarily generated the generally preferred type of income, money.

The monetary income

In general terms, and as has been pointed out earlier, the income of the children is very low, lower than that of the adults in the same activities and in many cases the children do not receive any income at all for their work. As has already been discussed, the income of the children in the urban informal sector is difficult to calculate because of sector characteristics with respect to forms of employment, the nature of the activities, and the existence of different types of income. With the exception of a few cases where the children were employees, and performed a specific activity located at a well identified place of work, it has not been possible to establish the size of the income with any accuracy. This has been true of other studies as well, and the solution has usually been either to address the problem in very general terms which produces only imprecise conclusions, or, in strictly economic terms, which often leads to conclusions with a large margin of error. In spite of the difficulties, it is important to try to get an idea of the income of the child workers in absolute terms, even though that information could not be used to calculate their monthly or weekly income size. In the present study, the absolute size of the monetary income was analysed in an attempt to establish possible relationships between size of income and the activity types and occupational categories of the children. In addition, an attempt was made to classify the income of children in terms of regularity and reliability.

The size of children's daily income

As was shown above, a large number of the interviewed children said that they had two types of income: monetary income and income in kind. Also, a number of children stated that they had two activities at the time of the interviews, a principal and a secondary one. In this chapter, the "size of income" is related only to the daily monetary income resulting from the principal activity. The children were asked to give information about the monetary income during "the last day of work" before the day of the interview, which in most cases coincided with the day before the interview. As it turned out, all the children remembered very well how much they had earned.

The dependent child workers who worked with a member of the household—all sellers—could not give an account on their own income, since they handed over all their daily earnings to their parents or relatives, often immediately after they received it or at the end of the day. Some of these children declared that some days they got a share of their earnings back; other children said that they never received any payment at all. A small group said that they sometimes received some money, e.g. when they wished to buy something special.

The dependent sellers that worked for another person outside the household, however, could give an account on their income. They worked directly subordinated to either a vendor of food products or of lottery tickets and other games, and received their payment on a daily basis, either as a percentage of the sales or on the basis of a previous agreement. These children said that they felt they were very badly paid since they had to sell a lot in order to get a satisfactory daily income.

The independent sellers sold products which either required very low investment capital or no capital at all. They were incredibly quick in calculating the real value of their daily income, after reducing the investment costs. This was done without problems since they were running their own businesses, as vendors of ice water, newspapers sellers, or food products and used newspapers.[1] The vendors of used newspapers did not need any capital at all to run their activity; they collected the newspapers from private houses and sold them afterwards at the market; their income thus equalled the sales. The children in service activities sold their labour by performing direct services to the customer without investing any capital. The car wards and those

---

[1]. The vendors of ice water were among those who had to invest their own capital in order to keep their activity going: they did not pay for the water, since they obtained it from public water taps at the places of work, but they had to buy ice and plastic bags in which the water was served. The size of the investment on these two items depended on the daily profit: the "really bad" selling days did not give enough profit for buying ice and therefore they simply sold water in plastic bags. They expressed their concern about this, since water without ice was very difficult to sell and their earnings dropped and investment opportunities as well. They knew which days were the best selling days, and some preferred not to have any income on the bad selling days, in order to keep the investment capital required for keeping up the activity.

Figure 29   Children's mean daily income in Cordobas[a] by occupational category and activity type

Activity Type	Employed	Self-employed
Seller (food prod.)	10	18
Seller (lotteries)	14	–
Seller (newspapers)	–	20
Seller (used newspaper)	–	13
Diverse tasks	5	5
Shoe-shiner	–	11
Car ward/washer	–	10

a. In July 1994, the exchange rate of the Cordoba was 6.74 per one US dollar. One pound of beans was 2.67 cordobas and one pound of rice 1.94 cordobas.

who washed cars, the loaders, and those who performed diverse tasks, had no difficulty in estimating how much they earned. The total earnings of one working day was the equivalent to their net incomes.

At first glance figure 29 seems to indicate a considerable difference between the lowest and the highest mean daily income, 5 and 20 cordobas. There are indeed great variation in individual incomes from a low of 1 cordoba to a high of 40 cordobas. Clearly the group of activities labelled "diverse tasks" generated the lowest mean income, regardless of the occupational category of the children. The highest mean income was found among the "sellers" of both categories, and this is where the largest daily incomes were found, in some cases amounting to 40 cordobas/day. This is obviously the reason why so many children expressed the wish to become independent sellers. The sellers themselves knew very well that they were earning more than the children in other activities. The poor incomes from car warding reflects the low status of that activity and in a way confirms the validity of the complaints of the children about the attitude of the customers towards this activity and their reluctance to pay for the service given.

Returning for a moment to the findings about incomes in kind, one can observe a negative relationship between frequency of income in kind and size of the monetary income. The children who received a share of their earnings in kind, had the lowest monetary income, in two thirds of the cases below 10 cordobas/day. Those without income in kind had the highest monetary income, in all cases above 10 cordobas and up to 40 cordobas/day. In sum, the children who had the highest monetary income were those who were self-employed and had no complementary income in kind.

In spite of the complexity of the issue, it is possible at this stage to draw some general conclusions about the income situation of the children. On one hand a clear relationship was found between the size of the monetary income and the type of activity, regardless of the children's occupational category. The best paid children were the sellers and the lowest paid were those with "diverse tasks". The activities, rather than the occupational category, seems to be what determines the size of the monetary income. The median income for both groups—dependent and independent workers—was the same, 10 cordobas, and the difference between the mean value for these two groups was minimal (10,56 for the dependent and 11,60 for the independent). On the other hand, the range of incomes in both groups, 1-40 cordobas for the independent and 5-20 cordobas for the dependent, shows that self-employed children had a better chance of earning good money than those working for another person. The income level of the latter group was presumably kept down, because they were dependent upon the good will and of course the profit interest of the employers themselves.

It is not possible to undertake a complete comparison between the income levels for different activities since not all the activities are represented in both occupational categories, self-employed and employed child workers. However, it is possible to say something about the income of those engaged in the most common activity, i.e. selling. Firstly, with respect to the relationship between income size and activity type, it was possible to conclude that selling was the activity that led to higher incomes, regardless of the occupational category of the children. Secondly, from an occupational category perspective it was quite clear that the lowest paid child workers were those who worked for another person. Not only did they have the lowest monetary income of all, they also received very little (20 per cent) additional remuneration in the form of payment in kind. That this group had the lowest income of all raises the question of the incidence of exploitation of children working as employees in the urban informal sector.

Income classification

Among other things, the previous analysis of income size indicated that the children were facing uncertainties with respect to the size of their income and its regularity. On the basis of this analysis, and additional information submitted by the children about their incomes, it was possible to group them into three different categories with respect to the criteria of reliability and frequency of their monetary income. A first group includes the children in the category "unpaid family workers"; although they earned money through their activities they did not really have an income of their own, since they primarily were suppliers of income to the household, handing over their earnings to the adult member of the household with whom they worked. A second group includes the children who also were family workers and handed over their earnings at the end of the working day, but in contrast to the first group received some payment for their work. Their income was variable both in frequency and in size, and therefore on the whole highly uncertain. A third group includes the majority of the children who had a monetary income resulting from their work as employees or self-employed. Many of these children would hand over part or all of their earnings to their mother or the head of the household, but they nevertheless considered these earnings as their personal income. Even if the income of these children was a little more constant in frequency than that of the former groups, there was no evidences that it was more reliable. Figure 30 represents an attempt to classify children's income situation along a range of income categories spread from "no personal income", at one end, to "uncertain income" at the other end of the scale.

In sum then, the children's situation was one of considerable uncertainty with respect to their daily monetary income, both in terms of size and reliability, as many as one third of them not having any income at all of their own.

The destination and use of the monetary income of the children

The magnitude of the income that children earn is significant in itself, but an equally important question is how their income is being used—

Figure 30   The income of the children

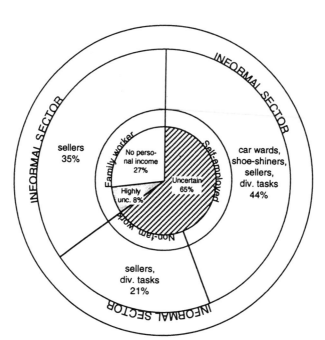

by the children themselves or their households. In fact, one of the myths of child work in the urban informal sector is that the money the children earn through their work is used primarily to satisfy superfluous needs rather than to improve the economic conditions of the household. Children are assumed to spend their earnings on candies, sodas, cookies or other consumption goods which are not really necessary for them or their households. Therefore, in the present study, a particular effort was made to clarify this subject by focusing on two aspects of this matter: the destination and the use of children's monetary income.

The term destination is used to indicate where the children's income goes, in the case when it is not kept by themselves, i.e. which person or persons will receive the children's earnings. By use is meant the purposes for which the children use the income from their work, if and when they keep all or a part of their earnings.

The children were asked two complementary questions about the monetary earnings they obtained through their economic activities.[1]

Figure 31   Sellers at the Roberto Huembes market

Firstly what they did with their earnings, in order to differentiate between those who gave all their earnings to another person and those who kept all or part of their earnings for themselves. Secondly, those who kept all or part of their earnings, were asked to tell how they used them.

[1.] In this chapter, both the principal and the secondary activities of the children are included in the analysis.

The results show, as has been the case in other studies of child work, that the main receptor of the children's income was their mother regardless of whether there was a father in the family or not. As many as 69 per cent of the children gave everything they earned to their mothers. The account of Diesenia, who sold vegetables at El Mayoreo market, is typical of most of the children of this study. She said:

> All the money, all of it, I give to my mother so she will be able to buy us food.

Other children said that they gave their income to the head of the household. All in all as many as 73 per cent of the children did not keep their incomes for themselves. However, a smaller number of children, mostly boys, did keep a portion of their earnings, and shared the rest of their income with the mother, father or another relative who was the head of the household. The proportion of the income that they kept for themselves varied a good deal depending upon the current economic situation of the household. However, most children claimed that as a rule they used to give half of their income to the household. As Juan at the Galeria Internacional parking put it:

> From whatever I earn, I give half to my mother and I keep the other half for myself. With my half I buy food, a soda, but sometimes also things that I need for school.

An interesting finding was that as many as 12 per cent of the children, all boys, kept all their earnings for themselves. From the point of view of gender differences it is interesting to note that the boys disposed of their income themselves to a greater extent than the girls did. As many as one third of the boys kept all or a part of their earnings for themselves, while no girl kept all the income for herself and only 5 per cent kept a part of their income. Contrary to other findings, which suggest that the older the children the more likely it is that they keep their income for themselves, in the present study no such relationship was found. Children of all ages were found in all categories. It is perhaps worth noting that the lowest age of the children who kept their income for themselves was 10 years.

The occupational category of the children apparently did not have any significant effect on the destination of the income. The percentage

Figure 32   The destination of the children's monetary income

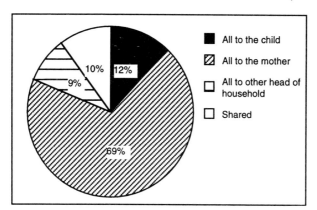

of the children who gave all or part of their income to the mother or another head of the household was approximately the same across all the categories—family worker, employee and self-employed—and did not vary with age. However, the younger family workers to a larger extent shared their earnings with the head of the household. These children were in reality given back a part of their earnings as payment for their work. As José Antonio at Roberto Huembes market said:

> Everyday I have to give all the money I earn to my father; it is he who gives me the vegetables for selling. But afterwards he pays me whatever he thinks I deserve for my work and depending on his earnings for the day.

The ways in which the children who kept all or a part of their income used it can be a good indicator of the importance of children's income for the children themselves and for the budget of the household. In some cases it became clear that the children depended very much on their own income for satisfying basic needs such as food. To this group belonged all the children who kept all their income for themselves. In fact they were responsible not only for getting their own clothes and school materials but in some cases also their food. Other said that their earnings were used exclusively to buy food for

Figure 33   Car wards at Galeria Internacional

themselves and their families at the end of the working day, before they went home. This was so in the case of Terner who said:

> I buy our food here at the market after selling the newspapers, and I give it all to my grandmother. Oil, or rice...She is at home and my grandfather has no job. We all eat of that food and of whatever my brother brings home.

In general the answers revealed that, with very few exceptions, the income was used to cover essential needs. If not directly used to buy food or to cover other basic needs such as clothes and shoes, it was used to buy a variety of other articles, e.g. things needed for attending school such as uniforms and books. Juan Carlos, who guarded cars at Galeria Internacional parking, told me how he used his income:

> With my money I use to buy all I need for school, and my clothes and everything else. When I have some money left, I give it to my aunt so I can help to pay for part of my food at home.

The exceptions to this general picture were some of the older boys who used a part of their earnings in arcade games and for other diversions. In contrast to the findings of Alarcón (1991), no children in the present study said that they saved part of their income on a more long-term basis.[1] The necessities they bought were mostly basic and instantly needed, and the children who said that they saved some money, did so for a certain short-term purpose, e.g. to buy a pair of shoes.

In sum, all the children who obtained an income in money through their work handed over all or a part of that money to their mother or another head of the household, or bought basic and essential things for themselves or for their families, thus contributing to the household budget. The girls did not dispose of their own income themselves to the same extent as the boys. In fact, whereas the girls said that they gave all their earnings to the mother so that she could afford to buy them school materials, clothes and other things, many of the boys kept everything or a share of what they earned, although they also used it to buy the same type of things or, in a few cases, spent some of the money on diversions.

---

[1]. Glasinovich, W.A. (1991).

Chapter 11

The households of the children in an economic perspective

So far, the household has been dealt with as a social unit to which the children belonged, whether they were living together with their natural families or not. In this section the household will be analysed as an economic unit composed of economically active individuals which participate together in the procurement of resources needed for their common everyday life. Different households have different needs depending on a number of economic and social factors, and the economic activities of the household members and the income generated by these activities is the context within which the work of the children must be put. So far, the analysis has concentrated on the economic characteristics of working children. In the following the focus will be on the economic characteristics of household heads and their partners. The purpose of this chapter is to establish to what kind of households the working children of this study belonged, and to identify aspects that would permit the construction of a typology of the households whose children are working in the informal sector in Managua.

The activities of household heads and their partners

Without exception, the children could describe which activities the heads of the household (a parent or another relative) and their partners were engaged in.[1] The procedure used was to first ask the children to distinguish between the economically active members in a household and the inactive ones. Several questions were then asked about the economically active household members, regarding work both within and outside of the household. The children were asked to name the place of work of the persons they said were working, as well as how much they worked and for or with whom they worked.[2] This information made it possible to establish not only the actual activity of adult household members at the time of the interview, but also to identify occupational categories and places of work. Figure 34 list occupations and places of work of heads of households and their partners, for women and men respectively.

It is obvious that there are significant differences between men and women both in terms of occupation, and geographically with regard to type of place of work. First of all the range of occupations was much greater for men than women. Many of the men had jobs which required a certain degree of training in the formal education system, as in the case of drivers and security guards, or special skills as in the case of bricklayers and car repairmen. Their places of work showed great variation as well; they worked both in the public and the private sector, either in locationally fixed working places or simply in the streets. The women's occupations, on the other hand, normally were extensions of domestic or household work, in the service sector, illustrated by such tasks as working as domestics in private homes, washing and ironing clothes at home or in private houses, and preparing food at home for sale. As a consequence, the places of work of the women tended to be much less diverse in terms of type and location than those of the men. In fact, almost all of the women worked either at home, in their own selling stall, in private houses or at the market.

[1.] The question of the economic activity of the head of the household as well as of his/her partner, was posed with great care due to the importance of obtaining a correct classification. The method used was that of exploratory questioning. The children were first asked what their mother, father or other relative head of the household and her/his partner did for a living. The category of "unemployed" was carefully probed by posing the question whether the person in question had had a job before and if she/he was actually looking for a job. The category of "housewife" was dealt with in the same way.

[2.] By asking who the employer was, it was possible to establish if the person was active in the formal or in the informal sector of the economy.

Additional information received from the children also revealed stark dissimilarities in the occupational situation of men and women. In both cases, the majority were self-employed workers, but as many as one third of the men worked as employees, which was twice as many as in the case of women. Women were employed in private houses, and in many cases worked on a part-time basis. It was really quite remarkable to find that all the men who were employees were employed as workers in the formal sector, at banks, schools, ministries or, factories with full-time jobs and apparently jobs of a permanent kind.

Substantial differences were also found within the category of "self-employed" with respect to the type of activities that men and women were engaged in.[1] It was twice as common that men were running their own businesses as that women did. Almost invariably, these business activities required only small investments of capital, such as retailing or production of food for sale. With the exception of a few women who ran their businesses outside the home in small stalls of their own, the manufacture and sale of food was located at home[2] or at the market. The activities of the self-employed men who ran their own businesses partly resembled the businesses run by women. In fact, a substantial number of sellers were men, but they usually sold other products than the women did, such as clothes and shoes and which required larger and more frequent investments of capital. In addition to selling, the self-employed men were engaged in other activities,

---

[1.] As discussed earlier, the occupational category of "self-employed" includes those persons who worked independently, in the sense that they were not employees of another person. In this study, a distinction has been made between independent workers who performed economic activities which needed no/very low investment of capital, and those who performed such economic activities which involved substantial investments of capital or specific skills acquired through formal education or training. The former are labelled self-employed and the latter self-employed with their own business. Car wards and sellers of ice water, e.g., belong to the first category, whereas persons selling clothes, shoes or food products would fall in the second category.

[2.] Always when the food products were sold at home, the children used the term "venta" (stall, selling place) referring to the home as the working place. They usually said: "She makes the "tortillas" at home, and then she sells them at the stall, at home". This statement shows that the children were well aware of the type of economic activity performed by adults, even when these activities were performed at home.

Figure 34   Occupation and place of work of female and male household members [a]

	OCCUPATIONS	PLACE OF WORK
FEMALE	Seller Maid Washing and ironing Food manufacturing	Home, own stall, street, market Private houses Private houses Home, market
MALE	Seller Car ward Driver Security guard Industrial worker Construction worker/bricklayer Car repairman Welder Rural worker Non specific tasks	Street, market. own stall Street, market Private houses, ministries, companies Schools, banks, factories Factories Factories, private buildings Informal workshops, private houses Factories Private/state production units Market

a. The class "female household members" includes female heads of household and the female partners of the heads of household. By "male households members" is meant male heads of households and the male partners of female heads of household.

including car warding, loading, ambulatory vending of low capital value products such as fruits, vegetables and water.

Income classification of heads of household and their partners

The children were not able to divulge the incomes of their parents and/or relatives, but this did not present a major problem, since the income situation of household heads and their partners could be classified with sufficient accuracy by other means. The data that had been collected on activities, places of work and occupational category provided enough information to allow me to determine income characteristics. Basically the income of the adults was estimated by using the same criteria that were employed in the determination and analysis of the income of the children, namely, the regularity and reliability of income earned.

About 25 per cent of the women had no income of their own. They were economically inactive, or had worked earlier but were unemployed at the time of the interview. All the gainfully employed women were active in the informal sector, which implies variable size and frequency of income. However, two groups were identified as having a modest margin of security in terms of the regularity of income inflow. One group consisted of those employed in private houses as housekeepers or maids, the other group of self-employed women who were running a business of their own at fixed places of work. Some women combined part-time jobs as maids with the manufacturing and selling of food at home. About one third of the women can be described as being in what might be called *less uncertain* income situations. The other women were self-employed and worked as vendors, either in a fixed place or as ambulatory sellers, and their incomes were characterized by uncertainty both in terms of regularity of earnings and size of income. Thus, only one third of the women who headed households, or were partners of heads of household, had an income that, though not completely certain, was relatively stable. The rest of the women only had irregular incomes or no income at all. The income situation of the women is summarized in figure 35.

The income situation of the men was quite different from that of the women, the most significant difference being that as many as one third had regular incomes in terms of size and timing, as they were employed in institutions or at places of work in the formal economic sector. Of course, even for these men there were no guarantees for security of employment, but they could at least count on earning a regular income of a known size for the duration of the employment. A second group consisted of self-employed men who had a vocational occupation or were sellers running their own business. Just as the women with the same characteristics, these men had what I would consider a "less uncertain" income. Lastly, we have the group of men whose economic activities greatly resembled the activities of the working children. As in the case of the children, these activities implied an uncertain income both in terms of regularity and size. The classification of the men's income situation is summarized in figure 36.

In sum, close to one third of the male household heads had regular

Figure 35   The income of female household members

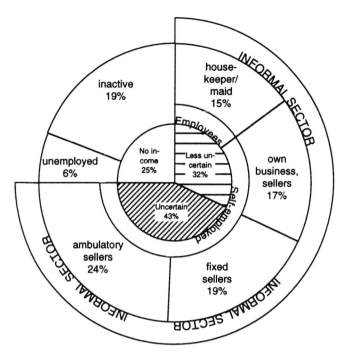

incomes since they were employed in the formal sector.[1] Despite the lack of information about the size of their income, which was undoubtedly low since they worked in low-paid occupations, the fact that their income was constant and certain permits us to conclude that these households do not, strictly speaking, belong to the poorest households of the city, with high rates of unemployment and consequently the smallest contributions of adult earnings to the household economy. In fact, the level of open unemployment among both women and men in this group was below the average estimated for the city, about 21.9 per cent in 1993.[2] Even if these incomes are not

[1.] Although information about the rate of employment and about unemployment of the men is available, an equally important factor is not taken into account here, namely the rate of underemployment which is calculated on the basis of the number of working hours and income. That rate, in spite of its significance, was not possible to include in this chapter because of lack of information. One can perhaps assume, however, that the households of the children followed the same pattern of high rate of underemployment that was characteristic of the households of the city with the same socio-economic characteristics.

[2.] Source: MITRAB (1995).

Figure 36   The income of male household members

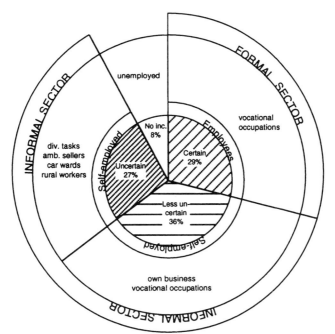

high, the great majority of the household heads who worked in the formal sector and had regular earnings had children who were working in the informal sector. This finding runs counter to another myth regarding child work in the urban informal sector of Third World cities, namely that the children engaged in that sector come exclusively from households where parents are engaged in the urban informal sector.

Is there a typical "working child household" in Managua?

Since child work in the urban informal sector, for obvious reasons, so often is discussed in the context of, and even is justified by the existence of extreme poverty, a key question to explore in this study has been to find out if child work was restricted to the poorest strata of the population of Managua.

The previous analysis of the housing conditions and places of residence of the children showed that they did not live only in the poorest districts of the city. However, the economic situation of the children's households was not discussed. This is the question that will be addressed in this section in an attempt to find out whether these children came from households with similar economic characteristics or not.

This chapter focuses upon two questions: firstly, whether the households were similar from a socio-economic (labour force) point of view, and secondly, to what extent households were dependent on the income earned by the children. The hypothesis is that it might be possible to identify a "typical" household of working children, a household type from which working children are most likely to come.

In the previous chapter the destination and use of children's income was discussed. It was shown that most of the children handed over all their earnings to the head of their household, usually the mother. It was also shown that in most cases the income was used to buy essential or basic products such as food and school materials. However, the significance of such contributions in quantitative terms was not explored. It is reasonable to assume that the importance of the income from children's work varies a good deal, depending on the economic situation of the household. To determine the significance of such contributions is not easy, however, because of the difficulties one faces in any attempt to calculate the absolute value of incomes from the urban informal sector. In her study of Asunción, Espínola limited the discussion of the contribution of children solely to monetary income.[1] She distinguished between direct contributions, when the children gave all their earnings to their families, and indirect contributions, when they first bought whatever they needed for their own consumption. Alarcón used the same distinction between direct and indirect contributions, but extended his definition of children's contribution so as to include other forms than cash or monetary income.[2] He differentiated between unpaid work and income resulting from the acquisition by

---

[1.] Espínola, B. et al. (1989). p. 38.
[2.] Glasinovich, W.A. (1991).

the children with their own money, of products for self-consumption; he defined the former type as direct contributions, and the latter as an indirect form of contributions.

It is my assumption that since the children's families sent their minors to work outside their homes, or allowed them to do such work, the income so generated has to be significant for the household economy. Consequently, not only paid or unpaid work performed outside or inside the household must be regarded as economic contributions, but also all other activities that release adults from domestic work and enable them to engage in some other economic activity. Furthermore, the children who received payment in kind, often food, for their work have to be considered as actively contributing to the family's budget. Through their work they reduce expenses and save money. The form that these contributions take—direct or indirect—is perhaps less significant than their importance in relative terms. My position therefore is that all the working children actively contribute to the household economy, as long as they are engaged in activities which exclude sleeping, playing, studying, personal care or leisure time.

Starting with this assumption, the next question to address is the issue of how significant these contributions by the children are to the household economy. There are several ways of measuring the importance or weight of such contributions. The focus here will be on four main indicators: (i) the total number of adults with an income; (ii) the number of working children in the household; (iii) the type of income earned by the adults; and (iv) the destination of the income of the children.

A first classification of the households was made on the basis of the total number of adults with an income in the household; this resulted in three categories of households:

i. households with no adults with incomes
ii. households with one adult with an income and,
iii. households with two adults with incomes.

Despite the fact that in some households the number of adults was greater than two, no household was found which had more than two adult incomes. The presence of a grandmother or grandfather who was economically inactive, in the extended and composed family types, can partly explain that the number of adult incomes is lower than is suggested by the absolute number of adults in the household. It perhaps also indicates a higher rate of unemployment among household members other than the household heads and their partners. The previous classification might also indicate that the degree of dependence of households on the income of their working children is relatively high.

A smaller number of the households (7 per cent) included no economically active adults at all, and these families therefore depended completely on the income earned by the children. On the whole these households were small in size, in fact far below the average household size in Managua.[1] They were nuclear families where both the mother and the father were unemployed or the mother was a housewife. In such households, all the children gave their income to the mother. One perhaps extreme case that illustrates the situation of these households was that of Juanas. She and her oldest brother sold lemons at San Judas market for a lady seller. Their father was a casual worker but had been unemployed during the month before the interview was made. He supported the activity of the mother who made tortillas for sale, but when lack of money made it impossible for them to buy the flour needed to prepare the tortillas, she also became unemployed. There were eight children in this family, including a one month old baby, but most of them were too young to work, and the family was sustained by the work of Juana and her 13 year old brother. The accounts given by other children about their situation varied from case to case, but common for these households was that they lived solely on the income of the children.

The second category of households, those having only one adult with an income, made up as many as 48 per cent of the studied households. Both the nuclear and the single parent-headed family types were equally represented in this category, which partly explains why they included only one adult with an income. If one combines the nuclear families with the extended families, the proportion of households with more than one adult member rises to 57 per cent, which indicates a high unemployment level among the adults of the house-

---

[1.] The average household size in Managua was 5.8 persons, in 1994. Source: FIDEG.

holds of this group. The largest households, with 7-12 members, belonged to this group. The average number of working children was two, which is higher than for the first category or type of household (1.75). On the whole, the mother received or collected the income earned by the children, but a significant proportion of the children—as many as one third—kept all or a share of their income for themselves. In this category, 21 per cent of the adults had a regular income, and most likely this indicates how many of the fathers (male heads of the households) that worked in the formal sector. Since they were not single parents, but part of households with at least two adults, one can assume that their partners were either unemployed or housewives.

Finally, some households were supported by two adult incomes. 85 per cent of these households were nuclear families. They were larger than the average household size for Managua, and the average number of adults was greater than in any other category. Although the dominant adult income type must be characterized as equally irregular as in the previous category, there was in this household category a greater share (39 per cent) of adults with relatively certain incomes. As in the other categories, the mother was the main receptor of the total income of the children (in 85 per cent of the cases). Figure 37 summarizes the characteristics of the households according to the classification by the number of adult incomes.

If one examines the distribution of the adults' income in relation to that of the children by type of household and in relation to the number of adults earning an income, it would appear that the children's contribution is important in all the cases. In fact, household dependence on the income of the children was total in the first category, since no adult worked. In the second category, two children were economically active and provided income for the household, whereas one adult did so. In the third category, the participation rate of the children was even slightly higher.

It was shown in a previous section that in this study, almost all of the children, irrespective of the type of adult income in their household, gave their incomes, partially or totally, to the mother or another household head. In spite of the incidence of "regular" income across the households, income from the children's work certainly must have been important for the households.

Figure 37   Socio-economic characteristics of the households

	No. of Adult's Income		
	None (n=4)	One (n=29)	Two (n=27)
Type of Adult Income			
- Certain	-	21	17
- Less certain	-	14	22
- Uncertain	-	65	61
Total	-	100	100
Destination of Children's Income			
- Mother	100	73	85
- Shared	-	17	11
- Self	-	10	4
Family Type			
- Nuclear	100	43	85
- One parent	-	43	4
- Extended	-	14	4
- Composed	-	-	7
Total	100	100	100
Working Children (average)	1.8	2.0	2.2
Household Size (average)	5.8	7.1	6.9

The answer to the question, whether there exists a *typical* household from which the majority of the working children in Managua come, is "no". It has been shown that child work is found in households with rather different economic and demographic characteristics. One can not say that child work is restricted to the lowest strata of the population of Managua. The low real value and the decline in the purchasing power of the salaries, in the formal as well as in the informal sector, is resulting in a continuing and increasing pauperization of the households in the city, even including those which given their economic and demographic characteristics one would not expect to be among those most affected by poverty. That is the reason why the children from these families have to work. That is also why only a few children could keep their earnings for their own consumption, since other members of their households depended on them. Paradoxically, the work of the children in this sector has been systematically belittled and the importance of their income has been denied as a factor which is essential for the welfare of the children themselves and for their households as well. Instead, it has been seen as a sporadic activity intended to support superfluous consumption. This study has shown that this is not the case.

Chapter 12

The working children's everyday life

Thus far, the study has been concerned mainly with just one of the activities of the children: their work in the labour market. However, the everyday life of these children, like that of other children, is made up of many types of activities, performed at different times and at different locations. As children all over the world do, the children interviewed in this study also play, do their homework, help at home, sleep, and move around between different places, and between a variety of activities. It is the everyday life of the working children that is the subject of this chapter.

Human life is organized in time and space, but no one can organize his or her time-space completely at will; we are all constrained by a number of social, economic, cultural, and temporal factors. The major difference between the lives of adults and children is perhaps the fact that children are not as able as adults of organizing their own lives completely at will because their status as children puts them in a subordinate position vis-a-vis adults who can and do exercise a relatively great control over their lives. As shown earlier, most of these children were compelled to work because their contribution of income was important to their families and themselves. The obligation to work by necessity leads to competition with other activities which we think of as proper child activities, such as going to school and playing. The purpose of this chapter is to try to provide a picture of how the everyday life of the children is organized in time and space. The principal question addressed here is: in which order of priority are the daily activities of the children organized and performed in terms of time allocation, duration and location? Such information would allow us to contextualize child work within a more complete matrix of the everyday life of the children, which in turn should enhance our understanding also of their working life.

Classification of activities

There is no problem in classifying those activities which are easy to distinguish a priori from purely economic activities, such as studying or playing. There are, however, other activities which are more difficult to classify, especially those performed within the household and/or at home. It may be recalled that the criteria used for the classification of "work" is a matter of importance in this study. Several criteria were used in order to define "work", and the primary criterion was the children's own evaluation and judgement of whether the activity took place outside the household or not, and whether the "work" involved was directly and exclusively related to the production and/or sale of goods and services in the labour market, irrespective of whether the children could or could not keep an income for themselves. However, everyone knows, of course, that children "help out" in many different ways at home, but in general such tasks are not considered to be "work"—either by the children or by the parents or other relatives with whom the children live.

The problem of classifying the activities of children at home as work or not is not only confined to child work, but is a central issue in the discussion of women's work as well (especially in developing countries). In the case of work done by women (and also in the present case by children) at home the basic problem is how to draw the line between activities, or work, of an economic or non-economic type. Usually, the categories of "domestic work" and "reproductive activities" have been used to distinguish non-economic from economic activities. But as several authors have demonstrated, these definitions have major shortcomings, are ambiguous and difficult to implement in practice. A major problem is that they fail to distinguish clearly between different activities and often include in the same category activities which actually are quite different. Often activities performed inside the household are multifaceted in the sense that one and the same activity may have different objectives. One example that illustrates the ambiguous nature of certain activities rather well is the manufacture of food at home. A case in point is the widely spread manufacture and sale of tortillas in Central America. The mother who makes them at home, and the child who usually sells them in the street, also eat them at home, as do other family members. When is the production of tortillas to be considered productive work for a market? When is it domestic work? And is it not also a reproductive activity?

The difficulties encountered in the classification of the production and selling of tortillas are typical of many of the activities generally considered as domestic work: cleaning, cooking, child-care, firewood gathering. In my opinion, Richard Anker, has provided a very comprehensive discussion of this problematic that captures the difficulties arising from the ambiguity of definitions used in estimations of women's work in the labour force. His observations can in many respects be extended to the problem of defining "work" in the case of child labour.[1] Besides focusing on the methodological problems that arise from the use of deficient concepts and definitions in collecting information, Anker alerts us to the problems that emerge in processing and analysing data as well. To begin with, he emphasizes the need for clarification in the use of what he calls "key" words, such as "work", "job", "main activity", "main occupation". Often, the use of such words in research questionnaires only results in incomplete answers, which makes the interpretation and analysis of data difficult. He mentions the internationally accepted definitions of labour force activity by ILO as a case in point. ILO has defined "work" as,

– Persons who perform some work for pay or profit (ILO, 1954).
– All persons of either sex who furnish the supply of labour for the production of economic goods and services (ILO, 1966).

[1.] Anker, R., Khan, M.E. and Gupta, R.B. (1987): *Women's participation in the labour force: A methods test in India for improving its measurement.* Women, Work and Development. No. 16. ILO. Geneva.

- All persons of either sex who furnish the supply of labour for the production of economic goods and services as defined by the United Nations systems of national accounts and balances (ILO 1982).

Anker points out that these definitions denote activities which are "economic" in character, but adds that statisticians and economists hold different opinions about what it is that makes an activity economic or non-economic. Anker notes that:

> International recommendations of the Conference of Labour Statisticians on "economic" activity defer to the United Nations system of national income account statistics (SNA). Thus, activities which—according to the United Nations—result in goods or services which are included in SNA (i.e. included in GNP statistics) are considered to be economic (and therefore labour force) activities; all other activities are considered to be non-economic (and therefore non-labour force) activities. As a result, market-oriented activities related to wage or salary employment and/or enterprises are clearly considered to be labour force activities. In theory, so are many activities oriented to self-consumption such as subsistence agriculture, home construction and improvement, milking animals and processing food.[1]

Further he quotes ILO, 1982:

> "According to these systems (of national income accounts) the production of economic goods and services should include all production and processing of primary products, whether for the market, for barter or for own consumption".[2]

And United Nations, 1968:

> "All production of primary products should, in principle, be included in gross output (in national income) whether for own

---

[1] Anker et al.. (1987) p. 6-7.
[2] ILO (1982): *Thirteenth International Conference of Labour Statisticians. Resolution concerning statistics of the economically active population, employment, unemployment and underemployment.* Official Bulletin. Series A. No. 3. Geneva.(Quoted by Anker, R. (1987).

consumption, for barter or for sale for money. It is also desirable to include in gross outputs: (i) the output of producers of other commodities, which are consumed in their household and which they also produce for the market and (ii) the processing of primary commodities by the producers of these items in order to make such goods as butter, cheese, flour, wine, oil, cloth or furniture for their own use though they may not sell any of these manufactures".[1]

However, Anker points out that for several reasons there are difficulties in implementing these recommendations. One reason is that national practices differ from country to country, another that the recommendations exclude several subsistence-type activities from the category of labour force activities. The lack of consensus and disparity in the criteria employed, and in the interpretation of the recommendations, has often led to incompatibility between the statistics from different countries, and thus difficulties in comparing research results. Because of such shortcomings and ambiguities in the definitions of economic and non-economic activities, Anker states that:

> The truth of the matter is that among the Third World poor virtually all adults and sizeable numbers of children engage in "economic activities" in order to help the family meet its basic needs; much of this work occurs outside the market place. Among the poor, it is not so much whether or not men, women and children are economically active, but how hard they are working and what activities they are doing. Under such circumstances, there is clearly a need for several labour force measures that indicate the type (e.g. paid, not paid) and level (e.g. part-time, full-time) of labour force activity based on different definitions of "economic" activity. In our opinion, there can not be one correct definition of labour force activity, as a simplistic distinction between labour force/non-labour force activities. In addition, all aspects of labour supply and labour markets cannot be covered by one definition.[2]

[1.] United Nations (1968): *A system of national accounts*. Studies in methods. Series F. No. 2. New York. (Quoted by Anker, R .(1987).

[2.] Anker et al. p. 8.

He proposes, therefore, four complementary labour force definitions: (i) paid labour force, (ii) market labour force, (iii) ILO labour force, and (iv) extended labour force. An examination of these definitions shows that it is no longer necessary to use "domestic work" as a concept, and that some of the activities usually included under "domestic work" can be incorporated within one of the four new definitions.

Let us examine these in brief:

> (i) "*Paid labour force*, includes persons in wage or salary employment for which they are paid in cash or in kind. These people who have "jobs"... and "for whom planners generally feel they must create a sufficient number of jobs" *(ii) "Market-oriented labour force,* persons in "paid labour force" plus persons engaged in an activity on a family farm or in a family enterprise or business that sells some or all of its products: The following are included : employers, own-account workers; unpaid family workers; and members of producers' co-operatives"... *(iii) "ILO labour force,* persons engaged in activities whose products or services should be included in the national income accounts statistics according to United Nations recommendations...includes persons engaged in the production of economic goods and services, irrespective of whether these goods or services are sold...for example all activities associated with primary products—such as food "production", and food "processing", including animal tending and milking, ...unpaid gathering of food and fruits, threshing in the home compound, are considered labour force activities here, whether or not market-related exchanges occur. And (iv) "*Extended labour force* includes persons engaged in activities not included in the most recent United Nations recommendations on the SNA, but which none the less contribute to meeting their families' basic needs for goods and services which are generally purchased in developed countries ...includes activities such as gathering and preparing fuel (e.g. gathering sticks and wood), water fetching, etc".[1]

With regard to child work and children's activities within the household and/or at home, a review of the literature shows that the concept

---

[1]. Anker et al. (1987) p. 29.

of "domestic work" has not been questioned, but rather accepted uncritically by students of child labour. Instead, the discussion has focused on whether these activities are "economic" or not. In other words, opinions with respect to whether domestic work is or is not work (in the sense that it is an economic activity), have been quite divergent. Rodgers and Standingwere the first to develop a typology for the analysis of child work, which tried to distinguish economic from non-economic activities.[1] On the basis of this typology, the activities of the children include:

1. Domestic work
2. Non-domestic work, non-monetary work
    a) in subsistence production
    b) in market production
3. Tied or bonded labour
4. Wage labour (alone or a family group, including apprenticeship)
5. Marginal economic activities
6. Schooling
7. Idleness and unemployment
8. Recreation and leisure
9. Reproductive activities

Although this classification was important because it was the first of its kind, the authors did not delve further into the grey zone of what is productive work and domestic work, despite the fact that they established the usage of domestic work as a general concept, still broadly in use today by researchers, in official documents and in the reports of international and regional organizations. Several authors have pointed out the difficulties in distinguishing between "work" of these two types, since they tend to be compounded. Other authors have tried to use the relative weight of domestic work in relation to other activities in order to determine whether an activity should be classified as work or not. That is, when a child uses most of his or her time in domestic work, it has to be considered as work.

---

[1] Rodgers, G. and Standing, G. (1979): *The economic role of children in low-income countries: a framework for analysis.* Population and Labour Policies Programme. World Employment Programme Research. Working Paper. No. 81.

To distinguish between domestic work, reproductive activities and work is even more complicated. For some authors, "domestic work" performed by children is, in fact, an economic or labour force activity, because when children stay at home and perform domestic tasks, they make it possible for adults to be economically active in the labour market. They argue, therefore, that children who do domestic work must be classified as workers. Although aware of the economic value of such activities, other authors, like Glasinovich, differ in opinion and argue that children who do domestic tasks within the household are better off in terms of their personal development than children working in the streets or at other places of work, and that therefore they can not be considered to be workers (he never says, though, that those activities are not work).[1] To conclude, it seems that there is no consensus about how to classify the set of tasks that children are engaged in within the household or at home and whether these activities should be considered as work or not.

In the present study it became important to know what the time budgets of the children looked like, after deducting the time they spent working in the labour market. To that end, a classification of the activities that the children engaged in at home was necessary in order to account for their time allocation. Fully aware of the difficulties noted above, I avoid using the concepts of "domestic work" and "reproductive activities". It is my opinion that those activities performed by children inside the household which do not specifically involve personal care, eating, leisure, play and study, have to be regarded as work. In this sense, I agree with Anker's concept of the "ILO labour force" class. Still, I believe that it is also important to make some distinctions between activities on the basis of who "benefits" from the child's work. Put differently, it is essential to consider whether the work performed is primarily oriented towards the satisfaction of the child's own needs, or the needs of other members of the household. Consequently, the children were asked to provide as detailed a description as possible of the kind of activities they "helped" with at home. Based on this information, the activities performed by

---

[1]. Glasinovich, W.A. (1991): *Entre calles y plazas. El trabajo infantil de los niños en Lima.* ADEC/ATC. Instituto de Estudios Peruanos. UNICEF. Lima.

the children inside the household or at home were classified into five categories: (i) self-directed work such as washing their own clothes and cooking their own food; (ii) household-directed work[1] such as washing the clothes of family members, cooking for the household, cleaning the floor, fetching water; (iii) activities involving personal care such as eating, leisure, bathing; (iv) playing; and, (v) doing school homework. Outside the household, the main activity was work in the labour market, with school as the second major activity for most of the children in this study. Other common activities in the daily life of the children were play, sports and commuting to and from various activities. The activities performed outside the household have been grouped into four types, viz., (i) work in the labour market, (ii) school, (iii) play and sports, and (iv) mobility.

Place and time allocation of activities

Some of the activities, for instance play and sports, were performed at several locations and at different times of the day. Likewise, work was also performed at different places and times, whereas schooling as expected took place at a fixed place according to a predetermined time schedule. Depending upon what activities the children took part in, and where they took place, different sets of constraints with respect to the children's movement during a day emerged.

The places: the children referred to four places between which they moved in their daily time-space trajectories: (i) home (residence); (ii) working place (markets and parking lots); (iii) school; and, (iv) the street, (in the neighbourhood, in another district or at intermediate locations). The locations of these places in the city are key components in the analysis of the allocation of time for different activities and for the analysis of the spatial pattern of activities. The household or the "home" is of course particularly important since it is the point of

---

[1] This category also includes the situation when the child itself uses the product or service that the activity results in.

departure and return in the everyday trajectories of children in urban space.

Time: the children were asked about the starting and finishing times for each activity that they performed during a normal day of work. They were reminded to refer to "yesterday", if they worked then, as the reference period. In general, the children had a very clear idea about the exact times, such as the time when they left home in the morning, the time they began and finished work, school and so forth. They had relatively precise ideas about the time it took them to get to different places and activities. The youngest children found it more difficult to estimate times, but it was easy to check their information, since both the locations where the activities took place and the means of transportation used by the children were known.[1] However, the principal difficulty encountered had to do with the time spent at home. The children´s perception of home was that "it was always there"—a place permanent in space and static in time—and therefore they could not account for the exact time spent on each of the various activities that they did at home.

Playing and sports

To play is what children all over the world like to do most. Play is an important part of children's personality development and socialization, and also one of the basic rights of the children. Unfortunately that right is not guaranteed for all children, at least not to the extent that they would wish. This was illustrated also in the present study.

The children were not asked to specify the type of games or sports they played. Instead, they were simply asked to state whether they used to play or not, when they played and where and for how long they played on each occasion. Some of them also told me what kinds

---

[1.] The information about time spent on each activity and between activities was carefully double-checked both by asking other questions in the course of the interview and by using information given by other children who were present during the interviews; in case of inconsistent information, the subject was discussed until the matter was settled.

of games they played or which sports they engaged in, but that information is not included here. Irrespective of sex, all but one of the children declared that they used to play, many of them everyday either after school or after work. However, a substantial number of children (close to one third) and specially the girls, complained about the lack of time for play, or that they only had time for play on weekends or during school recesses.

The most common place for playing was the home or the residential neighbourhood. Some of the oldest boys, however, played ball elsewhere in the city, e.g. in municipal sport courts, and others played electronic games. Even at or around the home, the girls had less time for play and fewer places to play in than the boys. Over half of the girls said that, if they had time to spare, they played at school or at home. Many children (20 per cent) were unable to give accurate information about the time spent on every play occasion. Of those who could make an approximate estimate, however, almost 60 per cent said that they either played for brief periods of up to half an hour, during intervals between different activities at home, or during school recesses, for between 10 and 15 minutes. Some children said that they were forbidden to play or could not afford to play, since the weekends were the best selling days at the market and they then had to work longer hours than during weekdays. Only just over 20 per cent of the children said that they played every day, usually for one or two hours each day. Here as well there was a clear difference between girls and boys, with almost 80 per cent of the girls playing only for short periods of time at home or at school, compared to 50 per cent of the boys. With respect to the distribution of playtime by age, it was found that the children who played longer per play occasion and had better opportunities for play, were in the seven and eight year age group.

Although the majority of the children declared that they did play, it was obvious that most of them engaged in play for only short periods of time, either at home, between other activities or during school recess, with the exception of those who declared that they played every day after work or after school. On the whole, girls seem to have stricter space-time constraints and lower playtime budgets than boys, as play could only take place as an extension of other activities which the girls were compelled to do, such as school and tasks at home. Only one boy, Marvin, seven years old, said that he also played at the market in the afternoons; he worked as an employee of a lady seller and worked only until noon, but his sister worked at the market all day and he stayed there until she finished work.

With that exception no one declared that he or she played at the place of work even though I explicitly questioned the children on that point. The children were very conscious of their "duty" to perform the various work activities and thought that play was an activity clearly confined to certain well defined places such as school, home or the neighbourhood. Although the children's behaviour at the place of work might have looked like play to adults, the children categorically maintained that they did not play there as they had to be on the alert all the time in order to attract more customers or sell more products.

Mobility

Moving between the various activities which one performs in cities is usually a time-consuming and demanding activity, in 'developed' as well as in 'developing' countries. Travelling in Managua is not an easy task, due to the poor infrastructure which badly lags behind public demand for transportation within, to and from the city. Many people prefer or are forced to walk to different places and activities, as the children in this study mostly did. Although the daily trajectories of the children varied in space and time, depending on where the different activities were performed, all had at least one thing in common—they all had to travel or walk through the city. Two trips per day was the minimum for children who did not attend school, four for the majority who both worked and attended school, and six trips per day for those who worked both before and after school. Obviously, the start and end points of these daily trajectories were common to all children, their home, but in other respects the individual trajectories during a day were quite different. The children either walked or took the bus to and from their working places.

For most of the children, the school they attended lay in the vicinity of their home and this explains why they usually walked to school.

The majority of the children walked to school everyday, a trip which lasted no more than between five and fifteen minutes one way. Only a few children had to take the bus to a school that was far away from their home, either because they went to a special (confessional) school, lived in new squatter settlements with no school, or because they lived in a rural area with no school nearby and had to travel to a school far away from home. In these cases, the one way bus trip varied from fifteen minutes to one hour.

The journeys to the place of work varied in duration, depending both on the location of the place of work in relation to the residences of the children and on the means of transport used. Almost half of the children walked to work, but some lived in districts on the opposite side of the city from their place of work and in those cases the one way journey to work lasted from thirty minutes up to an hour. Other children who journeyed to work came from the predominantly rural districts of Managua, such as Villa El Carmen, or from distant districts, such as San Judas or Asentamiento Carlos Blae. In a few cases, children journeyed from adjacent municipalities such as Ticuantepe and Masatepe, or from municipalities in other cities such as La Concha and Masaya. The mean journey times for children who walked or travelled by bus was 15 and 30 minutes, respectively. However, even those who lived in the city in some cases had to walk long distances that took as much time as it took to travel by bus to the city from other municipalities or nearby towns. Keeping in mind that these are one way journey times only, it is obvious that many of these children spent a good deal of their daily lives moving from home to work and back home again.

If we change perspective and focus on the work places in an attempt to establish the possible relations between means of transport and average transport time, it is interesting to note that certain work places only attracted working children living in the same neighbourhoods, while other places of work attracted children who came from quite far away in the city and even from other cities or municipalities. All but two of the children came to the El Mayoreo market by bus (the others walked). Children came to this market from quite a number of districts in the city—near and far—as well as from other municipalities and cities. Some children had very short travelling times—from five to seven minutes—while others had to make very long trips of between one and one and a half hour. The children came on foot to the smaller work places, of the San Judas market and the Galeria Internacional parking lot, since they all lived in adjacent districts. The average walking time was fifteen minutes, and there were some children who lived only five minutes walking time from the market. Almost all of the children who worked at the large Roberto Huembes market came by bus from other municipalities or from rural Managua, and in general journeyed over quite long distances, with an average travel time of thirty-five minutes. A few children lived nearby, within just ten minutes walking time from home. Finally, the Israel Lewites market place attracted mostly children from the rural districts of Managua, and from other districts in the city located quite far away, such as Monte Fresco, Villa el Carmen and Camilo Ortega. In spite of the long distances, the majority of the children who worked at this market walked to work. Their trip averaged twenty-five minutes; those who travelled by bus had the longest travel times of all, averaging fourty minutes.

Activities at home

Both before and after work at the market, the parking lot or at school (for those who attended school), the children engaged in various activities at home, some of which had to do with "personal care" such as bathing and eating and, "night sleep", others with recreation, described as "leisure" and "play", or education—"homework"—but others involved additional work at home. Let us take a look at the work performed by the children at home.

Self-directed and household-directed work

Self-directed and household-directed activities together cover all the work performed by children at home. As indicated earlier, the main criterion used to distinguish between these two types of activities was who benefits mostly from the activities of the children. Self-directed activities would thus include all tasks performed by children for the purpose of satisfying their own needs, as when they cooked for themselves or washed their own clothes. All other tasks performed at home and intended to supply other members of the household with goods and/or services were classified as household-directed work, such as washing the clothes of other household members, cooking food for the family and the like. In this context, a question of primary interest is whether there were any distinct gender and age patterns in terms of the conduct and frequency or intensity of both types of activities.

All the children in this study, save the five who maintained that they never "helped", in one way or another, worked at home on a daily basis. The children enumerated a series of tasks that they performed regularly, and on the basis of this information it is possible to distinguish between two groups. Some children were "assigned" or were responsible for one or two tasks which they always performed at home, after work, school or before leaving home in the morning, such as mopping the floor, watering the patio, washing dishes and emptying trash. Other children had a broader range of chores to do, such as cleaning house and making beds, cooking, and fetching water and firewood, but they were not directly responsible for them on a daily basis.

There was no indication of a relationship between the number of tasks performed and the age of the children. On the other hand, there was evidence of some gender division of tasks, with girls doing a broader range of chores than boys. The information obtained from the children does not, however, allow any definitive conclusions about the existence of any clear-cut gender division of household chores. The only task that seemed to be more typical for boys than for girls was running errands. Otherwise, the type of household work performed did not differ significantly with respect to the age or sex of the children. It was surprising to hear teenage boys state that they did their own laundry or fed their young cousins in the morning before leaving home. At the same time, it was evident that activity types were clearly related to place of residence; children who lived in rural areas or new squatter settlements that lacked basic infrastructure, for instance, more often had to fetch water, fill barrels with water and gather firewood. Most of the children who were engaged in activities defined as household-directed, were sharing the workload with other children or adult members of the household. Some also helped adults get ready for their work in the labour market, often a time-demanding task. Nine year old Jessica, for instance, prepared the meat that her mother used in making "tacos" for sale. Although household-directed work predominated the tasks that children performed at home, such chores were mostly done alongside or in combination with self-directed tasks.

Daily life inside a household, with all kinds of activities succeeding each other over time, meant that the children experienced these activities as occurring in continuously time. Hence, they could list activities in the order they were usually performed but could not specify exactly the time spent on each of these tasks. As a result, information about the time spent on the various activities at home, will be presented later in the study, but only as aggregate values of total time spent on all activities at home, without specifying the time used on each activity.

Schooling

Education has been declared to be one of the Human Rights,

> Everyone has the right to education. Education shall be free, at least in the elementary and fundamental stages. Elementary education shall be compulsory.[1]

and specially it is one of the Rights of the Child,

> The education of the children is intended to develop their personality, abilities and capacities to the maximum, will teach them the respect for the human rights, to their parents, to them selves and to their country. The boys and the girls will be educated to assume a responsible life, including the respect for the environment.[2]

However, many children have no access to education even though it has been declared to be compulsory and free in their country. The reasons for this are manifold, but in most cases poverty is the principal factor, i.e. the children's families can not afford schooling. All the

---

[1] Universal Declaration of Human Rights. Article 26.
[2] Articles 28 and 29 of the United Nations *Convention on the Rights of the Child*.

countries of Central America have decreed that education is compulsory and free, although there are variations in terms of the number of years required. In Nicaragua, education is compulsory between the ages of seven and twelve. It is the lowest national standard in the region, and only covers primary education, whereas in Costa Rica and El Salvador compulsory schooling extends to the whole or a part of secondary education. According to a report from the Central American Seminar on Child Work from 1993, Nicaragua seems to be the country that faces the greatest problems in education.[1] According to non-official statistics, the illiteracy rate in Nicaragua has increased from 13 per cent in 1985 [at that time among the lowest in the region after Costa Rica (7.2 per cent) and Panama (11.9 per cent)], to 23 per cent in 1993.[2] The school drop-out rate was 45 per cent in primary education, and the country had the lowest proportion of children in the region, who completed their primary studies (29 per cent). In the rural areas, the rate was as low as seven per cent.

Among other things, the report mentions high costs and technical problems related to the educational system as factors behind the poor record in education. The report points to the costs of education for low income families as the chief factor behind the high drop-out and non-attendance rates in Nicaraguan schools. Although all countries in Central America have formally declared that the provision of primary education is free of charge, in reality things are very different. In Nicaragua, in particular, the policies enacted by the government in recent years, in an attempt to transfer the burden of social costs from the state to the people, has had a very negative impact on the resources available for education. Currently, the state only covers the supervision and technical aspects with minimum economic support and the children's families have to pay for school uniforms, books and so forth.

The number of young children in school age per household is quite high in Nicaragua, and highest in low income families which means that the costs for schooling incurred by low income families can easily be unbearable. In the document quoted above, this situation is illus-

---

[1] IPEC (1993): *Documento del Seminario sobre el trabajo Infantil en América Central*. (Programa Internacional sobre la Abolición del Trabajo Infantil) OIT. Ginebra.
[2] Ibid. p. 78.

trated by the finding that 17 per cent of the households had to take their children out of the school due to lack of resources.[1] Other problems were also pointed out, some of which had to do with the qualitative aspects of education. In 1993 for instance, 65 per cent of the primary teachers (so-called empirical teachers) in Nicaragua had not completed any formal primary teacher training. The schools had very poor teaching materials and in many cases were in very poor physical condition. In some schools, children had to take their own chairs to school and back home every day. Moreover, the low salaries of teachers meant that incentives to improve teaching were lacking for most of the teachers, and the teachers were often absent from school.

Given this situation, it is not surprising that there is a public debate about the urgent need to reform the educational system. A new intensive primary education programme, and one that is more adapted to the realities of life of the low income population, has been proposed. However, throughout 1993-94 the programme left much to be desired in terms of implementation. The introduction of flexible time schedules that reflect the needs of the children has also been an issue on the school reforms agenda. This would be a significant improvement for working children who would thus have a better chance to attend to their studies while still being able to work. Furthermore, some of the NGOs which are engaged in the problems of working children, are fighting for the approval of special primary education programmes intended for children which have so far been excluded from the formal education programmes because of their age. These children—often teenagers—do not feel comfortable in attending classes with much younger children, but might be willing to join such special programmes.

The report compared the educational situation of working children in five countries in Central America. Due to lack of information Nicaragua is not included in the final analysis. Nevertheless, because of the general relevance of the results, the findings will be presented briefly. It was shown that, with the exception of Panama, there is a high drop-out rate throughout the region. Dropping out, and the fact that many children have to remain one or more years in the same

---

[1]. Ibid. p. 80.

Figure 38 Relationship between the drop-out rate, illiteracy and work in Central American countries (Nicaragua excluded) [a]

Country	Activity	Drop-out Rate, %	Illiteracy, %
Costa Rica	Working children	76.2	2.9
	Non-working children (FwithWCh)[b]	31.7	1.9
	Non-working children (Fwithout WCh)[c]	17.6	2.1
El Salvador	Working children	37.3	10.6
	Non-working children (FwithWCh)	7.6	4.5
	Non-working children (Fwithout WCh)	4.7	2.5
Guatemala	Working children	33.3	26.3
	Non-working children (FwithWCh)	13.1	24.9
	Non-working children (Fwithout WCh)	10.0	12.7
Honduras	Working children	34.3	21.9
	Non-working children (FwithWCh)	11.3	11.1
	Non-working children (Fwithout WCh)	6.7	6.1
Panama	Working children	8.5	0.7
	Non-working children (FwithWCh)	6.9	3.3
	Non-working children (Fwithout WCh)	1.5	0.9

a. The information in this table was extracted from table III.8 on p. 85 from IPEC (1993):*Documento del Seminario sobre el trabajo Infantil en America Central.* (Programa Internacional sobre la Abolición del Trabajo Infantil). OIT. Ginebra.
b. (FwithWCh) = Non-working children living in families with working children
c. (Fwithout WCh) = Non-working children living in families without working children

grade, are the two major problems encountered in primary education in Central America, and particularly for children from low income households. Among the working children who do not drop out but continue to study, the majority trail two or more grades behind the norm for their age.

The report concludes that the drop-out and illiteracy rates were four to five times higher among working children than among economically inactive children, and that working children who succeeded in combining school and work at the same time did so at the cost of trailing two or more years behind in their grades. Finally, the great majority of the working children who did manage to finish their compulsory education did not continue their studies. The report states, however, that irrespective of the presence of working children and despite lower drop-out and illiteracy rates, in the final analysis the educational accomplishments of non-working minors from low income families are very similar. In his comprehensive analysis of the educational situation of children in Lima, Glasinovich showed that the performance in school of working and non-working children in Lima was equally poor.[1] Additional evidence from countries all over Latin America shows that most working children, especially in the urban areas, do attend school but often with poor results.[2]

The educational situation of the interviewed children

Most of the interviewed children attended school. Only one girl and thirteen boys (23 per cent) did not attend school at the time of the interview. Of those, eight had never attended school, and because most of them were between ten and thirteen years old (with the exception of a seven year old boy), the chances for them to enroll in the formal educational system must be regarded as minimal. The remaining six children had started going to school but dropped out because they were too old for the grades they were attending. Only two children, aged nine and eleven, had started school one year later than normal. All these children, who did not attend school, regretted this very much, and when asked why not, gave two main reasons: the poverty of their families or lack of time because they had to work. Thus, ten year old Eric said that "...we did not have money for the uniform", and 14 year old Juan said that "...they (the parents) could not afford the registration fee." For Antonin, on the other hand, lack of time for the studies was the obstacle. As he put it, "...I have no time; I have to work." Another boy, Julio, simply said "...my parents did not want me to study." The most tragic aspect was that these children had

---

[1]. Glasinovich, W.A. (1991): *Entre calles y plazas. El trabajo infantil de los niños en Lima*. ADEC/ATC. Instituto de Estudios Peruanos. UNICEF. Lima.

[2]. Comparing four surveys from Latin America, Myers (1989) found that 77 per cent of the children in Asunción claimed to be attending school, 82 per cent in Brazil, 84 per cent in Lima and 49 per cent in Cochabamba, Bolivia. ILO. International Labour Review.

been attending school earlier and would have liked to continue, yet some of them now were too old.

When looking at some socio-economic characteristics of this group, it became clear that they made up almost half of the children whose families had migrated from rural areas to Managua; in some cases they still lived in the rural areas. The children came from all the different types of households although the nuclear family type was slightly over-represented; the average household size was 6.3 persons. On the other hand, the number of children younger than fourteen was generally high, whereas the number of working children was low in these households. This finding brings to our attention a characteristic strategy of low income households, pointed out in the IPEC report and in other studies, namely that poor and very poor large households choose to invest in the education of one or two of their children, usually the younger ones and preferably the boys, at the expense of the studies of the other children, usually the older boys and girls who have to work in the labour market.[1] Another characteristic common to these children, was the occupations of their parents, which (with the exception of two fathers with vocational occupations), belonged to the irregular income group, most of them working as sellers. Perhaps the combination of these characteristics can in part explain the school drop-out rates of children, and why, regardless of their current age and the age at which they began at school, they had not completed their primary compulsory education. Nevertheless, over three fourths (77 per cent) of the working children in this study said that they attended school regularly, which is surprising especially when we take the long work days of many of them into account. It should be pointed out that a few of those children who claimed that they attended school on a regular basis, were not in school at the time of interview, as they should have been according to the information they provided. When asked why, they said that sometimes they had to work extra and therefore did not have time to go to school. This clearly suggests that school attendance was subordinate to the need for earning an income, and that the children's difficulties in fulfilling their educational plans were due to work.

[1.] IPEC (1993): *Documento del Seminario sobre el trabajo Infantil en América Central.* (Programa Internacional sobre la Abolición del Trabajo Infantil). OIT. Ginebra. p. 85.

In an attempt to extend the analysis of educational success, based on three indicators—the drop-out rate, school starting age, and the number of years that children had to remain in the same grade—by looking at the spatial patterns in educational performance, a distinction was made between children who were born in and lived in Managua and those who came from migrant families or still lived in the rural areas of Managua or other municipalities.

With respect to the school starting age, the analysis showed that children who had migrated to Managua or still lived in rural areas on average had begun school two years later than those born and residing in Managua—8.2 and 6.4 years respectively. On the other hand, it was surprising to find that the children from Managua on the average had poorer school results in terms of the grade they attended relative to the age they began school. On average they lagged behind by two grades, compared to only one for children from outside Managua. This suggests that migrant children, although they had begun school two years later, performed better in their studies. It is difficult to establish the reasons behind this difference; whether it solely reflects that the children in the former group had to remain one or more years in the same grade, or on other factors about which information is not available here, such as partial or temporary non-attendance because of illness or for other reasons.[1] On the other hand it is interesting to note that the children in both groups began to work at the same age—8.6 and 8.8 years respectively, which is above the official age of starting school of seven; in these cases work was not the main reason for not starting school at the normal age.

About 44 per cent of the children lagged behind the normal grade age by a year, and 40 per cent lagged behind two or three grades. In other words, only six children or 15 per cent, were in a grade corresponding to their age. These are discouraging results and show how difficult it is for the children to do well in school and to complete

---

[1]. The example of the child who told me that he had to stop going to school because he did not come in time for registration when the family moved to Managua, illustrates one reason for non-attendance that can be interpreted as drop-out or grade repetition. Another is the case of the child whose family had moved to another district so that he had to change school; he was forced to repeat the same grade as there was no place available in the grade he should have been attending.

their formal compulsory education. I did not specifically ask the children what they thought about their poor school results. Yet, many of them ventured to mention that they were usually tired and could not concentrate fully on the lessons, that they had neither the time nor the proper conditions at home for doing their homework, and that this explained why they did not do so well in their studies.

Glasinovich discusses the work-school relation and suggests that there is no support for the presumed incompatibility of these two activities.[1] He based this conclusion, that work does not substantially affect school performance, on the fact that the performance of non-working vis-a-vis working children was similar in Lima. At the time of the present investigation, there was no adequate comparable information available to confirm or refute Alarcon's claim with regard to Managua. As noted above, many of the factors behind the poor school results of the children in most Latin American countries are definitely related to weaknesses in the formal educational system. Many of the children were aware of some of the deficiencies in the school system, and among other things complained about the lack of teachers, the lack of time and the associated burden and difficulties of doing homework. The children working at the Israel Lewites market spoke of a nearby school where the children had a school schedule more adapted to a combined school-work time budget with the last two hours reserved for doing "homework" at school. According to the children that was much better than doing homework at home. The shortcomings of the educational system and teaching schedules, in my opinion impact more on working than non-working children. However eager they might be to attend school, it is clear that the children in this study have to work in the labour market, and this will directly or indirectly affect their performance in school. Most working children in the cities in Latin America attend school and receive a modicum of basic though incomplete primary education, and it is thus difficult to claim that school and work are mutually exclusive. Rather, the issue is to what extent work is a detriment to good school results and the extent to which it impedes the children from progressing smoothly through the formal educational system. Attending school does not necessarily

---

[1.] Glasinovich, W.A. (1991).

mean gaining from the education that the schools offer. In this study, work was the main reason given by children who never went to school or had to drop-out of school. For them there was no choice—they had to work.

When I related the school results of the children in this study to their workload, defined as the number of workdays per week, the result speaks for itself. The only children who were in grades which corresponded to their age, were those who only worked on weekends. Although only 12 per cent of the children fell into this category, their case shows that it is possible to combine work and school and get good or at least acceptable results, if the intensity of work is moderate. On the other hand, the children who worked all days of the week plus one or two days during the weekends were between a year and half to two and half years behind in grade.[1] There was a clear relationship between work intensity in terms of working days per week and school results.

As mentioned above, the children were not asked directly about how work impacted on their studies. Yet they often made spontaneous references to lack of time as the main impediment to regular school attendance and good study results. The time children spent at school did not vary significantly from case to case since most children attended regular schools, where the school day averaged 4.30 hours.

In sum, what can be learned about the schooling situation of the children of this study? First of all, most of them attended school while working at the same time. Secondly, the immediate economic needs of the children's households were given priority when a decision had to be made between having to work or going to school. There was plenty of evidence for this conclusion in the stories told by the children who never went to school or who had had to drop out because they had to work instead and could not afford school expenses. Furthermore, some of the children stated that they attended school while in fact they were working at times when they should have been in school. But as they put it, "sometimes I can not go to school, I have

---

[1]. Among the children who lagged far behind their "normal"grade, there were three teenagers who because of their age were attending adult courses, between six and nine o'clock in the evening.

to work all day" or " yesterday the earnings were bad, so today I have to work all day".

It was not possible to establish with any precision how many of the children who worked all through the week as well as on weekends, that attended school on a regular daily basis. Taking their poor study results into account, however, it is very obvious that it was extremely difficult for them to combine school and work. Those children who worked only during weekends and who were able to continue their studies with satisfactory results, despite long days and weeks of school and work—they were the exception. When only such a small proportion of the children could conduct school with success, it is quite evident that work has negative effects on the educational performance of children. On the other hand, work in some cases makes it possible for the children to attend school; even if it meant that most children were one or two grades behind in their school carrier, work was undoubtedly the decisive factor in making it economically possible for them to go to school, in contrast to the children who failed to attend school because they could not afford it. Thus, in my opinion the relationship between school and work is quite complex and can be better described as a paradox than as a dilemma, as it is commonly presented. Put differently, we know that many children drop out of school because they have to work, but who knows how many children work because they could never afford to begin school. But even more important is the fact that many children work in order to earn the money needed to attend school, money that otherwise their parents could not afford. This was the situation of many of the children interviewed in this study, who said that they worked to pay for their uniforms, school materials and so forth.

This study has shown that work is not only a factor that discourages schooling, but that, on the contrary, work may be a factor that helps to keep children in school. Undoubtedly school attendance also has an indirect regulating role in terms of reducing the workload for children in the lower grades. Children who both worked and attended school, on the average worked three hours less per week than those who only worked and did not attend school. Readjustments in the educational system and regulations of working time would I believe, permit the working children in the urban sector of Managua to avail themselves of what is in fact an obligation stated in the national law: primary education.

Work in the Labour Market

Finally, I will discuss the time allocation of the activity that is the focus in this study: work in the labour market. The work load of the children varied a great deal in terms of weekly and daily working time. From a first look at the weekly working time (total days of work/week), two main patterns emerged: a dominant one, including the majority of the children (60 per cent), who worked as much as seven days a week; and a second one, including 12 per cent of the children who worked two days, often at weekends. Between these two "extremes" was a group consisting of the children who worked three to five days/week. With respect to the nature of work, in terms of permanent or temporary/seasonal work, all the children worked all year round. Those who worked only during weekends told me that they also worked all week during holidays. Figure 39 summarizes the weekly pattern of work in terms of which days of the week the children worked and the total number of workdays.

The majority of the children had very long weeks of work; just over 70 per cent of the children worked six or seven days/week. Within this group were found all the children who also were engaged in a secondary activity, as well as most of those who did not attend school. If one compares these children with the next biggest group (20 per cent), who worked two or three days/week, two different and quite contrasting patterns can be identified with respect to the significance of work in their weekly time budget. At one end of the scale are those children who spent most of the week working in the labour market, sometimes engaged in more than one activity, and for whom no time was left for other more "child-fit" activities such as school. If they tried to combine work with school, the latter activity came second and their school work suffered badly. At the other end of the scale are the children who came from families who could afford to keep them in school, but still worked on weekends and holidays. Although

Figure 39   The weekly work schedule of the children

Days of Week	Days of Work	Number of Children	
All days	7	36	(60%)
All days except Sunday or Saturday	6	7	(11%)
Weekends or weekends + one day	2 or 3	12	(20%)
Five working days, or three working days + weekends	5	4	(7%)
No information		1	(2%)
Total		60	(100%)

the workload was different, in both cases the children had very full weeks with no days of rest. Even though many of the reasons behind individual variations remain unknown, the children's stories indicated that they had had very little influence on their parents' or other adults' decisions about the organization of their weekly and daily lives.

A second aspect of interest here is the number of hours that children work in a day. The criterion used in establishing "hours of work" was the total time that children were present at the place of work including so called "dead time", which is typical of many activities such as warding and washing cars and shoe-shining. Hence, working time is here defined as the sum of the time spent on the activity itself and the time children were active in the sense that they were waiting for work.

On average, the working day of the children was 6.15 hours, but with great individual variations. The information gathered from the children referred to the last day of work, but most of them regarded that as a pretty "normal day of work". This means that most children had working weeks of between 36 and 43 working hours. Some children in fact worked between eight and twelve hours every day. On the other hand it is also relevant to point out that a few children, although they worked all days of the week, did so for much shorter time periods, between 2 and 4 hours per day, often before school. Children who worked only on weekends were among those who worked long days, on average seven hours. Figure 40 summarizes the allocation of the working time of the children in terms of hours of work by number of days of work.

Boys spent more of their time for work in the labour market than girls did, on average seven hours and five hours and twenty minutes,

Figure 40   Distribution of children's working hours/day by working days/week

Working Hours/Day	Working Days/Week			
	Two or three	Five	Six	Seven
- Minimum	3.30	3	3.30	2
- Maximum	10	11	10	12
- Median	7	5	5.50	6.15
Number of children[a]	12	4	7	36

a. One missing observation.

respectively. This result is in accordance with other investigations which have indicated a similar difference between the sexes, mainly reflecting a greater burden of work in the home for the girls; in the present study there was not enough evidence to test whether that explanation was relevant. With respect to age, the hypothesis of a positive relationship between age and the number of working hours was tested, but no clear-cut relationship could be established; age did not seem to influence the number of hours of work in any significant way.

Daily working time varied between different activities. The number of hours of work was significantly higher for car wardens and car washers than for other occupations, which partly reflects the fact that this occupational group was the lowest paid of all and these children thus had to work longer hours in order to increase their earnings. In fact, the car warders and washers on average worked eight hours while the sellers, e.g., worked seven hours and the shoe-shiners and those engaged in "diverse tasks" on average worked five hours.

In sum, the study of the time allocation of children's work provides insights into the organization of children's lives in both a weekly and daily perspective, and reveals life patterns composed of different activities performed on different days, at different times and in different places. These time-space patterns can certainly be said to require great efforts on the part of the children in order for them to successfully carry out all the activities they are expected to do. The time used by children in their work in the labour market proves that for the majority of them—and contrary to yet another "myth" concerning work in the urban informal sector—work was their main activity. They did not work just to satisfy superfluous needs. Rather, they should be described as workers, contributing necessary income for themselves and for their households, but—sadly enough, it must be said—at the same time depriving themselves of educational opportunities and time for play and sleep.

Chapter 13

The spatial organization of the everyday life of the working children—a missing link?

The previous discussion of how the activities of the children could be classified provides the background for this chapter in which I will attempt to show how these activities were organized and combined in a time-space context. To put it simply, the purpose is to shed some light on the possible patterns of everyday life of the children. Although the children were engaged in a great variety of activities, the simple "work-school dichotomy" will be used to structure the analysis of how their lives are organized, because as children they are supposed to have a right to get a formal education, and as participants in the labour market work is obviously an activity of fundamental importance in their lives.

This study has shown that the working children came from households which differed a good deal in terms of their socio-economic characteristics. However, it was also found that significant differences in the work intensity of the children and in the rate of school participation could not be fully explained by reference to household characteristics. For instance, children from apparently quite similar households in some cases worked only two days a week and attended school, whereas in other cases they worked seven days a week and did not attend school at all. Such inconsistencies raise questions about what other factors, besides the socio-economic ones, that play a role in shaping such very different patterns of everyday life.

A first step in this attempt to identify everyday patterns was to consider the number of days per week that the children engaged in work, respectively went to school. Several alternative ways in which to group the activities performed by the children on a weekly basis were explored, but the one that was eventually chosen identified three quite distinct patterns of the everyday life of the children: (i) children who worked five, six or seven days of the week and attended school, (ii) children who worked all seven days of the week and did not go to school, and (iii) children who worked on the weekends (or three days of the week) and attended school during the week. The purpose of this grouping was to bring to light everyday patterns which reflected as clearly as possible "contrasting" conditions of life for the children, differing with respect to allocation of time not only to work and school, but also with respect to other activities that children were engaged in, namely self-directed and household-directed activities performed at home and in their leisure time. In summary form, the three patterns were labelled:

A "the everyday life of the full-time student and weekend child worker"
B "the everyday life of the full-time student and daily child worker"
C "the everyday life of the full-time child worker"

As was demonstrated in a previous chapter, the children lived, worked and attended school at different, sometimes far-between places in the city, and even outside the city. The locations of home, place of work and school, the time needed for travel between these places, and the time allocated to the various activities of the children, together make up spatial and temporal context, within which these everyday life patterns have to be organized. The purpose of the following sections is to search for configurations in the resulting time-space activity patterns which might contribute to an understanding of why so many dissimilar everyday life patterns can be found among working children from similar households.

I have chosen to introduce the discussion of each type of life pattern by sketching an impressionistic portrait of a child with that kind of life.

The everyday life patterns

A - The full-time student and weekend child worker
Freddy is thirteen years old and lives in Masatepe, an adjacent municipality, with his parents and younger brothers. During the week he does not work, he only goes to school. He gets up at 5 a.m. It takes him twenty minutes to walk to the school that begins at 7 a.m. At 1 p.m. he returns home. In the afternoon he helps his mother at home with various tasks, does his homework, and plays with friends near the house. He goes to bed at 7 p.m.

Freddy works on the weekends. In the morning he gets up at 5 a.m. as usual, and takes the bus to Managua. He sells ice-cream at the Roberto Huembes market. Freddy began to work when he was eight years old, together with his father in the fields, but that work did not give enough money, he says. About a year ago his father started to sell ice-cream in Managua, and Freddy has been helping him in that business since then. The bus trip to the market takes one hour, and he begins work at 8 a.m. and works until 6 p.m. On those days he has no time for playing. He goes to bed at 9 p.m. He gives everything he earns to his father, and thinks that it is right that older children work in order to help their families. However, he is quite afraid of working at the market, he says, because he is not so used to the city.

The typical feature for the twelve children of this group is that they combined school and work by performing these activities on different days of the week: school on weekdays, and work on the weekends. In terms of weekly time, school came first, but, in terms of everyday life, the days when they worked were longer than the days they went to school. In fact one can talk about two different everyday life patterns, one for the days the children "only" go to school, and another for the days when they "only" work.

Most of the children who belonged to this group lived in Managua, but quite often far from the place of work; some, like Freddy, did not live in Managua. All of them, however, lived near the school they went to and on the average had a ten minutes walk to school. They spent between four and five hours a day in school which corresponds to a normal school day. During the week, after or before school, the children had a good deal of "free" time when they could do their home-

Figure 41 Time allocation in the everyday life of children in pattern A during school days and work days

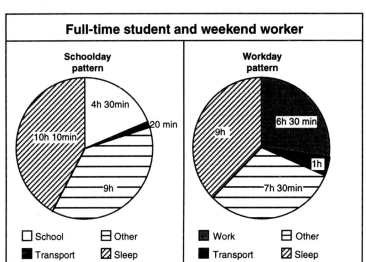

Note: The category "other" includes self-directed and household-directed work, homework, personal care, leisure, play, and in some cases a secondary activity.

work and play. All of them were also engaged in all kinds of "household-directed" work – cleaning, emptying trash, watering the patio, fetching water – and to a less extent in "self-directed" work.

On the weekends, their days were dominated by the work and the trips to and from the place of work. They worked between six and ten hours per day. The majority of them travelled by bus, one and a half hour on the average. Those who walked to their place of work had a mean walking time of forty minutes. These children worked as sellers and car wardens or car washers, and either worked together with a member of their household, as self-employed or as employees. With respect to the income of their families, there were great variations, with incomes characterized either as "certain" and "less uncertain", and on the other hand as non-existent and "uncertain", many in the latter group had female heads of household, either housewives or unemployed. The work place where children with this double pattern of everyday life were most common was the Roberto Huembes market. Figure 41 illustrates the everyday life patterns of these children.

B - The full-time student and daily child worker

Her name is Cristel and she is nine years old. She lives with her mother and two sisters - seven and ten years old - and a brother. She gets up at 6 o'clock in the morning. She lives near the market in a new squatter settlement and in the morning she only has to walk ten minutes to get to the Israel Lewites market where she works together with her mother and one sister. She starts work at 8 a.m., selling candies and cookies that she gets from her mother who has a permanent stall at the market. Cristel spends almost all day working at the market, weekdays as well as Saturdays and Sundays. She gets quite tired, she says, because she moves around in the market all day long. In the middle of the day she takes a break, she eats together with her mother and sister, changes into her school uniform, and walks to the school that is situated next to the market. There she stays between noon and 4.30 p.m. She plays during the recesses. After school she returns to the market and continues to work until 7 p.m. Then, together with her mother and sister, she walks back home. Once at home she helps her mother with the evening meal and the washing up, and finally washes her own clothes and her school uniform. She goes to bed at 9 o'clock.

Thirty-four of the children interviewed in this study worked five, six, or, in the majority of the cases, seven days of the week, like Cristel, and attended school at the same time. They all lived in Managua, and most of them within walking distance of the school; on the average it took them 20 minutes to get there. Only a few lived in districts far from their place of work and had to take the bus; their journey time varied but on average was 40 minutes in total.

Their everyday life was characterized by one work period - relatively speaking shorter than that of the children in the other two life patterns - and a school day as long as that of the full-time students. These two important activities dominated most of their day. Once at home all these children took part in "household-directed" work, and most of them also in "self-directed" work such as washing up their own clothes or preparing their own food. Also, more than half of those children which were engaged in a secondary work activity were represented in this pattern. Since they were engaged in quite a number of activities at home other than play and study, the leisure time of the children in this pattern was much reduced. In terms of their work, these children were engaged in all the occupations studied, although

Figure 42   Time allocation in the everyday life of children in pattern B

Full-time student and daily worker

- 4h 30min — School
- 9h — Sleep
- 5h 30min — Work
- 4h — Other
- 1h — Transport

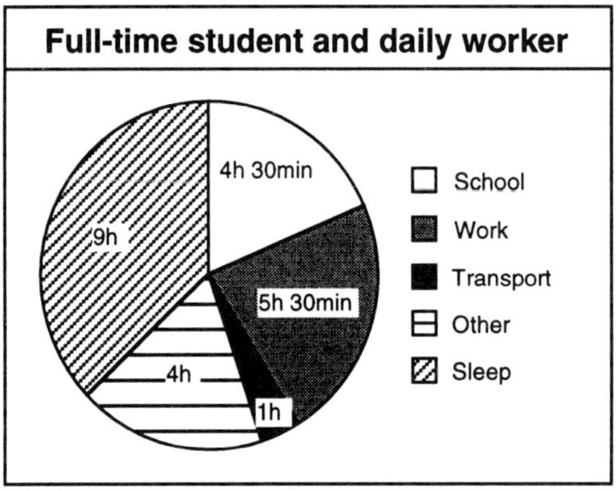

Note: The category "other" includes self-directed and household-directed work, homework, personal care, leisure, play, and in some cases a secondary activity.

sellers were over-represented, and all the shoe-shiners happened to belong to this group. In most cases, the children lived with their nuclear family, but some of them in one-parent and composed families. The majority of the children came from households which were relatively well-off; among the adults in these households incomes of the types previously classified as "less uncertain" and "certain" dominate. In figure 42 the organization of the everyday life of children in pattern B is illustrated.

C - The full-time child worker
Antonin sells ice water at El Mayoreo market. He was not born in Managua but lives there now. He is eleven years old and lives with his mother, an older sister and two younger brothers. He does not attend school because he has not got the time, he says, but he works everyday including the weekends. He gets up at 5 in the morning and begins work at 6 at the market. It takes him 15 minutes to get to the market by bus. There he spends almost all day, working until 4 o'clock in the afternoon. One of his younger brothers works there too and they usually travel back home together. Antonin has been working since he was seven years old, earlier at the Oriental market, where he helped load rice and beans together with his father who lived with the family at that time. After work, when he has returned home, Antonin helps his mother with heavy tasks

such as fetching water and filling the water barrels. Afterwards he plays with some friends in the streets near home. He goes to bed at 7 o'clock.

Fourteen of the children interviewed for this study did not attend school, and all but one of those were included in this pattern. They all worked at least five, but mostly seven days a week, on average 9 hours/day, so obviously the pattern of their everyday life was dominated by the time they were engaged in work. Most of the children in this pattern lived in Managua but their place of residence generally was situated far from from the place of work. With the exception of two children, all had to take the bus to the markets where they worked all day long. Their travel time was on average 40 minutes. The other two children walked to work, which took them one hour and twenty minutes and thirty minutes, respectively. Eleven of these children came from families which had moved from other regions to Managua. They lived either with their nuclear families, with one parent or together with relatives, and their households must be described as relatively poor – few of them had "less uncertain" and "certain" incomes. They worked mainly as sellers but also as car wards, either together with a member of their household or as employees of someone else. Many of the children were also involved in a secondary activity. They were concentrated to the biggest markets, i.e. the Roberto Huembes, the El

Figure 43   Time allocation in the everyday life of children in pattern C

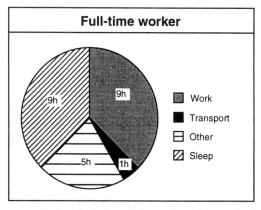

Note: The category "other" includes self-directed and household-directed work, homework, personal care, leisure, play, and in some cases a secondary activity.

Mayoreo, and the Israel Lewites markets. This third everyday life pattern is illustrated in figure 43.

Combining school and work

The patterns of everyday life of the children show that the children indeed lived under very different circumstances with respect to the share of their daily time that the activities "work" and "school" demanded.

The organization of the everyday life of the children in pattern B very clearly shows what the consequences are of trying to combine work and school in such a way that it is possible for the children to take part in both activities on a full-time basis. Work and school together took up eleven hours of these children's fifteen hour long days, leaving very little time for play and homework. If we add that many of them had a secondary work activity that they had to do after returning home, and also were engaged in household-directed work at home, one can not but characterize these children's lives as very strenuous. Their weekly time of work was almost forty hours and they spent more than twenty hours a week in school, which adds up to at least sixty hours of time taken up by these activities. The poor school results of these children are not difficult to explain with reference to the difficulty of combining full-time work and full-time school.

Figure 44 illustrates how the children allocate their time during the week to work in the labour market and to school.

Another way in which work and school were combined was that illustrated by pattern A. These children in principle lived two different daily lives. During schooldays they had plenty of time left to study, play and participate in work at home. During workdays they worked for many hours, but they still had a good deal of time left for play and rest. On the average they got more sleep than other children. This pattern gave the children the chance to attend to their studies in a more normal way, because not only could they attend school, but also had time to do their homework. However, they had to devote the whole weekend to work which means that they had no day of rest. In this respect these children's situation did not differ from that of the majority of the children in this study.

Figure 44   The three patterns of weekly time allocation

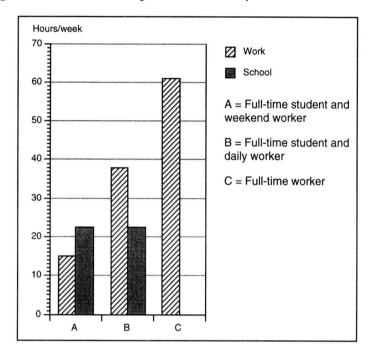

Lastly, the organization of everyday life reflected in pattern C was aimed at maximizing children's engagement in work in the labour market, and did not leave any time for school. Including travel time, the normal workday of these children was ten hours, leaving only five hours for other activities. Many of these children were also engaged in secondary activities which further reduced the time available for leisure and play. As full-time workers, usually working seven days a week, most of these children had a workload amounting to about sixty hours a week.

It is difficult to say which one of the two life patterns, in which both school and work feature, that best complies with the children's right to follow and ability to complete a normal school career, as well as the need to work so as to improve the economic situation of themselves and their households. My data clearly indicate that a combination of both on a daily basis greatly reduces the time left for leisure and sleep and jeopardizes the children's school-work. The children very often talked about how tired they were and that they did not have time to do

Figure 45 Time allocation of each child in the everyday life pattern B

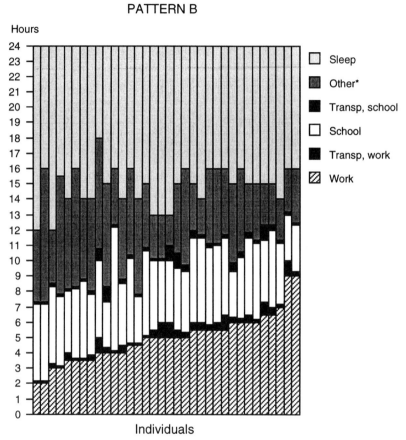

*The category "other" includes self-directed and household-directed work, homework, personal care, leisure, play, and in some cases a secondary activity.

their homework. Only when work and school were scheduled on different days did the children have more time for leisure, study and play, than the time they devoted to work and school. It is worth noting that the children who did not go to school were the ones that worked the longest days, and, as it turned out, had approximately as much time for leisure and sleep as those who worked and went to school at the same time.

Which of the two "school and work" patterns that best suits the interests of the children is not so easy to say, even if, as here, we narrow the question down to a question of how to improve the living sit-

Figure 46 Time allocation of each child in the everyday life pattern C and A

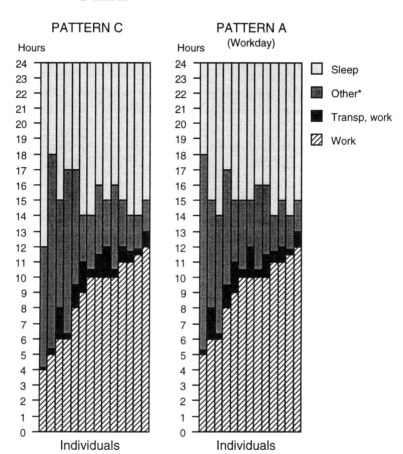

*The category "other" includes self-directed and household-directed work, homework, personal care, leisure, play, and in some cases a secondary activity.

uation of the working children in the urban informal sector. It should be added that some factors, which have not been sufficiently explored in this study, also have to be considered, such as the dangers the children face in their work and the existence of work that is detrimental to the physical and psychological development of the children. However, access to a meaningful education must be regarded as a minimal requirement if the quality of life of these children is to be improved. It is time that the majority of the children of this study is given the opportunity to combine school and work - but at what price?

The role of the spatial patterns of activities in shaping everyday life patterns

An inspection of the socio-economic characteristics of the households which become a part of each child's everyday life pattern, confirms what has been noted earlier in this study, namely that variations in children's work intensity and in their school attendance are not necessarily directly related to the socio-economic situation of their households. In fact, across the three patterns, all types of households were found - in terms of their size, composition, family type, and type of income of the heads of household and their partners. Some of those characteristics made the inclusion of the children in certain patterns easy to understand, especially the incidence of certain types of income of the heads of the household and their partners, but we are left with the question why other children living in the same type of household were part of other life patterns.

Of course, each individual everyday life pattern was accompanied by a specific pattern of spatial behaviour. The location of home, place of work, and the travel time and means of transportation used between the places, differed from child to child. As was mentioned earlier, decisions about the children's participation in work vis-à-vis school, or in both activities at the same time, were mainly taken by the head of the household or his/her partner. Such decisions may be so important for the household that economic considerations prevail over all other things, such as the children's schooling. However, the assumption that the spatial aspects, in one way or another, may have influenced such decisions, and consequently may have contributed to shape the children's everyday life pattern, called for a closer analysis of the everyday life patterns in a spatial perspective.

First of all, the distance between home and place of work seems to have been a very important factor for decisions about children's school attendance. In fact, the great majority of the children who lived near their places of work also attended school. They did both things on a full-time basis. That was the case of more than half the children included in pattern B. They all had short journeys between school and home - twenty minutes on average in both directions - and between home and work - on average thirty minutes in both directions. In this situation, the socio-economic characteristics of the children's household seem to have been less relevant, since all categories of households were found in this pattern. The characteristics of the places of work was apparently of some importance as well, since these children were found not only in the smallest places of work - Galeria Internacional and San Judas market - but in the largest markets as well.

In sum, proximity of the place of residence to the place of work seems to be a primary prerequisite condition for children's school attendance, because the "price" to be paid is acceptable in terms of travel time to the school as well as to the place of work, and both activities are therefore compatible with each other in space and time.

However, for those children who did not live near their place of work the situation was different. It was no longer that evident that the children could engage in both activities at the same time and thus a choice had to be made. That choice was obviously made by the household of the children, and meant that priority had to be given either to work or school, such as in the cases of children in pattern C or pattern A.

When "work" was regarded as more important than "school", as in pattern C, the main reason was that the household was not ready to pay the price of children going to school to because in that case it had forgo the necessary income from the work of the children. If, because of their spatial location, both activities were not compatible in terms of full-time engagement in work and in school at the same time, in these cases the economic situation of the household weighed heaviest in decision-making, but at the same time it was still subordinated to the spatial factor. Actually, other children in households with similar socio-economic characteristics both worked and attended school, if they lived near the place of work. But, all the children in the C pattern lived far from their place of work, eleven of the thirteen had to travel by bus for about one hour in both directions, and two children had to walk on average one hour and twenty minutes.

Once the decision to choose "work" has been taken, it seems that the spatial location of the place of work is no longer so important. The children's households are ready to support the temporal and monetary costs needed for the children's transportation to and from the place of work. The highest price for that decision was paid by the children themselves; they had the longest days of work in comparison with the children in the other patterns, and did not get an education. These children were concentrated in the biggest places of work, the Roberto Huembes and El Mayoreo markets, where the flow of possible customers was greater and the odds of earning good money were better.

When "school" was given priority, the households were prepared to pay the price of the education, i.e. to forgo the income that would have come from the children's work during the week. The school was near the home, so not too much time or money was lost in transportation. On the weekends, however, the children worked. On those days, distance to the place of work did not seem to be a restriction on children's participation in work. Most of them took the bus to their place of work and travelled on average one and a half hour; in other cases the children walked for forty minutes. Their work days were a little longer than those of the children in pattern B, who both worked and went to school.

In conclusion there is some evidence that the spatial pattern of the activities in terms of the relative location of home, place of work and school, had an impact on the organization of the everyday life of the working children of this study. Proximity to the place of work permits the children to work and at the same time to attend school, regardless of the socio-economic situation of their households. This is so because the two activities are spatially and temporally compatible, which means that the household can count on some income from the children whether they attend school or not. When the place of residence and also the school are located far from the place of work, it is much more likely that the children will not be going to school because of the incompatibility of the two activities in space and in time. In that situation the crucial question is whether the household can dispense with the income from the work of the children. The children's income is necessary for all these households, but in some cases, the income from a few days of work is sufficient to improve the economic situation of the household and therefore the children can attend school. If the households can not dispense with a daily income contribution from the children, they have to work all week and thus can not go to school. One cannot say that the location of work and school by themselves and all alone can explain the different patterns of everyday life of children in similar socio-economic situations, nor can the socio-economic characteristics of households. However, this discussion of how households adapt their decisions about the work of the children to the spatial pattern of home, place of work and school suggests that these spatial relationships must be included in the analysis if we are to get a better understanding of the complex set of factors that shape the everyday life of the working children of the informal sector in Managua.

Chapter 14

Risks at work

When I meet a child working at a market, in a parking lot or simply in the street, the first thought that goes through my mind is that this child is constantly exposed to many risks. Without parents or other adult relatives within easy reach, these children are in frequent contact with people that they do not know, they are generally vulnerable, and easy targets for those who are on the lookout for recruits to criminal activities, drug use and prostitution. The street is a violent environment and the children are often drawn into dangerous situations where they risk to be harmed not only physically but also psychologically, not just for the moment but perhaps for life. The problem of how to minimize the risks that threaten the working children is a complex one, and especially because of the characteristics of the places where children in the informal sector work. Whereas working conditions in a factory or a workshop, for instance, can be improved and rectified by regulations, or improvements to tools and machines, the large work place of the street, or other open places, by its very nature is much more difficult, if not impossible, to modify or regulate so that it becomes a secure place.

In their recent book, Bequele and Myers included those children engaged in the activities that this study focuses upon, in the list of children working in hazardous circumstances.[1] They suggest that these children's hazardous situation tends to be ignored, because there are so many of them that the general public has become indifferent to their

---

[1] Bequele, A. and Myers, W.E. (1995): *First things first in child labour. Eliminating work detrimental to children.* UNICEF. ILO. Geneva.

presence. In defining work that must be regarded as hazardous to children, the authors stress that it is most important to keep in mind the differences between children and adults, because work hazards that affect adults often affect children even more strongly:

> Children differ from adult workers most importantly, however, in that they are still in the process of growing up, and their normal development can be severely endangered by conditions that may not appear to adults to constitute a peril. When speaking of children, therefore, it is necessary to go beyond the relatively limited concept of "work hazard" as applied to adults, expanding it to include the development aspects of childhood. Because they are still growing, children have special characteristics and needs that must be taken into consideration when defining work place risks to them. This means that, in the case of child labour, the concept of "work hazard" needs to be child-centred, focusing not only on factors of immediate jeopardy, but also those that menace child development over the long term.[1]

The authors group the different dimensions of child development - physical development, cognitive development, emotional development, social and moral development - into two categories, physical and psychosocial, and discuss at length the different hazardous situations that children face in their work and which might jeopardize their development in these two respects. Among other risks, they stressed that violence from adults is the most important physical hazard that children at work face, and that the most common psychosocial hazard is the fact that work often arrests children's intellectual development, by making it difficult or even impossible for them to get an education.

To be sure, the health of working children has been on the agenda of WHO and ILO for some time. In December 1985, a WHO Study Group on Special Risk Factors of Children at Work met in Geneva and proposed that a serious attempt should be made to identify the special risks to which children at work are exposed, taking into consideration that the risks that the children face are different from those

---

[1]. Ibid. p. 6.

faced by adults and thus call for special measures; the aim was to achieve health for all by the year 2000.[1] The report with the findings and proposals of that study group was completed in 1987, and included, among other things, a WHO-sponsored review of studies on the social and psychosocial problems of children at work. In that study four groups of children were considered: (i) children working in other people's homes in Kenya, (ii) children working on plantations and farms, (iii) children working in the streets as bootblacks, newspaper vendors, messengers, sweepers, vendors at markets and food stalls, as well as accomplices in illegal activities, and (iv) children working i factories. The report refers to the children in group three as follows:

> There is much anecdotal evidence to show that the conditions described in Clopper's book *Child Labor in City Streets*, first published in 1912, are still prevalent today in some parts of the world. The effects of street work on children, according to Clopper, include: (i) distaste for regular employment, (ii) excessive fatigue, (iii) use of coffee, cigarettes and liquor, (in) venereal disease (v) defiance of parental control, (vi) recruitment into criminal activities, and (vii) bodily deformation and stunting.[2]

This report produced some valuable findings, although it did perhaps not add very much to Clopper's conclusions about the health condition of that group of working children, nor about the risks they face at work.

Much more recently, UNICEF's "The State of the World's Children 1997" report finally focuses on the necessity to distinguish between the different forms and nature of child work in order to identify work that is hazardous and exploitative. By its definition, that work involves:

- full-time work at too early an age
- too many hours spent working
- work that exerts undue physical, social or psychological stress
- work and life on the streets in bad conditions
- inadequate pay

---

[1]. WHO (1987): *Children at work: special health risks*. Report of Study Group. Technical Report Series. No. 756. World Health Organization. Geneva. p. 5.
[2]. Ibid. p .31-32.

- too much responsibility
- work that hampers access to education
- work that undermines children's dignity and self-esteem, such as slavery or bonded labour and sexual exploitation
- work that is detrimental to full social and psychological development.[1]

This definition is still very vague and wide and it is pertinent to ask how one might find implementary measures to protect children from all these situations, based upon such a general frame. For instance, in the case of the work of children in the informal sector, this is clearly by this definition a hazardous and exploitative form of work, but no specific reference is made to this particular form of work.

When the present study was designed, there was no intention to make an evaluation of the health conditions of the children. Nevertheless, it is important to mention - as I have already done in previous sections - that fatigue and concentration problems in school were often mentioned quite spontaneously by the interviewed children. It is hardly rash to suggest that these problems are related to their situation as child workers, keeping in mind their often long working days, often combined with school-work, and sometimes with an engagement in a secondary activity.

However, an attempt was made to explore the problem of risks at work, but this time from a different perspective, namely by trying to get some insights into how the children themselves perceive the risks that they are exposed to when they work, and trying to relate the findings to the characteristics of the places where they work.

The children were asked a direct question: "Are you afraid of working here"? Twenty children said that they were indeed afraid, and thirty-nine that they were not.[2] The reasons given by those that said that they were afraid were:

- I am afraid of thieves and of being robbed
- I am afraid of "bad guys", rapists and kidnappers

---

[1]. UNICEF (1997): *The State of the World's Children 1997*.
[2]. One child said that he did not know how to answer that question, and is therefore not included.

- I am afraid of the night
- I am afraid of being alone
- I am afraid of going back home alone
- The reasons given by those who said that they were not afraid were:
- I am not afraid because I have many friends here (at the place of work)
- I am not afraid because my mother/father/relative is here too (at the same place of work)
- I am not afraid because I am used to work

It was interesting to note that only one of the children who said that they were afraid, was unable to explain why not. Most of the other children could give several reasons and told me about different hazardous situations that they had witnessed or heard about. In contrast, many of those who said that they were not afraid could not explain why they felt that way. No relationship was found between the age of the children and the way they answered the question. There was, however, a certain relationship between the answers and the different places of work, although it was not obvious how that could be explained in terms of the characteristics of the places. None of the children at Galeria Internacional, for instance, said they were afraid of working there, which seemed to make sense because of the small size of the parking lot and the calm work milieu there, whereas most of the children at San Judas market, also a small and apparently calm place of work, said that they were afraid of being there because of thieves that they knew could come. In the biggest market, El Mayoreo, half of the children said that they were afraid and the other half that they were not, and a similar situation existed at the Roberto Huembes market. Curiously enough, almost all the children at Israel Lewites said they were not afraid of working there, despite its large size and the hustle and bustle at this market. These results seemed to indicate that it was not primarily the characteristics of the different places of work that influenced children's perception of the risks they were exposed to.

When I searched for other possible explanations of such different feelings among children in apparently similar situations and at the same places of work, it was rather obvious, and perhaps not surprising, that the presence of an adult from the household of the child was a factor that very definitely contributed to the child's feeling of security at work. In fact, when the children worked together with a member of their household, were employees, and also when they were self-employed but a relative also worked at the same place, the children said that they were not afraid at work. This factor largely explains the difference in attitudes between the children at the Galeria International and San Judas, respectively. Although in the Galeria most children worked independently, most of them had parents or relatives who worked in the same place or close by. At San Judas, a small and peaceful work milieu, the children were afraid at work, because they had no adult relative working there with them.

It would be dangerous to draw any comprehensive conclusions from these findings. They suggested, however, that the children's perception of the risks they were facing at work was not directly related to the characteristics and general work milieu of their places of work, but primarily had to do with whether they were working alone, or could feel that they were under the surveillance or just in the presence of an adult member of their household. This might explain why only one child mentioned traffic as a risk at work, although there is plenty of evidence that shows that it is precisely traffic accidents that cause most of the deaths of children who work in the street and other open places. The reasons given by the children to explain why they were afraid show, however, that children are very much aware of the fact that they risk to become victims of the widespread violence in the urban environment, and their fears confirm that violence from adults is still the most common threat against children at work. It also became clear that the girls were very conscious of their particular vulnerability, and almost all of them said that they were afraid of rapists and "bad guys".

Figure 47   The children really enjoyed to use the tape recorder!

Chapter 15

What the children think about child work

I have tried to remind myself, constantly throughout this study, that each one of the interviewed children is an individual with his or her unique characteristics and situation of life. Most of the time the individuals have had to be invisible in the interests of more general analyses; still, each particular child has been present behind the figures. In this chapter, however, the children will get a chance to speak for themselves. Here the purpose is to bring to light their opinions and feelings regarding child work as well as their perception of their role as child workers.

This was the last part of the interviews, and the rationale for this was that I hoped that by that time a certain level of confidence between myself as the interviewer and the respondents would have been built up. Three introductory, but to my mind crucial questions were asked in order to start the conversation about these matters, each one followed by a "why" question which allowed the children to openly express their points of view. Firstly, the children were asked if they liked to work; secondly, what their opinion was about the fact that so many children worked, not only in Managua but all over the world; and, finally, they were asked to talk about what they would do if they suddenly would find themselves in a situation where they need not work.

Beginning with the first question, all the children, without exception, declared that they liked to work. Not all of them, however, were able to elaborate upon their answers. The younger children, in particular, could not explain why they liked to work; they simply said:

"because it is nice" or "it is boring when I am not working", or used some cliché phrases, such as, "it is good to learn to work while one is a child", "it is better to work than to be involved in robbery and other mischiefs", "working is good because otherwise one would become lazy". Those more able to qualify their answers, presented various reasons, often related to their personal and family situation. Actually, two reasons for why they liked to work were very dominant: (i) because they were able to help their mothers or to contribute to improve their household economy in general, and (ii) because they could earn money that they would otherwise not get in order to cover their own expenses for food, school, and personal care.

The second question aimed at giving the children the chance to reflect more deeply upon their situation as child workers, and yet without asking them directly about it. I tried to put the question in a more subtle way by asking the children what they thought about the fact that so many children worked. The answers about the situation of that "conceptual" child worker necessarily have to be understood in part as a reflection of the children's own experiences and thoughts about their own situation as workers, but at the same time, the answers presumably represented their views about child work in general.

Only a few children were unwilling to express an opinion; these children felt the question was too difficult and said that they never had thought about that subject. As many as 20 per cent of the children strongly believed that working was not good at all for any child. On the other hand, the great majority (68 per cent) were of the opposite opinion and maintained that work was good for children.[1] The main reasons given to justify either view or attitude could be summarized as follows:

A - *I think work is good because...*
   ...children can help their mothers
   ...children can help their mothers to buy food

---

[1] It was interesting to note that even though this question was intended to allow the children to express themselves freely (it was an open question), the children always began by qualifying work according to the dichotomy "good" and "not good", and then proceeded to express their opinions.

...children can help their families
...children can help their families with money
...children can get enough to eat
...children can learn that to work is good for life

B - *I think it is not good...*
...because the children can get hurt
...because of the murderers, rapists and thieves
...because the children are victims of adults on the street
...because the parents should have enough money so that their children need not work
...because it is not fair to the child
...because it is not fair, but if the family needs it, they have to
...because these children have no childhood
...but better than loafing away time

The differences between these attitudes can partly be accounted for by some of the circumstances which have been discussed in this study, but a deeper understanding obviously would require much additional information about the children's family life, their experiences at school and in their life as workers.

At first glance, it would appear that the age of the children could be a primary explanatory factor. In fact, the children who said that work was not good for the children, all were among the oldest interviewed children, between eleven and fourteen years. Certainly age would seem to explain in part the high degree of awareness and concern reflected in the responses of the children who talked about social injustice and the dangers that working children are exposed to in their work milieu. The justice-injustice dichotomy was evident in the statements which blamed society for failing to provide adequate resources for families, so that they were forced to send their children to work. As fourteen year old Luis Alberto put it:

> Working is not good for the children. The parents should have enough money and food to provide for their families so the children did not need to work.

In spite of the strong criticisms directed at society, the solidarity of the children with their families is evident, as could be surmised from most comments, such as that by José:

> To work is not good for the children, but if their families do not have anything, they have to work anyway.

It was also evident that the older children made a clear distinction between younger and older child workers, when they stated that they did not consider work to be harmful to the older children like themselves, but very bad for the young ones; they admitted, however, that they were forced to work out of sheer necessity in order to support their parents and families. Some added that working children had no childhood. Such statements reveal a certain feeling of hopelessness about the situation of the younger working children, and can be interpreted as reminiscences of the older children's lost childhood and their own "careers" as child workers which began at very low ages. The element of danger was frequently mentioned in the conversations. The children were not asked if they had been involved in the kind of dangerous situations that they mentioned, but some of them commented on authentic cases that they had witnessed or had heard of. In sum, the reasons given by those children who were critical of child work were mostly of a humanitarian nature, focusing on social injustice, solidarity with young child workers and the family, as well as on the hazardous work environment.

The main arguments of those who defended child work were mostly related to the different states of poverty of the children's families. Some children talked about poverty in more general terms as when they stated that "it is good that the children work so that they can help their mothers" and, "...to help their families with money". More specifically they referred to situations of urgent need of basic resources, in statements such as "to help their mothers to buy food", and "it is good so the children can get enough to eat". In sum, the reasons given by those who defended child work were mainly of an economic character, and focused both on the economic situation of the family and the children's own economic needs. These answers supported the findings presented in a previous chapter regarding the destination of the income of the children and the importance of their work for the economy of poor households and for the children themselves. Some of these children declared very definitely that they were dependent on their work for eating, and that this was one of the reasons why they liked to work.

Apart from age, I tried to search for other characteristics that might help me understand the two contrasting views that the children held towards child work. Common to all those who thought that work was not good for children, was the fact that they had begun to work at very low ages, most of them between the age of five and seven and some when they were eight or nine years old. It turned out that more than 60 per cent of them had a secondary activity at the time of the interview and that almost all of them were independent workers. All these children attended school. In sum, not only did they have long careers as workers behind them, they also carried the burden of combining work and school. It is not surprising that their opinion about child work was negative.

In stark contrast to that group, the great majority of the children who were in favour of child work were family workers. They usually had begun to work later in life at the ages of nine to eleven years; at the time of the interviews most of them had had only a short working carrier, and almost none had a secondary activity. Another significant aspect, and one that may partly account for their positive attitudes toward child work, was the fact that many of them had migrated with their families to the capital. Their working situation could perhaps be perceived as being better in comparison with what their life was like before they moved to the city.

Finally, the question about what the children would do, in case they did not have to work, was intended to give an idea about the extent to which children were content with their status as workers, whether they preferred to work rather than to engage in any other activity. The answers showed that only seven per cent of the children said that they would work even if they did not need to, because they had always been working. The great majority of the children (86 per cent), however, said that they would prefer to stay at home. Only two alternative activities were named, independently or jointly, (i) to help the mother with domestic work, and (ii) to study more. Finally, some children said that they just wanted to stay at home doing nothing, playing or resting.

What general conclusions is it possibly to deduce from these answers?

First of all that there was no consensus among the children about the benefits of child work for the children themselves, but there was an implicit and common understanding of the benefits that accrued to the children's families. Despite the divergent opinions that emerged, when they were asked whether child work is good or not good for children, in effect the children revealed a common awareness of the fact that, either for purely economic reasons or for socio-economic reasons of a humanitarian character, child work is a must. In both cases, the perception of the children about their own role as workers was unequivocal: their work was of vital importance for their families and, in many cases, for their personal upkeep. Finally, it has to be concluded that, in spite of the fact that all the children declared that they liked to work, in reality only a few would continue to work if they had the choice not to do so. If it was possible, the great majority of them would stay at home and replace work by other more "child-fit" activities, such as studying or simply playing or relaxing. The majority said that they would also help their mothers with domestic work at home. In sum, the findings indicate that for most of the children, work was not a hobby, but a necessity. They did not work voluntarily, but rather were compelled to work because of the economic conditions of their families and in extreme cases in order to get their own food. In reality their options with respect to choosing between work and other activities apparently were non-existent since otherwise the great majority of them would not have been child workers.

...and dreams of the future?

After their reflections about child work, the children were asked to talk about their hopes and aspirations for their lives as adults. The question put when discussing the future was "what do you want to be/do when you have become an adult"? The answers to that question were meant to give a glimpse, if no more, of the kind of future the children expected to have for themselves. Another aspect of interest in the context of this research was whether the children's aspirations with regard to future occupations would indicate any intentions of continuing with the occupations they were engaged in at the time of the interviews, or if, on the contrary, they wished to work in totally different occupations. Once again, the children's awareness of the economic situation in which they and their families found themselves became very apparent from their first spontaneous responses and throughout the conversations. To have a "decent" job or to simply be able to work was the principal desire of the majority of the children. Some qualified this by adding "a good job" or "a well paid job so that my children need not work". At the same time, the children were also fully aware that the economic situation of their families could thwart such aspirations for the future. Hence, their answers were often qualified by such expressions as "...if I can..." or "...if I could afford..."

The importance of education as a means of acquiring better jobs was an idea that was present in the conversation with most children. The majority mentioned vocational education and training in particular, rather than higher education, as the best means of obtaining a good job. With the exception of a few very young boys who maintained that they had never thought about their future lives, and others who said they simply wanted to have a job in the future, the great majority of the children even specified the type of occupation they wanted to have as adults.

The preferred occupations and the proportion of children aspiring to such jobs can be grouped into four types: (i) jobs in the informal sector (13 per cent), (ii) professional (17 per cent), (iii) vocational (48 per cent), and (iv) agrarian (7 per cent). All the boys in the first category aspired to be sellers as adults, and the girls said that they wanted to be domestic servants. If we compare their responses with the current or actual activities of the children and of their parents or relatives, in both cases selling was the predominant activity. The high incidence of sellers among members of the children's families, and of children working as sellers, may in part explain their desire to continue to work as sellers as adults. A more obvious correspondence between the children's aspirations for an occupation in the future and their parents' occupations is found in the case of those who aspired to be rural workers. They were all boys and their wishes are not surprising if we take into account that these children were either rural-urban migrants or that they lived in the rural districts of Managua and travelled to the city every day to work. Moreover, the fathers of almost all the children who wanted to work in rural occupations as adults were rural workers. They talked very warmly about how they wanted to work in the fields with a "machete", some specifying that they wanted to work in a sugar plantation, others claiming in more general terms that life in the countryside was better than in the city. Only one of these children attended school, which partly had to do with the long trips they had to make everyday, in some cases close to three hours. In sum, the aspiration of this particular group of children was to take up an occupation after their fathers, as they could more easily identify with these activities because of their rural background, than with the activities they performed in the city.

Nevertheless, most children aspired to work in other occupations than those they were engaged in at the time of the interview. The main motives behind such a choice was clearly the desire to improve their lives through professional training that would guarantee them a better economic situation, as well as the desire to attain a higher social status than that of their parents or other relatives they lived with.

As many as 65 per cent of the children neither wanted to carry on with the same informal activities that they were engaged in now, nor wanted to do the kind of work that their fathers or mothers were doing. Most of the children preferred occupations that required short educational programmes and/or vocational training. Others aspired to professions requiring higher studies. Only two of these children did not attend school. It was evident that in general the children were very much aware of the value of education if they were to get better jobs in the future, a theme often brought up during the interviews and informal conversations.

There were very clear-cut differences between the occupational preferences of girls and boys, respectively, which to some extent reflected what the children considered as "typical" male and female occupations. The first choice occupations for the girls were those of primary teacher, nurse, and secretary, but also medical doctor. Secretarial and teaching professions were those mentioned most often. In contrast, the boys mentioned a broader range of professions, including that of engineer, medical doctor, lawyer, architect, manager, bookkeeper, car mechanic, technician, teacher, bricklayer, security guard and policeman. Book-keeping and working as a car mechanic were the favourite careers for the boys. Since many of the children had some knowledge of vocational jobs, either through their fathers or other relatives, their future career horizons were not confined to the informal activities they performed.

In conclusion, the aspirations of the children about their future lives indicate a common desire to get a job that would guarantee that their basic needs would be satisfied. There was some evidence of a correspondence between the actual occupations of the children, those of their parents and the careers the children aspired to. That association was quite clear in the case of the children which belonged to the poorest households (i. e. sellers and rural workers), where both parents had irregular earnings and were engaged in the same activities as the children. On the other hand, the correspondence was not so self-evident in the case of the children which came from households with parents or relatives engaged in vocational occupations. Those children expressed their desire to have a vocational occupation as adults, but not necessarily the same professions as those of their fathers or other relatives.

Chapter 16

Summary and conclusions

The subject of this thesis is child work in the informal sector in Managua. This topic has many aspects, but this study has focused specifically upon two of these aspects. It attempts to unravel the interrelationships between the urban informal sector and child work, and, secondly, to illuminate the conditions of life of children at work through an intensive study of a sample of working children between the ages of 7 and 14.

More concretely, the specific objectives of the study concern two interrelated issues. The first has to do with the economic and social aspects of the work of children, in particular the role of children's work in the informal sector with respect to the characteristics and economic significance of their work, and the conditions that facilitate or restrict the entrance of children into the informal sector. The second issue concerns the living conditions of the children, and here the aim has been to describe and analyse the everyday life of working children, focusing in particular upon the relationship between school attendance and work in the labour market.

In the literature on economic and social development, the role of the informal sector in urbanization processes has been interpreted in various and sometimes diametrically opposite ways; the sector has been expected either to solve or to aggravate employment problems in the cities. At the present time, the existence of an expanding informal sector in many cities in Latin America generally seems to be accepted as an inevitable phenomenon, inherent in the process of urbanization, although governments do not seem to be particularly interested in trying to combat it; on the contrary, they seem to expect that it will continue indefinitely to absorb labour and thus solve employment problems in the cities. However, there are signs of a saturation process in the sector, which has resulted in a marginalization of the sector in terms of a general decline of incomes, changes in its occupational structure, an increase in illegal activities and criminality, and a diffusion of poverty to new groups of the urban population.

In the case of Managua, the links between poverty and employment in the informal sector are very obvious. The expansion of the sector has been characterized, among other things, by declining incomes and the integration of new groups into the informal labour force—workers from the formal sector and children. Child work in the sector has been increasing steadily during the last few years. Competition within the sector is stiff and hardening. Especially attractive are the activities for which investment capital, however trifling, is not needed—the visible activities in streets, markets and so forth—those in which the people most severely affected by poverty are engaged, and where the child workers are found. The emergence of new barriers which make entry into those activities more difficult has led to a permanent struggle in order to get access to places of work and jobs.

The theoretical discussion served as the basis for the analysis of specific research questions in the empirical study of Managua. Against that background, the work of the children in the informal sector has been understood as an integral component of this sector and of urban development processes in general. The work of the children has also been analysed in a household perspective, since child work is considered to be one of a set of strategies that households adopt in order to cope with lack of resources. Finally, the work of the children was analysed as a central factor behind the shaping of the conditions of life of the children in the broadest sense of that expression.

Some of the main findings of the investigation can be summarized in the following way.

- The work of the children in the informal sector is a well-organized activity, one to which the children are committed in a very serious and conscientious way.

– In the struggle to get access to the activities and places of work in the urban informal sector, children clearly are in a disadvantaged position, subject to discrimination by as well as support from the adults.

– There is a clear relationship between child work and poverty in terms of the destination and use of the children's income. In general, the households were dependent upon the income from the work of the children, because of the low incomes of adults in the household.

– There is, however, no "typical" household to which working children belong. Working children came from households with varying socio-economic characteristics.

– Whether children attend school or not is not determinated only by the socio-economic characteristics of the households of the children. The spatial pattern of the activities, in terms of the relative location of home, place of work and school, also has a significant impact on the organization of children's everyday life with respect to whether priority is given to work or school.

– Work does not necessarily discourage schooling; on the contrary, income from work may be a factor that helps to keep children in school. School attendance, however, had an impact on the work of the children by reducing their work load.

– Regardless of whether the working children attended school or not, work was clearly the most important activity of the child workers, one that took precedence over other activities such as school, homework, play, leisure and sleep, or that occupied children's leisure time on weekends. This was true for all the three major patterns of everyday life organization which were identified in the study on the basis of the children's own account of what their weekly schedules looked like.

– Place-specific factors, such as organization of work, and exposure to threats and harassment, influence the gender distribution of the activities of the children, especially in the case of girls.

In the following, I will develop these general conclusions in somewhat greater detail, focusing in particular on the subordinate position of the child workers in the informal sector, the social and economic aspects of the work of the children, and on their living conditions.

The struggle over urban economic space. Child work in the visible activities of the informal sector has typically been regarded as sporadic and marginal, mainly undertaken in order to acquire capital for non-essential consumption, and children engaged in these activities have not been accorded the status of "real" workers. In Managua, the expansion of the informal sector has to a large extent been characterized by a growth in those activities and by increasing competition. At first sight, these "visible" activities may seem easy to undertake, since the city is seen as an open economic space. However, in the informal sector there are more attractive and less attractive places of work, and the competition for sites in urban economic space has created "barriers" which restrict the entrance of new workers into the sector. Some of these "barriers" have a spatial expression, and are directly related to the local organization of economic space at the places of work, where social networks and family relations often are more important than economic resources as determinants of access to or exclusion from places and activities. The child workers are at a disadvantage in such struggles since they very rarely can form social networks of their own which have any real power.

This study has shown that the child workers have to fight a daily battle for their right to work within the sector. One conclusion is that the support of adults (particularly relatives) is essential if children are to get access to places of work and activities, and makes it much easier for the children to organize their own work. Such support does not necessarily have to be active; it can simply be that an adult is present at the same place of work. Left on their own, the children were often kept out of or expelled from the attractive places of work, and if they could get in there, they were marginalized and poorly organized.

The low rate of occupational mobility among the working children can be interpreted as an indicator of the necessity to protect a secured position in the sector, and also highlights the constraints on entry into other activities. Only a few children had changed activity, and if so only once. The decision to change activity was not taken by the children themselves, but by adults in the household, either because the income from the former activity was regarded as too low, or because of a change in the place of residence. With but a few exceptions the children already had a long career as workers behind them. On average, they began to work at the age of eight, but many had started when they were only six or even five years old. For the majority of the children this meant that they had been working for between six and eight years, and in almost all cases within the same occupation and at the same place of work.

These findings clearly suggest that we should reject the assumption that child workers in the urban informal sector move haphazardly and capriciously between activities. On the contrary, in view of the restrictions on entry into the informal sector, and considering the importance of location rights and access to contact network and of holding on to a position, in an occupation, once it has been secured, it seems unlikely that children should venture to change occupation on their own.

The sample of working children was selected at five different places of work in the city, in an attempt to capture the impact of place-specific characteristics on the work of the children. These five places were selected mainly on the basis of dissimilarities between them, in terms of their location in the city, their functional character, types of activities, size and work milieu. It became clear that those characteristics indeed influenced the work of the children and their situation as workers in various ways. Apart from differences with respect to how difficult or easy it was to get access to the places—as discussed above— they also differed in drawing-power vis-à -vis the child workers. It turned out that the small but not necessarily peripheral places of work were characterized by fewer types of child work activities and primarily attracted child workers from surrounding neighbourhoods. Larger places with many urban functions offered opportunities for a more varied range of activities and attracted child workers not only from the neighbourhoods but principally from more distant urban districts, from the rural areas of Managua and even from other cities and villages.

Another feature of child work that turned out to be influenced by place-specific characteristics was the gendered differentiation of children's activities, and in a limited way this study might make a contribution to the debate about the reproduction of gendered activities. The assumption that there are typical "girl activities" and typical "boy activities" is widespread in the literature, and usually taken for granted. As far as the present study goes, it turned out that the prevailing gendered distribution of the types of activities in which the children were engaged, was largely due to place-specific factors. The spatial organization of work, the work environment, and the social networks at the places of work were determinants of gender variations. At places where the situation made it equally possible for both boys and girls to work in the same activities, the girls were in fact engaged in the same activities as the boys. For example, warding and washing cars are usually considered to be typical boys' activities, but at certain places of work such tasks were performed by girls as well.

The characteristics of the work of the children. The analysis of the characteristics of the work of the children showed that this was a well organized activity within the informal sector, and similar in several aspects to the work that adults do in the sector. All children worked on a permanent basis, in the great majority of the cases, for seven days of the week.

In terms of occupational categories, there were also similarities between children and adults. Most of the children were self-employed and family workers, only a few worked as employees. There was a tendency that children moved into self-employment as they grew older. Boys mostly worked independently as self-employed workers, whereas the great majority of the girls were dependent workers, working together with a parent or another relative.

There was a clear relationship between occupational category and activity type. Almost all of the dependent child workers were confined to selling, whereas the independent workers were found in all the activities in which children were engaged—selling, shoe-shining, guarding and washing cars, and so forth.

In the context of this case study it is not possible to speak of any one activity as "child-specific", since those activities in which the children were engaged also were performed by adults. However the range of activities in which children were engaged was more limited than that of the adults. For instance, there were no differences in type between the principal and the secondary activities of the children—they could all be classified into a limited number of job types.

The importance of the work of the children. A conclusion of this study is that the integration of children in the informal sector is in fact one among a set of strategies that households adopt in order to cope with the problem of scarce resources. The importance of the income for the children themselves, and for the households, was clearly demonstrated by the information that the children gave about the destination and use of their earnings. All the children had a monetary income through their work in the informal sector, but in many cases they also received an income in kind, usually as some kind of food. That income was often consumed at the place of work, and in most cases was the only food that the children consumed during their working day. In other cases, fruit or vegetables that children received as payment for their work were brought home and became merchandise that later could be sold by the mother.

The destination of the monetary income of the children was another indicator of the importance of the children's income. It was used to cover essential needs, such as food, clothes and shoes. In many cases, according to the children themselves, what food they would get depended on their own income. But even more significant was that a large number of children used their income to pay for a school uniform and other articles related to their school work. The main reason given by those children who did not attend school was, in fact that their families could not afford it.

The main recipient of the children's income was the mother or the head of the household, to whom the majority of the children gave all their earnings. Only a small number of the children kept their income for themselves, but in that case they also had to buy things for themselves and/or were responsible for school expenses. In this respect there was a clear gender differentiation since the boys to a greater extent disposed of a part of or the whole income for their own expenses, while the girls, in contrast, gave all their income to the household.

The importance of the children's monetary income for the economy of their households is highlighted when put in the context of the dependency of the household upon the number incomes from adults and children. In a few cases, the households were totally dependent upon children's income since no adult was economically active. In almost equal number, there were households with one respectively two adult incomes, and where the average number of children's incomes was two or more.

In some households, the children, boys as well as girls, worked both in a principal activity and in a secondary activity; the latter was often an activity located in the neighbourhood of their home. Most of the households of those children were headed by a single parent, usually the mother, who in almost all the cases prepared food at home for selling. These households also accounted for half of all the households of the study who had moved from rural areas to Managua.

In conclusion, the study has shown that the work of the children was essential not only for the welfare of the child workers themselves but also for the economy of their households. Furthermore, children of migrant families, headed by the mother, were those most affected by poverty; they worked most and did not attend school. These findings are in accordance with findings from other studies which have shown that female-headed households of the informal sector in Managua are those most severely affected by poverty.

The child workers and their families. Because the streets and other open places in the city are common places of work for the children engaged in the activities investigated in this study, this is where the working children are visible, and for that reason they are often regarded as homeless, with little or no contact with a family. This study shows that this is not necessarily true. In fact, no child in the sample was homeless. All the children belonged to a household to which they returned at the end of the day, and most of them lived in nuclear families, in many cases with both their natural parents. In general they were in permanent contact with both natural parents or at least one of them. Some children lived with only one parent—in almost all such cases with the mother—but that number was unexpectedly low in view of the large number of female-headed households in Managua.

Most of the children were born in Managua and came from families which were not first generation migrants. However, a surprisingly large number of children had been sent by their families from rural areas to Managua in order to work, and they lived there with their relatives. A few of the children in the sample did not live in Managua but travelled to the city everyday to work. These findings indicate that the composition of the child labour force in the informal sector is not homogeneous, but includes children from the city, children from other nearby villages and cities and in-migrant children. In this respect it is similar to the composition of the adult labour force in the informal sector.

One of the principal questions at the outset of this study was whether the working children come from households with similar socio-economic characteristics. Lack of regular employment and lack of regularly paid jobs held by the heads of the households and their partners certainly were the dominant characteristics of the households of the children. However, in many cases, and contrary to expectations, children also came from households which—judging by their socio-economic characteristics, especially in terms of the realibility of income—would not be expected to send their children to work. In particular, the fact that in several cases the male heads of household held jobs in the formal sector with reliable and regular incomes supports the conclusion that the working children do not belong exclusively to informal sector households.

In addition, the place of residence of the children showed that they did not live exclusively in slums and squatter settlements but also in traditional neighbourhoods with acceptable housing standards. Both the standard of housing and the occupation of the heads of the children's households thus support the conclusion that child work in the informal sector is not restricted to the lowest socio-economic stratum of households in the city. Rather, the expansion of child work in the informal sector to other types of households should be interpreted in the context of general trends in the economy. Because of the low real value and the decline in the purchasing power of salaries, in the formal as well as in the informal sector, during the last few years, there has been a continuing and increasing pauperization of the households in the city, and poverty has been extended to a broader range of urban households, including those which by their characteristics should be considered to be above the line of poverty.

The everyday life of the children. The analysis of the activities of the children showed that the children were engaged not only in work in the labour market, but also in work at home, in "self-directed" and "household-directed" activities. Here there was clear evidence of a gender division of work, not in terms of types of activities—boys and girls did the same things at home—but individually the girls performed a broader range of tasks than the boys. Other differences simply had to do with whether the place of residence of the children was situated in rural or urban areas.

After work, school was the next most important activity for those children who attended school. Play was clearly a kind of "residual" activity in the children's daily life—regardless of whether they attended school or not—and was often restricted to short spells between the dominant activities, and to recesses at school. Time for travel varied considerably depending on the spatial location of the various activities that the children engaged in, and was of course related to the type of transport used.

Thus, the principal and telling conclusion with respect to the allocation of time for different activities is that work in the labour market was a central activity, in relation to which other activities were subordinated in terms of time demand. It reinforces the earlier conclusion, with respect to the destination of the income of the children, that the work of the children was of fundamental importance for the economy of the households.

The "work-school dichotomy". One of the purposes of the study was to analyse how the everyday life of the children was organized, focusing especially on which factors restricted or facilitated the participation of the working children in school education.

The analysis of the time-space organization of the children's everyday life brought to light three different patterns, which clearly showed that very significant variations in the conditions of life of the children could be attributed to the priority given to different activities. The dominant pattern was that of the children who worked all days of the week, and at the same time attended school on a full-time basis. Another pattern was characteristic of the children who were full-time workers, working five to seven days of the week, but did not attend school. A third pattern was formed by the children who worked on weekends and went to school on week-days. A comparison of the three patterns suggests some general observations about what the life of those children looked like.

School attendance clearly meant a lighter work-load in terms of daily and weekly hours of work. The children who both studied and worked on a weekly basis worked significantly fewer hours than those who did not go to school, although when school work and work in the informal sector are added up their days were long. The children who worked full-time, and did not attend school, not only had the heaviest work-load but because some of them commuted into the city they also had to travel longer distances to their places of work.

An analysis of the location of the activities—work and school— and of the place of residence of the children, showed that this spatial pattern had an impact on the organization of the everyday life of the children. Proximity to the place of work made it possible for the children to work and attend school at the same time, regardless of the socio-economic situation of their households. When the place of residence and school were distant from the place of work, it was much more likely that children did not attend school.

The implications of that analysis are that when both activities—school and work—are spatially and temporally compatible, the household can count on the income from children's work whether they attend school or not, and if this is so the children are more likely to attend school. If, on the other hand, the two activities are not compatible in space and in time, school attendance will depend on the household's evaluation of how important the income of the child is, and that evaluation will determine whether the child will have to work full time and not be able to go to school or, alternatively, will go to school and work on the weekends.

This study thus has demonstrated that variations with respect to children's work intensity and school attendance can not be explained solely by the socio-economic characteristics of their households. In some cases children from households in a very difficult economic situation attended school, while children from households which were better off did not. Spatial relationships must be included in the analysis, together with other factors, if we are to understand how the everyday life of the child workers in the informal sector in Managua is shaped.

A final conclusion from the analysis of the time-space activity patterns is that it required great efforts on the part of the children to successfully carry out all the activities they were expected to do. There was little time for leisure and rest. Play, sports, school homework, school and sleep came second in the life of the children. They occupied the time that remained after the children's main activity—work in the labour market.

Pride in work, fear in work. The children were very conscious of their role as workers and of the fact that their income was important for their families and not just for themselves. They were proud of being workers instead of vagabonds or just "kids drifting about" in the streets. They were also very aware of the risks associated with the kind of work they did. Violence from adults, thieves and rapists were often mentioned as things they were afraid of. However, to be alone was what the children were most afraid of, independently of age and sex. This partly explains why there was no direct relationship between what the children said they were afraid of and the specific environment in which they worked. In fact, one might say that the things that the children feared were not so much place-related as they were associated with the presence or absence of a relative at the same place of work.

When asked about the future, the declarations of the majority of the children showed that they had no intention of remaining in the activities they performed at the time they were interviewed. Work in the urban informal sector is not chosen because it offers opportunities for a life style free from restrictions and pressures; it is something that people are compelled to do in order to make a living. To work in the formal sector is still regarded as the best way to achieve a secure future in terms of a regular and better paid job. In this perspective, the reproduction of the urban informal sector can not be viewed primarily as the result of a free choice on the part of the workers involved. Who knows how many of these children will succeed in realizing their hopes for a better future and how many of them will continue, as adults, to do the same things they are doing now? Be that as it may, the children themselves have given evidence that allows us to conclude that it was not their innermost desire to take up jobs in the urban informal sector-jobs which are risky, difficult and unrewarding.

Child work: a new field for geography

This study has shown how complex the study of child work in the informal sector is. Besides the usual difficulties associated with child work research, which have been partly discussed earlier, the multifaceted nature of the urban informal sector also requires a combination of theoretical approaches and methods from several scientific disciplines.

Geography is a discipline that can provide new insights into the problematic of child work in the city. The study of urban processes is a geographical tradition of long standing, and within those processes the dualistic structure of the urban economy is a well explored research field, which yet, however, has not taken the work of the children into account. What was attempted in this study, through an analysis of the spatial patterns of the activities of the children and the study of their everyday life, is a quite modest example of what a geographical approach can contribute, but one that perhaps can contribute to the implementation of urban planing projects that would be better adapted to the realities of life of the working children. For instance, the location of schools closer to the places of work where many children are found would make it much easier for them to combine school and work in comparison with the present situation when they normally have to attend a school in their residential district.

To map the activities of the children in the city on a broad scale, for instance, might seem to be an ambitious project but it certainly would contribute to a better understanding of the position of the children as workers in the informal sector. A study of the unknown, "hidden" activities in the sector, where so many child workers are to be found—such as domestic work and apprenticeship in informal workshops—could certainly provide new scenarios of child work and illuminate the role that the work of the children plays for the existence of those activities and consequently of the informal sector in general.

The situation of children at work is a major concern of NGOs, IGOs, local and central governments, and not least the focus of study of an increasing number of scholars in different disciplines. I fear, however, that children in the informal sector will continue to be the group of working children whose problems are least addressed in policy making and programme implementation, not because of lack of interest or lack of conscience, but in part certainly because of a lack of knowledge about those children's situation as workers and about their living conditions as children.

If this study has made a contribution—however small—towards a better understanding of the life of the working children, I would be satisfied.

Bibliography

Aburto, R. and Chavarria, J. (1989): *El Empleo: Un Problema de los Sectores de la Economia*. Boletin Socio Económico. May/June. Managua.

Aburto, R. (1988): *Impacto de la Reforma Económica en el Sector Informal Urbano - Análisis de Casos*. Boletín Socio Económico. Sept/Oct. Managua.

Aguilar, R., Stenman, Å., and Aguilar, J. (1995): *A New Door Might Be Opened*. Macroeconomic Report. 1996:1. SIDA. Stockholm.

Agurto, S. and Renzi, R. (1992): *Empleo y desempleo en Managua, León y Granada (Urbano). Material para análisis económico*. FIDEG. Friedrich Ebert Stiftung. Managua.

Agurto, S. and Renzi, R. (1994): *Mercado de Trabajo: Situación del Sector Informal en las ciudades de Managua, León y Granada*. El Observador Económico. No. 35–36. FIDEG. Managua.

Agurto, S. and Renzi, R. (1995): *Mercado de Trabajo: Situación del Sector Informal en las ciudades de Managua, León y Granada*. El Observador Económico. No. 47–48. FIDEG. Managua.

Ahmed, A. (1990): *El trabajo infantil en Egipto: las curtiembres de El Cairo*. Bequele, A. and Boyden, J. (eds.): *La lucha contra el trabajo infantil*. OIT. Ginebra.

Alemán, M. (1986): *La Estrategia de Sobrevivencia de los Sectores Populares de Managua y el Impacto del Mensaje Económico Gubernamental*. Revista Encuentro. No. 29. Managua.

Anker, R., Khan, M. E. and Gupta, R. B. (1987): *Women's participation in the labour force: A methods test in India for improving its measurement*. Women, Work and Development. No. 16. ILO. Geneva.

Anti-Slavery International (1979-1987): Several Reports on Child Labour. London.

Åquist, A. (1992): *Tidsgeografi i samspel med samhällsteori*. Lund.

Balsonaro de Moura, E. (1982): *Mulheres e menores no trabalho industrial: os factores sexo e idade na dinamica do capital*. Vozes. Petrópolis.

Barrera, Y., Castiglia, M.A., Kruijt, D. and Menjivar, R. (1992): *Informalización y Pobreza*. FLACSO. San José.

Berg, M., Hudson P. and Sonescher, M. (1983): *Manufacturing in town and country before the factory*. Cambridge University Press. Cambridge.

Bequele, A. and Myers, W.E. (1995): *First things first in child labour. Eliminating work detrimental to children.* UNICEF/ILO. Geneva.

Bequele, A. and Boyden, J. (1990): *La lucha contra el trabajo infantil.* OIT. Ginebra.

Bossio, J.C. (1991): *Algunos planteamientos acerca del trabajo infantil en América Latina.* Seminario Regional Latinoamericano. OIT. Quito.

Bossio, J.C. (ed.) (1993): *El trabajo infantil en el Perú*. OIT. Geneva.

Boyden, J. with Holden, P. (1991): *Children of the cities.* Zed Books. New Jersey.

Boyden, J. and Myers, W. (1995): *Exploring Alternative Approaches to Combating Child Labour: Case Studies from Developing Countries.* Innocenti Occasional Papers. Child Rights Series. No. 8. ILO. Geneva. UNICEF. Florence.

Cain, M. (1978): *The Economic Activities of Children in a Village in Bangladesh.* Population and Development Studies.

Castells, M. (1977): *The urban question.* Edward Arnold. London.

Castells, M. (1983): *The City and the Grassroots.* Edward Arnold. London.

CEPAL (1995): *Nicaragua. Evolución económica durante 1994.* LC/MEX/R. 519.

CEPAL (1989): *Balance Preliminar de la Economia de América Latina y El Caribe.* Revista No. 485. Santiago de Chile.

Chatterjee, L. (1989): *Third World Cities. New Models in Geography.* Vol.2. Peet, R. and Thrift, N. (eds.). London.

Chavez, M. (1995): *Entre semaforos y parqueos, el trabajo de los niños, las niñas y adolescentes de Managua.* MILAVF. Managua.

Coordinadora Nicaraguense de ONGs que trabajan con la niñez (1995): *Segunda Consulta Nacional. Los niños, las niñas, los adolescentes y sus derechos en Nicaragua.* Imprimatur. Managua.

Cubitt, T. (1995): *Latin American Society.* (2nd ed.). Longman. Harlow.

Dahl, G. (1984): *Det nyttiga barnet.* Aronsson, K., Cederblad, M., Dahl, G., Olsson, L. and Sandin, B.(eds.): *Barn i tid och rum.* Liber Förlag. Kristianstad.

Datta, S. (1990): *Class Dynamics, Subaltern Consciousness and the Household Perspective. Third World Urbanization: Reappraisals and New Perspectives.* Urban Studies. Swedish Council for Research in the Humanities and Social Sciences. Stockholm.

Dejo, F. (1989): *Los hijos de la pobreza.* CISE. Rädda Barnen. Lima.

De Soto, H. (1991): *El otro sendero*. Mexico.(Primera edición peruana 1986. Instituto Libertad y Democracia).

De Soto, H. and Schmidheiny, S. (eds.) (1991): *Las nuevas reglas del juego. Hacia un desarrollo sustenible en América Latina*. Fundes. Colombia.

Dickens, C. (1965): *Great expectations*. Calder, A. (ed.). Harmondsworth Penguin. (First edition 1860-61). London.

Ennew, J. and Young, P. (1982): *Child Labour in Jamaica*. Anti-Slavery International. London.

Espínola, B., Glauser, B., Ortiz, R.M. and Carrizosa, S.O. (1989): *En La Calle. Menores trabajadores de la calle de Asunción*. UNICEF. Serie Metodológica. Programa Regional de América Latina y el Caribe. No. 4. Bogotá.

FIDEG (1993–1996): El Observador Económico. Several monthly issues. Managua.

Friberg, T. (1990): *Kvinnors vardag. Om kvinnors arbete och liv. Anpassningsstrategier i tid och rum*. Lund

Fyfe, A. (1993): *Child Labour: A guide to project design*. ILO. Geneva.

Fyfe, A. (1995): *Government initiatives through child labour legislation and education: the case of India*. IPEC/ILO. Innocenti Occasional Papers. Child Rights Series. No. 8. Florence.

Garcia, N. and Castillo, R. (1991): *Diagnóstico participativo de los menores trabajadores del sector informal del Barrio de Acahualinca*. Centro Dos Generaciones. Managua.

Garcia, R. (1989): *Incipient Industrialization in an "Underdeveloped" Country. The case of Chile, 1845-1879*. Institute of Latin American Studies. Monograph No. 17. Stockholm.

Geertz, C. (1963): *Peddlers and Princes: Social change and economic modernization in two Indonesian towns*. Chicago.

Gilbert, A. (1994): *The Latin American city*. Latin american Bureau. London.

Gilbert, A. and Gugler, J. (1982): *Cities, Poverty and Development. Urbanization in the Third World*. Oxford University Press. New York.

Gilbert, A. and Ward, P. (1985): *Housing, the state and the poor*. Cambridge University Press. Cambridge.

Glasinovich, W.A. (1991): *Entre calles y plazas. El trabajo infantil de los niños en Lima*. ADEC/ATC. Instituto de Estudios Peruanos. UNICEF. Lima.

Glasinovich, W.A. (1986): *Pobreza urbana y trabajo infantil en Lima metropolitana*. Rädda Barnen. Lima.

Gonzalez, A. (1990): *Informal Sector and Survival Strategies: An Historical Approach.* Datta, S. (ed.): *Third World Urbanization: Reappraisals and New Perspectives.* Urban Studies. Swedish Council for Research in the Humanities and Social Sciences. Stockholm.

Hägerhäll, B. (ed.) (1988): *Vår gemensamma framtid.* Rapport från världskommissionen för miljö och utveckling. Prisma/Tiden. Stockholm.

Hägerstrand, T. (1974): *Tidsgeografisk beskrivning. Syfte och postulat.* Svensk Geografisk Årsbok. årg. 50. Lund.

Hägerstrand, T. (1974): Studier i samverkans tids- och platsberoende. Svensk Geografisk Årsbok. 50. Lund.

Hart, K (1973): *Informal income opportunities and urban employment in Ghana.* Journal of Modern African Studies. No. 11.

Hernandez, V. and Henriquez, S. (1991): *Menores en estrategia de sobrevivencia.* Centro Nicaraguense de Promoción de la Juventud y la Infancia. Dos Generaciones. Managua.

Hudson, P. (ed.) (1989): *Regions and Industries.* Cambridge University Press. Cambridge

Hull, T (1981): *Perspectives and data requirements for the study of children's work.* Rodgers, G. and Standing, G. (eds.): *Child work, Poverty and Underdevelopment.* ILO. Geneva.

Hurtado, M. (1986): *Teeming cities: the challenge of the urban poor.* Latin America and Caribbean Review. World of Information.

ILO (1972): *Employment, incomes and equity - a strategy for increasing productive employment in Kenya.* Geneva.

ILO (1973): *Minimum Age Convention.*

ILO (1983): *Report of the Director-General. Part I: Child Labour.* International Labour Conference. 67th Session. Geneva.

ILO (1986): *Child Labour: A briefing manual.* Geneva.

ILO/IPEC (1995): *Strategies, priorities and lessons for the future: A summary.* Geneva.

ILO (1991): *The Dilema of the Informal Sector.* Report of the Director-General. Geneva.

ILO (1996): *Child labour targeting the intolerable.* Geneva.

INEC (1988-1990): Household Surveys: *Encuesta de Conyuntura y de Impacto.* Several reports. Managua.

IPEC (1993): *El trabajo infantil en América Central.* Documento del Seminario Centroamericano sobre el trabajo infantil. Organización Internacional del Trabajo. (OIT).

Littlejohn, C. (coordinador de equipo) (1991): *Impacto de la Deuda Externa y las Medidas de Ajuste Estructural en la Familia, la Niñez y la Mujer.* CAPRI. Managua.

Levine, D. (1987): *Reproducing Families.* Cambridge University Press. Cambridge.

Levy, V. (1985): *Cropping Patterns. Mechanization, Child Labor, and Fertility Behavior in a Farming Economy: Rural Egypt.* Economic Development and Cultural Change. Vol. 33. Chicago.

Lewis, O. (1970): *The Culture of Poverty. Anthropological Essays.* Random House.

Lewis, W.A. (1954): *Economic Development with Unlimited Supplies of Labour.* Agarwala, A.N. (ed.): *The Economics of Underdevelopment.* Oxford University Press. New York.

Lewis, W.A. (1955): *The Theory of Economic Growth.* Allen and Unwin. London.

Kanbargi, R. (1990): *El trabajo infantil en la India: la fabricación de alfombras en Benares.* Bequele, A. and Boyden, J. (eds.): *La lucha contra el trabajo infantil.* OIT. Ginebra.

Mabogunje, L.A. (1980): *The Development Process. A spatial perspective.* Hutchinson Publisher. London.

Mansilla, M.E. (1989): *Los niños de la calle. Siembra de hoy, cosecha del mañana.* ADOC. Peru.

Massey, D. (1987): *Nicaragua.* Open University Press. Philadelphia.

Mendelievich, E. (1979): *Children at work.* ILO. Geneva.

Mingione, E. (1987): *Urban Survival Strategies, Family Structure and Informal Practices.* Smith, M.P. and Feagin, J.R. (eds.): *The Capitalist City. Global Restructuring and Community Politics.* Basil Blackwell. New York.

Morales, G.P. (1990): *Ser niño en Colombia. Elementos de Sociología de la Infancia.* UNICEF. Serie Divulgatoria. Programa Regional de América Latina y el Caribe. No. 2. Colombia.

Musgrove, P. (1978): *Consumer behavior in Latin America.* Estudios conjuntos sobre integración económica Latinoamericana. (ECIEL). Washington.

Myers, W. (1989): *Urban working children: A comparison of four surveys from South America*. International Labour Review. ILO. Vol. 128. No. 3. Geneva.

Norlund, I. (1990): *Informal Work: Textile Women in Vietnam and the Philippines*. Datta, S. (ed.): *Third World Urbanization: Reappraisals and New Perspectives*. Swedish Council for Research in the Humanities and Social Sciences. Urban Studies. Stockholm.

OIT (1994): *El trabajo infantil en Argentina. Propuesta para un Programa Nacional de Acción*. Geneva.

OIT (1993): *El trabajo infantil en Venezuela. Bases para la adopción de un Programa de Acción*. OIT. Geneva.

OIT (1986): *Child labour: A briefing manual*. OIT. Geneva.

Ortiz, F. (1987): *Los negros esclavos*. Editorial de Ciencias Sociales. La Habana. Cuba.

Pahl, R. (1980): *Employment, work and the domestic division of labour*. International Journal of Urban and Regional Research. Vol. 1. London.

Pahl, R. and Wallace, C. (1985): *Household work strategies in economic recession*. Redclift, N. and Mingione, E. (eds.): *Beyond Employment: Household, Gender and Subsistence*. Basil Blackwell. Oxford.

Peattie, L. R. (1975): *Tertiarization, Marginality and Urban Poverty in Latin America*. Latin American Urban Research. Vol. 5. Sage Publications. London.

Portes, A. and Walton, J. (1981): *Labour, Class, and the International System*. Academic Press. New York.

Portes, A. and Benton, L. (1984): *Industrial development and labor absorption: a reinterpretation*. Population and Development Review.

Portes, A. and Castells, M. (1989): *World Underneath: The Origins, Dynamics, and Effects of the Informal Economy*. Portes, A., Castells, M., and Benton, L. (eds.): *The Informal Economy. Studies in Advance and Less Developed Countries*. John Hopkins University Press. London.

Preston, D. (1987): *Latin American Development. Geographical perspectives*. Longman. Harlow.

Quijano, A. (1974): *The marginal pole of the economy and the marginalised labour force*. Economy and Society. No. 3.

Quijano, A. (1975): *The Urbanization of Latin American Society*. Hardoy, J. (ed.): Urbanization in Latin America. Anchor Books. New York.

Renzi, R. and Agurto, S. (1992): *Pobreza en los hogares de Managua, León y Granada (Urbano)*. Material para Análisis Económico. FIDEG. Managua.

Renzi, R. (1996): *Condiciones de vida de los hogares urbanos de León, Granada y Managua (1992-1995)*. El Observador Económico. No. 49. FIDEG. Managua.

Roberts, B. (1978): *Cities of Peasants: the political economy of urbanization*. The Third World. Edward Arnold. London.

Roberts, B. (1995): *The making of Citizens: Cities of Peasants*. Revised. Edward Arnold. London.

Roberts, B. (1989): *Employment Structure, Life Cycle, and Life Changes: Formal and Informal Sectors in Guadalajara*. Portes, A., Castells, M., and Benton, L. (eds.): *The Informal Economy. Studies in Advance and Less Developed Countries*. John Hopkins University Press. London.

Rodgers, G. and Standing, G. (1979): *The economic role of children in low-income countries: a framework for analysis*. Population and Labour Policies Programme. World Employment Programme Research. Working Paper. No. 81.

Rodgers, G. and Standing, G. (eds.) (1982): *Child work, Poverty and Underdevelopment*. ILO. Geneva.

Rogers, E.M. (1969): *Modernization among Peasants*. Michican State University.

Roldán, M. (1987): *Yet Another Meeting on the Informal Sector? Or the Politics of Designation and Economic Restructuring in a Gendered World*. Proceedings from a Conference in Denmark. *The Informal Sector as an Integral Part of the National Economy. Research Needs and Aid Requirements*. Roskilde.

Rozenzweig, M. (1981): *Household and Non-household Activities of Youths: Issues of Modelling*. Rodgers, G. and Standing, G. (eds.): *Child Work, Poverty and Underdevelopment*. ILO. Geneva.

Safa, H. (1987): *Urbanization, the Informal Economy and State Policy in Latin America*. Smith, M.P. and Feagin, J. R. (eds.): *The Capitalist City. Global Restructuring and Community Politics*. Basil Blackwell. New York.

Saffron, W. (1995): *Latin American Society*. Cubbit, T. (ed.). Longman. England

Salazar, M.C. (1990): *El trabajo infantil en Colombia. Las canteras y hornos de ladrillos de Bogotá*. Bequele, A. and Boyden, J. (eds.): *La lucha contra el trabajo infantil*. OIT. Ginebra.

Salazar, M.C. (1994): *The social significance of child labor in Latin America and the Caribbean*. Paper prepared for the 48th International Congress of Americanists. Stockholm.

Santos, M. (1978): *O espaço dividido: Os dois circuitos da economia urbana dos paises subdesenvolvidos*. (Original title: *L'espace partagé. Les deux circuits de l'économie urbaine des pays sous-développés)*. Alves Editora. Brazil.

Schibotto, G. (1990): *Niños trabajadores. Construyendo una identidad*. IPEC. Lima.

Schildkrout, E. (1981): *The employment of children in Kano*. Rogers, G. and Standing, G. (eds.): *Child Labour, Poverty and Underdevelopment*. ILO. Geneva.

Schteingart, M. (1990): *Production and Reproduction Practices in the Informal Sector: The Case of Mexico*. Datta, S. (ed.): *Third World Urbanization: Reappraisals and New Perspectives*. Swedish Council for Research in the Humanities and Social Sciences. Stockholm.

Sethuraman, S.V. (ed.) (1981): *The Urban Informal sector in Developing Countries. Employment, Poverty and Environment*. ILO. Geneva.

Sethuraman, S.V. (1987): *The Informal Sector and the Poor in the Third World*. Proceedings from a conference in Denmark. *The Informal Sector as an Integral Part of the National Economy. Research Needs and Aid Requirements*. Roskilde.

Sethuraman, S.V. (1994): *The Challenge of Urban Poverty in Developing Countries: Coping with the Informal Sector*. ILO. Geneva.

Sharif, M. (1993): *Child participation, Nature of work, and Fertility Demand: A Theoretical Analysis*. The Indian Economic Journal. Vol. 40. No. 4.

Smith, M.P. and Tardanico, R. (1987): *Urban Theory Reconsidered: Production, Reproduction and Collective Action*. Smith, M.P. and Feagin, J. R. (eds.): *The Capitalistic City. Global Restructuring and Community Politics*. Basil Blackwell. New York.

Smith, M.P. and Feagin, J.R. (1987): *Cities and the New International Division of Labour*. Smith, M.P. and Feagin, J. R. (eds.): *The Capitalistic City. Global Restructuring and Community Politics*. Basil Blackwell. New York.

Talamante, A.A. and Mercado, M.R. (1991): *Análisis de Situación de los niños de la calle en la ciudad de Managua*. Instituto de Promoción Humana. Programa de Promoción de la Familia y la Comunidad. Managua.

The United Nations Convention on the Rights of the Child.

Tienda, M. (1979): *The Economic Activity of Children in Perú: Labor Force Behaviour in Rural and Urban Contexts.* Rural Sociology.

Tokman, V.E. (1978): *An exploration into the nature of informal-formal sector relationships.* World Development. No. 6.

Tokman, V.E. (1990): *The informal sector in Latin America: Fifteen years later.* Turnham, D., Salomé, B. and Schwartz, A. (eds.): *The informal sector revised.* OECD. Development Centre.

UNICEF (1989): *Lineamentos para la aplicación de la guia metodológica para el análisis de situación. Menores en circunstancias especialmente difíciles.* Serie Metodológica. No. 8.

UNICEF (1991): *Nicaragua: Desafíos y opciones en un pais de niños y mujeres.* Análisis de situación económica y social. Managua.

UNICEF (1997): *The State of the World's Children Report. A new era for children.*

UNITED NATIONS (1982): *Exploitation of Child Labour.* Final report submitted by Bouhdiba, A. New York.

UNRISD (1995): *States of Disarray. The social effects of globalization.* Report for the World Summit for Social Development. UNRISD. London.

Universal Declaration of Human Rights.

Valladares, L. (1990): *Family and Child Work in the Favela.* Third World Urbanization: Reappraisals and New Perspectives. Swedish Council for Research in the Humanities and Social Sciences. Stockholm.

Walton, J. (ed.) (1985): *Capital and Labour in the Urbanized World.* California.

WHO (1987): *Children at Work: Special Health Risks.* Technical report series. No. 756. Geneva.

World Bank (1995): *Republic of Nicaragua, Poverty Assesment.* Report No. 14038-NI. World Bank. Washington.

Appendix

Questionnaire guide

It is important to know that the interviews took the form of conversations rather than question-and-answer sessions. The intention was to ensure that a set of questions focusing on the central research issues should be covered in all the interviews. The questions, as it were, became embedded in the conversations with the children. In the course of the interviews, many other topics and questions were brought up, as well. The "questionnaire guide" is best described as a check-list for myself and the colleague who assisted me during the interviews.

- What is your name?
- How old are you? Have you had your birthday, already?
- Where do you live?
- What are you doing here?
- (If working) What kind of work do you do?
- (In the case of sellers) How did you get this product? Did someone give it to you, for you to sell, or have you bought it, or did you get it at home?
- Besides this job, are you working somewhere else?
- Where is that job located? What kind of job is it?
- How many days do you work in your job here? Which days?
- At what time do you start working?
- At what time do you stop working?
- Think of the last day you worked before today: At what time did you start working?; at what time did you stop working?; how much did you earn?: was that what you usually earn?; apart from money, did you get any other payment for your work?
- (If yes): Is it usual that you get paid in that way?
- What did you do with the money you earned the last day you worked?; is that what you usually do?; how did you get to work?; how long did it take you?; are you afraid of working here?; what do you do when you get home?; do you go to school?
- (If yes): In which grade are you?; what was your last approved grade?; where is your school located?; how long does it take you to get from your home to your school/from your place of work to your school?; how do you get to your school?; at what age did you begin school?
- (If no): Why are you not attending school?; have you ever gone to school?
- (If yes): How old were you when you first went to school?; why did you stop going to school?; in what grade were you when you dropped out of school?
- Do you have any time left for play during the week?
- Where do you play?
- For how long do you play each day?
- Do you play on Saturdays and on Sundays? In the morning/afternoon?
- What do you do when you play?
- How old were you when you first began to work?

- From that age, have you been working all time or have there been times when you did not work?; Did you have any other job before this one?
- (If yes): Why did you change jobs?; what did you do in that job?; how long did you work in that job?; how old were you?; where was that work located?; where did you live then?; when you worked in that job, did you attend school then?
- (If yes): Where was that school located?; with whom do you live?; specify all the persons who live in the same home as you; are there any children in your home who have not had their 14th birthday?; specify who they are and how old they are; do some of these children work like you do?; in the same or in another kind of job?
- (If yes): What kind of job do they do?; where do they work?; with whom do they work?
- What does your mother do? (or other female head of the household of the child). (If employed): Where does she work?
- What does your father do? (or other male head of the household of the child). (If employed): Where does he work?
- Have you always lived in Managua?
- (If no): Where did you live before?; when did you move to Managua?; did you move alone or with your family?
- Think of the last day you worked before today. At what time did you get up?; at what time did you begin your work here?; at what time did you end your work here?; when did you begin school?; at what time did you finish school?; when did you get home?; what did you did when you got home?; what did you do before going to bed?; at what time did you go to bed?
- Do you like to work?
- What do you think about the fact that children work?
- What would you like to do if you did not work?
- What would you like to be when you grow up?

GEOGRAFISKA REGIONSTUDIER

Utgivna av Kulturgeografiska Institutionen vid Uppsala universitet

Nr 1 Uppsala län med omnejd. (The County of Uppsala with Environs.) Del I: Gerd Enequist och Lennart Hartin: *Folkmängd, odling och industri. (Distribution of population, cultivated areas and manufacturing industries.)* 1958.

Del II: Björn Bosæus: *Resor till arbete och service. Regionindelning. (Travel to work and service. Regional division.)* 1958.

Nr 2 Uppsala län. (The County of Uppsala.)
Inga Söderman: *Jordbruksnedläggelse och storleksrationalisering 1951-1961. (Changes in number and size of farms in Uppsala County 1951-1961.)* 1963.

Nr 3 Maj Ohre: *Förorter i Mälar-Hjälmarområdet. (Suburbs in the Mälar-Hjälmar region.)* 1966.

Nr 4 Hans Aldskogius: *Studier i Siljansområdets fritidsbebyggelse. (Studies in the Geography of Vacation House Settlements in the Siljan Region.)* 1968.

Nr 5 Maj Ohre-Aldskogius: *Folkmängdsförändring och stadstillväxt. En studie av stora och medelstora stadsregioner. (Population Change and Urban Sprawl. A study of large and middle size city regions.)* 1968.

Nr 6 Hans Aldskogius: *Modelling the Evolution of settlement Patterns: Two Studies of Vacation House Settlement.* 1969.

Nr 7 Hans Ländell: *Marknad och distrikt. Metodstudier med anknytning till företagslokalisering. (Market and Market Areas. Some methods of Analysing the Location of Economic Activity.)* 1972.

Nr 8 Hans Ländell: *Analyser av partihandelns lokalisering. (Analysis of the Location of Wholesale trade.)* 1972.

Nr 9 Sune Berger: *Företagsnedläggning - konsekvenser för individ och samhälle. (Plant shut down - consequences for man and society.)* 1973.

Nr 10 Lena Gonäs: *Företagsnedläggning och arbetsmarknadspolitik. En studie av sysselsättningskriserna vid Oskarshamns varv. (Plant Shut-down and Labour Market Policy. A study of the employment crises at Oskarshamns shipyard.)* 1974.

Nr 11 Jan Strinnholm: *Varutransporter med flyg. Flygfraktstudier med empirisk belysning av flygfrakt i Sverige, utrikeshandel samt flygfrakt över Atlanten. (Goods Transport by Air. Air Freight Studies Empirically Illustrated with Data from Sweden Foreign Trade and Air Freight via Arlanda.)* 1974.

Nr 12 *Uppsala - Samhällsgeografiska studier.* Redigerade av Maj Aldskogius. *(Uppsala - Studies in social geography.)* 1977.

Nr 13 Jan Öhman: *Staden och det varjedagliga utbytet. (The City and the Everyday Exchange.)* 1982.

Nr 14 Magnus Bohlin: *Fritidsboendet i den regionala ekonomin. Vart fritidshusägarnas pengar tar vägen. (Second Homes in the Regional Economy: Where the Cottagers Money Go.)* 1982.

GEOGRAFISKA REGIONSTUDIER

Nr 15 Kulturgeografiska perspektiv. *Forskningsbidrag från Uppsala 1985.* Red.: Hans Aldskogius, Ragnar Bergling, Sölve Göransson. (*Uppsala Studies in Human Geography, 1985.*) 1985.

Nr 16 Mengistu Woube: *Problems of Land Reform Implementation in Rural Ethiopia: A Case Study of Dejen and Wolmera Districts.* 1986.

Nr 17 Ali Najib: *Migration of Labour and the Transformation of the Economy of the Wedinoon Region in Morocco.* 1986.

Nr 18 Roger Andersson: *Den svenska urbaniseringen. Kontextualisering av begrepp och processer.* (*The Urbanization of Sweden. Contextualization of Concepts and Processes.*) 1987.

Nr 19 Mats Lundmark och Anders Malmberg: *Industrilokalisering i Sverige - regional och strukturell förändring.* (*Industrial Location in Sweden - Regional and Structural Change.*) 1988.

Nr 20 Gunnel Forsberg: *Industriomvandling och könsstruktur. Fallstudier på fyra lokala arbetsmarknader.* (*Industrial change and gender structure. Case studies on four local labour markets.*) 1989.

Nr 21 Kjell Haraldsson: *Tradition, regional specialisering och industriell utveckling - sågverksindustrin i Gävleborgs län.* (*Tradition, regional specialization and industrial development - The sawmill industry in the County of Gävleborg, Sweden.*) 1989.

Nr 22 Naseem Jeryis: *Small-Scale Enterprises in Arab villages. - A Case Study from the Galilee Region in Israel.* 1990.

Nr 23 Inga Carlman: *Blåsningen. Svensk vindkraft 1973 till 1990.* (*Gone With the Wind. Windpower in Sweden 1973 until 1990.*) 1990.

Nr 24 Bo Malmberg: *The Effects of External Ownership - A Study of Linkages and Branch Plant Location.* 1990.

Nr 25 Erik Westholm: *Mark, människor och moderna skiftesreformer i Dalarna.* (*Modern Land Reforms in Dalarna, Sweden.*) 1992.

Nr 26 Margareta Dahlström: *Service Production. Uneven Development and Local Solutions in Swedish Child Care.* 1993.

Nr 27 Lena Magnusson: *Omflyttning på den svenska bostadsmarknaden. En studie av vakanskedjemodeller.* (*Residential Mobility on the Swedish Housing Market. A Study Using Markov Chain Models.*) 1994.

Nr 28 Göran Hallin: *Struggle over Strategy. States, Localities. and Economic Restructuring in Sunderland and Uddevalla.* 1995.

Nr 29 Clas Lindberg: *Society and Environment Eroded. A Study of Household Poverty and Natural Resource Use in Two Tanzanian Villages.* 1996.

Nr 30 Brita Hermelin: *Professional Business Services. Conceptual Framework and a Swedish Case Study.* 1997.

Nr 31 Aida Aragão-Lagergren: *Working Children in the Informal Sector in Managua.* 1997.